THE AWAKENING OF FAITH
IN THE MAHAYANA
AND
ITS COMMENTARY
THE PRINCIPLE AND PRACTICE
OF MAHAYANA BUDDHISM

Suzuki & Goddard

SMC PUBLISHING INC.
Taipei

ISBN 957-9482-18-7

ACVAGHOSHA'S DISCOURSE

ON THE

AWAKENING OF FAITH

IN THE

MAHAYANA

大 乘 起 信 論

TRANSLATED FOR THE FIRST TIME FROM THE
CHINESE VERSION

by

Teitaro Suzuki

SMC PUBLISHING INC.
Taipei

Original Edition Published:
The Open Court Publishing Co.
Chicago, 1900

PUBLISHER'S PREFACE.

AÇVAGHOSHA is the philosopher of Buddhism. His treatise on *The Awakening of Faith* is recognised by all Northern schools and sects as orthodox and used even to-day in Chinese translations as a text-book for the instruction of Buddhist priests.

The original Sanskrit text has not been found as yet, and if it should not be discovered somewhere in India or in one of the numerous libraries of the Buddhist vihâras, it would be a great loss; for then our knowledge of Açvaghosha's philosophy would remain limited to its Chinese translation.

Açvaghosha's treatise on *The Awakening of Faith* is a small booklet, a monograph of the usual size of Chinese fascicles, comprising in its Chinese dress no more than about 10,800 characters, and may be read through in a few hours. But the importance of this monograph stands in no relation to its brevity, and it is very strange that no translation of it has appeared as yet in any European language. I was therefore exceedingly glad that Mr. Teitaro Suzuki, a Japanese Buddhist and a disciple of the Rev. Shaku Soyen, the distinguished Abbot of Kamakura, who was one of the delegates of the Parliament of Religions at Chicago in 1893, undertook the work of rendering Açvaghosha's monograph into English form. I watched the progress of his translation and my interest in the work increased the more I became familiar with the thoughts of the great philosopher of Buddhism. Not only is my own interpretation of Buddhism, as stated in the *Gospel of Buddha* and elsewhere, here fully justified, but there are striking similarities between the very terms of Açvaghosha's system and expressions which I have used in my own philosophical writings. The main coincidence is the idea of Suchness, which is pure form, or the purely formal aspect of things, determining their nature according to mathematical and mechanical laws.[1]

[1] This coincidence of some salient points need of course not exclude disagreements in other important matters.

Suchness, according to Açvaghosha, is the cosmic order or *Gesetzmässigkeit* of the world; it is the sum total of all those factors which shape the universe and determine the destinies of its creatures. It is the norm of existence and is compared to a womb in which all things take shape and from which they are born. It is Plato's realm of ideas and Goethe's "Mothers" of the second part of *Faust*.

Suchness which in its absolute sense means the total system of the abstractly formal laws, including, the moral order of the universe, is contrasted with the realm of Birth and Death. This realm of Birth and Death, is the material world of concrete objects. While Suchness is the domain of the universal, the realm of Birth and Death is the domain of the particular; and it is characteristic of the Mahayana school that the bodily, the particular, the concrete is not rejected as a state of sin, but only characterised as impure or defiled, imperfect, and implicated with sorrow and pain, on account of its limitedness and the illusions which naturally attach to it.

Suchness and the realm of Birth and Death

are not two hostile empires but two names of the same thing. There is but one world with two aspects describing two opposed phases of one and the same existence. These two aspects form a contrast, not a contradiction. Suchness (or the good law, the normative factor) dominates the realm of Birth and Death, which latter therefore, in a certain sense, belongs to Suchness throughout in its entirety as well as in its details.

But sentient beings are apt to overlook the significance of the universal, for the senses depict only the particular. Thus to a superficial consideration of sensual beings, the world presents itself as a conglomeration of isolated objects and beings, and the unity that consists in the oneness of law which dominates all, is lost sight of. It is the mind (or spiritual insight into the nature of things) which traces the unity of being and learns to appreciate the significance of the universal.

Universals, i. e., those factors which constitute the suchness of things are not substances, not entities, but relations, pure forms, or determinants, i. e., general laws. Thus they are not things, but ideas; and the most important one among them, the suchness of man or his soul, is not a concrete self, an âtman, but "name and form."

It is well known what an important rôle the denial of the existence of the âtman plays in the Abhidharma, and we need not repeat here that it is the least understood and most misrepresented doctrine of Buddhism.

Thus the essential feature of existence, of that which presents itself to the senses, is not the material, but the formal; not that which makes it concrete and particular, but that which constitutes its nature and applies generally; not that which happens to be here, so that it is this, but that which makes it to be thus; not its Thisness, but its Suchness.

Particularity is not denounced as evil, but it is set forth as limited; and we might add (an idea which is not expressed in the Mahâyâna, but implied) that the universal would be unmeaning if it were not realised in the particular. Absolute Suchness without reference to the world of concrete Particularity is like a Pratyekabuddha, and the Pratyekabuddha, a sage whose wisdom does not go out into the world to seek and to save, is regarded as inferior to the Bodhisattvas, who with inferior knowledge combine a greater love and do practical work that is of help to their fellow beings.

How highly Particularity is considered appears from the Mahayana picture in which it stands contrasted to Universality on perfectly equal terms.[1]

The world-process starts in ignorance, perhaps through ignorance or at least through some commotion void of enlightenment, but from the start it is enveloped by the good law of cosmic order. Suchness, the norm of being, guides its steps. It is shaped in the womb of the Tathâgata and is in the progress of evolution more and more tinged, or, as Açvaghosha says, perfumed, with the cognition of Suchness. Thus life will necessarily march onward to Buddhahood, actualising in the course of its development the eternal in the transient, the omnipresent in the special, the universal in the concrete and particular, and unchange-

[1] See the frontispiece.

able perfection in the imperfect haphazards of the kaleidoscopic world of changes, in which things originate by being compounded, and perish according to the law that all compounds are doomed to dissolution. Hence it becomes apparent that the realm of Birth and Death is the realisation only of that which in itself is immortal; it is the appearance in time and space, the actualisation, the materialisation, the incarnation, of that which is everlasting and permanent in the absolute sense. Says Goethe:

> "Alles Vergängliche
> Ist nur ein Gleichniss,
> Das Unzulängliche
> Hier wird's Ereigniss."

The reading of Açvaghosha's treatise may in some of its parts present difficulties, and Western thinkers would undoubtedly express themselves in other terms than this thinker of India who lived almost two thousand years ago; but the underlying ideas of his philosophy will be found simple enough, if the reader will take the trouble patiently to consider the significance of every sentence in its relation to the whole system.

PAUL CARUS.

TRANSLATOR'S PREFACE.

THE study of Buddhism has recently made gigantic strides, on this side of the Atlantic as well as on the other. Not only is the importance of the science of comparative religion making itself felt, but the advance of our Pali and Sanskrit knowledge has greatly contributed to a better understanding of things Oriental. Even Christians who were without sympathy for "heathen" religions have now taken up the study of Buddhism in earnest. Nevertheless, it appears to me that the teachings of Sakyamuni are not yet known in their full significance and that they do not yet command just appreciation. Though intolerant critics lose no chance of vigorously and often wrongly attacking the weak points of Buddhism, which are naturally seen at the surface, clear-sighted people have been very slow to perceive its innermost truth. This is especially the case with the Mahayana school.

TRANSLATOR'S PREFACE.   xi

The main reasons for this are, in my opinion, evident. While the canonical books of the Hinayana Buddhism have been systematically preserved in the Pali language, those of the Mahayana Buddhism are scattered promiscuously all over the fields and valleys of Asia and in half a dozen different languages. Further, while most of the Sanskrit originals have been destroyed, their translations in Tibetan, Mongolian, and Chinese have never been thoroughly studied. And, lastly, the Mahayana system is so intricate, so perplexingly abstruse, that scholars not accustomed to this form of thought and expression are entirely at a loss to find their way through it.

Among the false charges which have been constantly poured upon the Mahayana Buddhism, we find the following: Some say, "It is a nihilism, denying God, the soul, the world and all"; some say, "It is a polytheism: Avalokiteçvâra, Târa, Vajrapâni, Mañjuçrî, Amitâbha, and what not, are all worshipped by its followers"; still others declare, "It is nothing but sophistry, quibbling, hair-splitting subtlety, and a mocking of the innermost yearnings of humanity"; while those who attack it from the historical side proclaim, "It is not the genuine teaching of Buddha; it is on the contrary the pure invention of Nâgârjuna, who devised the system by ingeniously mixing up his negative philosophy with the non-âtman theory of his predecessor"; or, "The Mahayana is a queer mixture of the Indian mythology that grew most freely in the Tantric period, with a degenerated form of the noble ethical teachings of primitive Buddhism." Though no one who is familiar with Mahayanistic ideas will admit these one-sided and superficial judgments, the majority of people are so credulous as to lend their ear to these falsified reports and to believe them.

The present English translation of Açvaghosha's principal work is therefore dedicated to the Western public by a Buddhist from Japan, with a view to dispelling the denunciations so ungraciously heaped upon the Mahayana Buddhism. The name of Açvaghosha is not very well known to the readers of this country, but there is no doubt that he was the first champion, promulgator, and expounder of this doctrine, so far as we can judge from all our available historical records. Besides, in this book almost all the Mahayanistic thoughts, as distinguished from the other religious systems in India, are traceable, so that we can take it as the representative text of this school. If the reader will carefully and patiently go through the entire book, unmindful of its peculiar terminology and occasional obscureness, I believe he will be amply and satisfactorily repaid for his labor, and will find that the underlying ideas are quite simple, showing occasionally a strong resemblance to the Upanishad philosophy as well as to the Samkhya system, though of course retaining its own independent thought throughout.

In conclusion let me say a word about the difficulty of translating such an abstruse religio-philosophic discourse as the present text. It is comparatively easy to translate works of travels or of historical events or to make abstracts from philosophical works. But a translator of the Mahayanistic writings, which are full of specific phraseology and highly abstruse speculations, will find himself like a wanderer in some unknown region, not knowing how to obtain any communicable means to express what he perceives and feels. To reproduce the original as faithfully as possible and at the same time to make it intelligible enough to the outside reader, who has perhaps never come in contact with this form of thought, the translator must be perfectly acquainted with the Mahayanistic doctrine as it is understood in the East, while he must not be lacking in adequate knowledge of Western philosophy and mode of thinking. The present translator has done his best to make the Mahayanistic thoughts of Açvaghosha as clear and intelligible as his limited knowledge and lack of philosophic training allow him. He is confident, however, that he has interpreted the Chinese text correctly. In spite of this, some errors may have crept into the present translation, and the translator will gladly avail himself of the criticisms of the Mahayana scholars to make corrections in case a second edition of the work is needed.

Teitaro Suzuki.

La Salle, Ill., May, 1900.

TABLE OF CONTENTS:

	PAGE
Introduction	1.

Date, 2; Nativity and Peregrination, 17; Appellations, 20; Conversion, 24; Lists of Patriarchs, 32; As an Artist, 34; Works in Chinese Translations, 36; Chinese Translations of the "Discourse on the Awakening of Faith," 38; Outlines of the "Discourse on the Awakening of Faith," 41.

Adoration 46

Discourse 48

I. Introductory, 49; II. General Statement, 52; III. The Explanation, 55; IV. Practice of Faith, 127; V. Benefits, 146.

Glossary 151

Index 155

NOTE.

The method of transliteration for Sanskrit words adopted in the present book is one used in Whitney's *Sanskrit Grammar*, but from lack of type sh has been substituted for s, r for the vowel r, n for all the different kinds of nasal n's, and m for m. Further, no distinction has been made in the footnotes between the dentals and the cerebrals; c and $ç$ are also often used indiscriminately there.

As to the method of transliteration for Chinese words, almost every Sinologue has his own; but the one used in this book is that of Sir T. Wade, which I think has been adopted more generally than others.

INTRODUCTION.

AÇVAGHOSHA, the first expounder of the Mahâ-yânistic doctrine and one of the deepest thinkers among the Buddhist patriarchs, is known to most Western Buddhist scholars simply as the author of the *Buddha-caritakdvya*,[1] the famous poem on the life of Buddha. The accounts of his life and of the significance of his philosophy are so few that the important influence exercised by him upon the development of the Mahâyâna Buddhism has been left almost entirely unnoticed. That he was one of the most eminent leaders among earlier Buddhists; that he was in some way or other connected with the third convocation in Kashmir, probably presided over by the Bhikshu Parçva; that he had a wonderful poetical genius which rendered great service in the propagation of Buddhism,—these facts sum up almost all the knowledge possessed by scholars about Açvaghosha. The reason why he is not known as he ought to be, is principally that the Sanskrit sources are extremely mea-

[1] *The Sacred Books of the East*, Vol. **XLIX**. Beal's English translation of the Chinese translation *The Fo sho hing tsan king*, *S. B. E.*, Vol. XIX.

gre, while the accounts obtainable from Chinese and Tibetan traditions are confusing and full of legends.

This fact has led Professor Kern to say that Açvaghosha was not an historical man, but a personification of Kâla, à form of Çiva.¹ But the sources from which the Professor draws his conclusion are rather too meagre and I fear are not worth serious consideration. In the following pages we shall see by what traditions Açvaghosha's life is known to the Buddhists of the East.

DATE

Let us first decide the date, which varies according to different authorities from three hundred to six hundred years after the Parinirvâna of Buddha.

1. The *Li tai san pao chi* (*fas*.. 1),² quoting the Record of the Sarvâstivâdin school, says: "Açvaghosha Bodhisattva was born a Brahman in Eastern India some three hundred years after the Nirvâna. After he abandoned his worldly life, he refuted all the doctrines held by the tîrthakas (heathen),³ and writing

---

¹*Der Buddhismus und seine Geschichte in Indien*, authorised German translation, Leipsic, 1884, Vol. II., p. 464.

²歷代三寶記 *Records of the Triratna Under Successive Dynasties*, compiled by 費長房 Fe Chang-fang, A. D. 597; 15 fasciculi.

³ Tîrthaka, which literally means "ascetics," was first applied to a definite sect, viz., the naked ascetics of the Jains, but was later on extended to all dissenters and has therefore been translated "heretics or heathen." The Chinese translation of the term literally means "[followers of] a doctrine other than Buddhism."

the *Mahâ-alamkâra-çâstra*[1] in several hundred verses (*ghâtâs*) greatly propagated the teachings of Buddha."

2. Hui-yuen[2] states in his commentary (*fas.* 1) on the *Mahâ-prajñâ-pâramitâ-çâstra*,[3] on the authority of Kumârajîva 鳩摩羅什 (A. D. 339-413), that Açvaghosha flourished about three hundred and seventy years after the Nirvâna.

3. In the *Life of Vasubandhu*,[4] Açvaghosha is mentioned as a contemporary of Kâtyâyana who is said in the same book to have been living in the fifth century after the Nirvâna.

4. The writer[5] of the preface to the second Chinese translation of the *Mahâyâna-çraddhotpâda-çâstra*[6] says that this Çâstra "is the deepest of the Mahâyâna texts. Five hundred years after the Nirvâna, Açvaghosha appeared in the world. He was numbered.

[1] Translated into Chinese by Kumârajîva, circa A. D. 405. 15 *fas.*

[2] 慧遠 A. D. 333-416. The leader of the Pai lien she (White Lotus Society), first Sukhâvatî sect movement in China.

[3] *Treatise on the Great Wisdom-Perfection*, by Nâgârjuna. A Chinese translation by Kumârajîva, A. D. 402-405. 100 *fas.*

[4] The original Sanskrit author is unknown. The present Chinese translation is by Paramârtha who came to China from Western India A. D. 546.

[5] The writer's name is not mentioned there, nor the date; but judging from the knowledge he shows in treating the subject, as we shall see later, he must have been living either at the time of this second translation or immediately after it.

[6] *Discourse on the Awakening of Faith in the Mahâyâna*, the principal work of Açvaghosha.

among the four suns [of Buddhists], and his teachings stood most prominently [among the doctrine prevailing] in the five countries of India."

5. Sang-ying[1] states in his preface to the Chinese translation of the *Mahâ-prajñâ-pâramitâ-çâstra* that Açvaghosha appeared towards the end of the period of Orthodoxy, i. e., five hundred years after the Nirvâna.

6. The *Fu tsou t'ung chi*[2] (Vol. V.) says that it was the fulfilment of the Tathâgata's prophecy that six hundred years after the Nirvâna the Dharma was transmitted to Açvaghosha.

7. This six hundred year prophecy is adopted as if it were an unquestionable fact, by Fa-tsang,[3] a learned commentator of the *Çraddhotpâdaçâstra* (*Discourse on the Awakening of Faith*).

8. Chih-k'ai 智愷, who was the copyist for Paramârtha when he translated the *Çraddhotpâdaçâstra*, also adheres to the six hundred year tradition in his preface to the book just mentioned, saying that some six hundred years after the Nirvâna of the Tathâgata, many devilish heretical leaders clamorously protested their false doctrines against the good law of Buddha,

---

[1] 僧叡 A. D. 362-439. One of the four famous disciples of Kumârajîva.

[2] 佛祖統記 A history of Buddhism, compiled by Chih-p'an 志磐, a Chinese priest, during the latter half of the thirteenth century. 54 *fas.*

[3] 643-712. A most prominent leader of the Avatamsaka sect in China.

when a Çrâmana of very high virtue, called Açvaghosha, thoroughly versed in the philosophy of the Mahâyâna Buddhism and highly compassionate for those ignorant people, wrote this Discourse (the *Çraddhotpâdaçâstra*), in order that he might increase the brilliancy of the Triratna, etc., etc.

9. The six hundred year tradition is very popular among Chinese and Japanese Buddhists. The *Fa tsu li tai tung tsai*[1] (*fas.* 5) also follows it.

10. The prophecy above referred to (see No. 8), which is doubtless a later invention, appears in the *Mahâmâyâ sûtra*[2] (*fas.* 2) as follows:

"After the death of Buddha, Mahâmâyâ asked Ânanda if Buddha had ever told him in his life anything concerning the future of Buddhism. Responding to this, Ânanda said: 'I heard one time Buddha say this with regard to the future decline of Buddhism: "After the Nirvâna Mahâkâçyapa with Ânanda will compile the Dharma-pitaka, and when it is settled Mahâkâçyapa will enter into a Nirodha-samâpatti in the Lang chi shan [i. e., Mount of Wolf's Track, Kukkurapadagiri], and Ânanda too obtaining the fruit

---

[1] 佛祖歷代通載 *A History of Buddha and the Patriarchs Through Successive Dynasties*, by Nien chang 念常, A. D. 1333. 36 *fas*.

[2] The Sûtra is also called the *Sûtra on Buddha's Ascent to the Trayastrimsa Heaven, to Teach the Dharma to His Mother* 2 *fas*. A second Chinese translation by Shih T'an-ching 釋曇景 of the Ch'i dynasty 齊 (A. D. 479-502). His nationality and life both are unknown.

of enlightenment will in turn enter into Parinirvâna, when the right doctrine will be transmitted to Upagupta who will in an excellent manner teach the essence of the Dharma.... When five hundred years are passed [after Buddha's death] a Bhikshu named Pao-tien [Ratnadeva?] will in an excellent manner teach the essence of the Dharma, converting twenty thousand people and causing all sentient beings in the eight creations to awaken the Anuttarasamyaksambodhicitta [most-perfect-knowledge-mind]: The right doctrine will then go to decline. When six hundred years [after Buddha's death] are expired, ninety different schools of the tîrthakas will arise and proclaiming false doctrines, each will struggle against the other to destroy the law of Buddha. Then a Bhikshu, Açvaghosha by name, will in an excellent manner teach the essence of the Dharma and defeat all the followers of the tîrthakas. When seven hundred years [after Buddha's death] are expired, a Bhikshu, Nâgârjuna by name, will in an excellent manner teach the essence of the Dharma, destroying the banner of false philosophy and lighting the torch of the right doctrine." ' "

11. Referring to the statement of the above mentioned Sûtra, Nâgârjuna, a famous Buddhist philosopher who wrote a commentary on Açvaghosha's work, called *Çraddhotpâdaçâstra*, claims that there were six Açvaghoshas at different times, to fulfil the prophecy of Buddha and that the author of the book on which

he writes a commentary¹ was one who appeared on earth according to the prophecy in the *Mahâmâyâ sûtra*. Nâgârjuna even states that he was a disciple of Açvaghosha, but the work itself is regarded as spu-

¹ The Sanskritised title is the *Mahâyâna-çâstra-vyâkhyâ*, trans. into Chinese by Pa-ti-mo-to 筏提摩多, an Indian priest, A. D. 401–402. 10 *fas*. The statements in full run as follows:

"In all there were six Açvaghoshas, owing to different predictions in the sûtras; each of them appeared to fulfil his mission according to the necessity of the time, and there is no contradiction in them."

The author then proceeds to make particular references to those sûtras:

"When we examine all different predictions in the sûtras taught by Buddha through his whole life, we find six different [personages all called Açvaghosha]. What are those six? (1) According to the 大乘本法契經 *Tai ch'êng pên fa ch'i ching* (*Mahâyânapûrvadharmasûtra?*) we have the following: When the peerless, great, enlightened, honored one was speaking about his intention of entering into Nirvâna, Açvaghosha rising from the seat knelt down, saluted Buddha's feet, and respectively joining his hands together turned towards Buddha, the world-honored one, and said this in verse: 'The peerless one whose heart is filled with great love and whose immeasurable virtues have been accumulated through æons which are like a boundless ocean, the Buddha, only on account of love and compassion for all sentient beings, now speaks about his entering into Nirvâna, and I and all the other members of the Samgha feel an unspeakable despair, utterly confused in mind and spirit. If even the world-honored one, full of great love, is going to another world, leaving his own children behind him, why then could not I who am not yet full of love and compassion go to another world following Buddha's steps? Who can blame me?' When finished uttering these words, Açvaghosha gazed at the pupil of Buddha's eye and gradually passed out of life. (2) The 變化功德契經 *Pien 'hua kung tê ch'i ching* (*Vikriyâpunyasûtra?*) says: Then the Bhagavat said to Açvaghosha: 'Three hundred years after my Nirvâna thou shalt obtain an inspiration from me and with various methods (*upâya*)

rious, on account of some obvious contradictions, though the followers of the Mantra sect (*Shingonshyu*) insist on its genuineness, because they are anxious to have an ancient authority for their own mystic doctrines, which are here supported.

benefit and make happy all beings in coming generations. When thou dost not have any inspiration from me, thou canst not do this by thyself. (3) The 摩訶摩耶契經 *Mahâmâyâsûtra* says as follows: 'When six hundred years are passed after the disappearance of the Tathâgata, ninety-six different schools of the tîrthakas will arise, and professing false doctrines, each will struggle against the other to destroy the law of Buddha. A Bhikshu called Açvaghosha, however, will in an excellent manner proclaim the essence of the Dharma and defeat all followers of the tîrthakas. (4) In the 常德三昧契經 *Ch'ang tê san mei ch'i ching* (*Sûtra on the Samâdhi of Eternal Merit*) we read: In the eight hundredth year after the Nirvâna there will be a wise man, Açvaghosha by name. Among the followers of the tîrthakas as well as those of Buddhism, he will refute all those who cherish heretical views and will establish the Dharma taught by Buddha. (5) In the 摩尼清淨契經 *Mo ni ch'ing ching ch'i ching* (*Manivimâlasûtra?*) is said thus: About one hundred years after the Nirvâna of Buddha, Açvaghosha Mahâsattva will appear on earth protect the right doctrine and safely hoist the banner of Buddhism. (6) In the 勝頂王契經 *Shêng ting wang ch'i ching* (*Crimûrdharâjasûtra?*) is said thus: On the seventeenth day after the enlightenment of Buddha there was a tîrthaka called 迦羅諾鳩尸摩 Chia-lo-no-chiu-shih-to (Kâlanakshita?), who transforming himself into the figure of a great nâgarâja (i. e., snake-king) with 86,000 heads and 86,000 tongues, simultaneously proposed 86,000 contradicting questions and asked the Tathâgata [for the solution]. He then gave him a triple answer explaining all those paradoxes. The nâgarâja then proposed tenfold questions, again asking the Tathâgata [for their solution], to which he gave a hundredfold answers and explained their paradoxes. When this dialogue came to an end, Buddha said to the nâgarâja: 'Very good, very good, O Açvaghosha Çrâmana! in order to guard the castle of the Dharma, thou hast assumed this form of destruction, estab-

Deeply absorbed in metaphysical speculation, the inhabitants of India paid very little attention to history, and whenever we endeavor to ascertain the date of important historical figures we are sure to find our way to certainty barred. So we cannot decide which of the conflicting traditions above enumerated is to be considered as authentic. When taken independently of other historical events which are connected with them and whose dates have been already fixed, they have no value whatever. Besides it should be observed, the chronology of Buddha, to which every one of the traditions makes reference, is as yet unsettled and must have been still more so at the time when those traditions were current in India as well as in China. If they differed as to the date of Buddha, they might have maintained the same date for Açvaghosha; no one can tell. We have to seek a light from another source.

Another group of traditions centering around Açvaghosha is his connexion with a most powerful king of Yüeh chih 月氏國, who established his extensive kingdom in Northwestern India. Who was this king? In the 雜寶藏經 *Tsa pao tsang ching* (*Samyuktaratna-*

lishing the doctrine of Buddha. Be patient, be patient, always discipline thyself in this way, always behave thyself in this way, do not go round in a small circle, but make a universal tour.' The nagârâja then abandoning his assumed beast-form revealed his own real character and approaching the peerless, honored one and saluting him said rejoicingly in verse, etc., etc. This is the sixth Açvaghosha."

piṭaka-sūtra?)[1], *fas.* 7, we read: "A king of Tukhāra, Candana Kanishṭha[2] (or Kanîta? Chinese 旃憻扇呢吒 *chan-tan-chi-ni ch'a*) had a close friendship with three wise men: the first one was a Bodhisattva, called Açvaghosha; the second, a minister of state called Mo-cha-lo (Maṭhara or Madara?); the third, an experienced physician called Chê-lo-chia (Caraka). With these three the king was on most intimate terms and treated them with the utmost cordiality, permitting them to approach his person. Açvaghosha said [one day] to him that if he [the king] would follow his advice, he would obtain in his coming life everything that was good, eternally put an end to all his misfortunes and forever be free from evil." . . .[3]

[1] *Sutra on the Casket of Miscellaneous Jewels.* The original Sanskrit author is unknown. Translated into Chinese by Chi-chia-yeh (吉迦夜 Kimkara?) of the Western country and T'an-yao 曇曜, A. D. 472. 8 *fas.* The original text is said to have existed at the time when the *Chêng-yüan Catalogue* 貞元錄 was compiled (A. D. 785-804) by Yüan-chao 圓照, a Buddhist priest of the Tang 唐 dynasty (A. D. 618-907).

[2] Does Kanishṭha, which literally means "youngest," refer to th youngest of the three brothers who successively governed the Tukhâra district of India? If so, there is no question about the identity of him and King Kanishka.

[3] The *Fu fa tsang ch'uan* (*Transmission of the Dharma-piṭaka*), *fas.* 5, also seems to refer to the same tradition, for it is stated that when a king of Tukhâra (probably Kanishka) was very much afflicted on account of his having committed many atrocious deeds in the war with Parthia (Eastern Persia), Açvaghosha told him that if he would follow the Dharma with a sincere heart, his sin would gradually be attenuated; and also that the same king had a physician called Caraka "who thoroughly understood phar-

Açvaghosha's relation with King Candana Kanishtha (or Kanîta? Chinese Chi-ni-ch'a) is told also in the *Fu fa tsang yin yüan ch'uan,*[1] *fas.* 5: "[At that time] the king of Tukhâra was very powerful. He was called Candana Kanishṭha [or Kanîta? Chinese Chi-ni-ch'a]. Being very ambitious and bold, and far superior in courage to all his contemporaries, every country he invaded was sure to be trampled down under his feet. So when he advanced his four armies towards Pâṭaliputra [Hua shih ch'êng in Chinese], the latter was doomed to defeat in spite of some desperate engagements. The king demanded an indemnity of 900,000,000 gold pieces, for which the defeated king offered Açvaghosha, the Buddha-bowl and a compassionate fowl, each being considered worth 300,000,000 gold pieces. The Bodhisattva Acvaghosha had intellectual powers inferior to none; the Buddha-bowl having been carried by the Tathâgata himself is full of merits; the fowl being of compassionate nature, would not drink any water with worms in it,—thus all these having merits enough to keep off all enemies, they are on that account worth macy, and who was clever, learned, intelligent, elegant, meek, and compassionate," etc.

[1] 付法藏因緣傳 *Accounts Relating to the Transmission of the Dharmapiṭaka.* 6 *fas.* The original Sanskrit author is unknown. The third Chinese translation now existent is by Chi-chia-yeh (Kimkara?) of the Western country, A. D. 472. The original text is said to have been existing when the *Chêng yüan Catalogue* (A. D. 785-804) was compiled.

900,000,000 gold pieces.[1] The king [of Tukhâra] was greatly pleased at receiving them, and immediately withdrawing his army from the land went back to his own kingdom."

We have the same legend stated in a brief biography[2] of Açvaghosha as follows:

"After that a king of the smaller Yüeh chih country [i. e., Tukhâra] in North India invaded the Middle country [i. e., Magadha]. When the besieging had continued for some time, the king of Central India sent a message [to the invader] saying: "If there be anything you want, I will supply it; do not disturb the piece of my people by thus long staying here,' to which this reply was given: 'If you really ask a surrender, send me 300,000,000 gold pieces; I will release you.' The [besieged] king said: 'Even this entire kingdom cannot produce 100,000,000 gold pieces, how can I supply you with 300,000,000?' The answer was: 'There are in your country two great treasures: (1) the Buddha-bowl,[1] (2) a Bhikshu of

---

[1] This is a comical feature of the legend, for if these treasures could ward off all enemies why did they not protect the unfortunate king of Pâtaliputra against Kanishtha?

[2] *Life of Açvaghosha* 馬鳴菩薩傳, translated into Chinese by Kumârajîva. Very short. The author is unknown. The original Sanskrit text is stated in the *Chêng yüan Catalogue* to have been existing at that time Cf. Wassijew's *Buddhismus*, German edition, p. 231 et seq.

[3] Fa-hien 法顯 states that Kanishka (which is transliterated by him into Chinese Chi-ni-chia 罽賦迦, corresponding to Sanskrit Kanika) as if a different person from the king of Yüeh chih

wonderful talent (i. e., Açvaghosha). Give them to me, they are worth 300,000,000 gold pieces.' The [besieged] king said: 'Those two treasures are what I most revere, I cannot give them up. Thereupon the Bhikshu said to the king in explanation of the Dharma:

"'All sentient beings are everywhere the same, while Buddhism, deep and comprehensive, aims at universal salvation, and the highest virtue of a great man consists in delivering [all] beings. As our temporal administration is very liable to meet obstructions, even your rule does not extend itself outside of this one kingdom. If you, on the other hand, propose a wide propagation of Buddhism, you would naturally be a Dharmarâja over the four oceans. The duty of a Bhikshu is to save [all] the people and not to give preference to one or the other. Merits lie in our heart; truth makes no distinction. Pray, be far-sighted, and do not think only of the present.'

"The king who was from the first a great admirer of him, respectfully followed his advice and delivered him to the king of Yüeh chih who returned with him to his own kingdom.

Comparing all these traditions, we are naturally led to the conclusion that Açvaghosha, who was numbered as one of the four suns[1] of Buddhism, must have

who invaded Gandhâra to get the Buddha-bowl. *Vide* Legge's translation of Fa-hien, pp. 33 and 34.

[1] Hsüen-tsang's 玄奘, *Records of Western Countries*, Beal's English translation, Vol. II., p. 302.

had a very powerful influence over the spiritual India
of the time, that the king who wished to have him as
a spiritual adviser must have been a very devoted Buddhist so as to accept a Bhikshu instead of an enormous sum of money, and that such a devoted Buddhist
king, ruling over the vast domain which extended
from the bank of the Indus towards the lower Ganges,
must have been living sometime between the third
and sixth century after the Nirvâna, whatever the
authentic date of Buddha might be. The next conclusion we can advance therefore will be the identification of this king who is called Candana Kanishtha
or Kanîta in the above stories, with Kanishka,[1] the
originator of the third Buddhist convocation in Kashmir.

As to the difference of the name, we have to say
this. While Hsüen-tsang's transliteration for Kanishka
is Chia-ni-shê-chia 迦貳色迦 which is quite an approximate reproduction of the original sounds, the Chinese
method of transliteration before his time by the so-
called "old translators" was rather irregular, loose
and therefore often misleading. Add to this the liability to error on the part of local dialects, and we do not
improperly identify Chi-ni-ch'a, with Kanishka, while
the former may be Sanskritised Kanishta or Kanîta.[2]

[1] A. D. 85-106, according to M. Müller.

[2] One objection to identifying Chi-ni-ch'a 罽呢吒 (Kanishtha
or Kanîta) with Kanishka 迦貳色迦 is a single Chinese character
appearing in the *Mahâlamkâraçâstra* (*Book of Great Glory*), the
work ascribed to Açvaghosha. In *fas.* 3 as well as *fas.* 6 of the

In further support of this view, we quote from the *Journal of the Buddhist Text Society*, Vol. I., Part 3, an article on King Kanishka, taken from a Tibetan source, which bears a more historical appearance than the legends above referred to. The abstract is:

"Kanishka, king of Palhâva and Delhi,[1] was born four hundred years after the Nirvâna. When he learned that Simha, king of Kashmir, abandoned the worldly life to become a Buddhist priest under the name of Sudarçana and obtained Arhatship, he went to Kashmir and heard a sermon delivered by Sudarçana.[2] At that time a Mahâyâna priest who held a most prom-

<small>same book referring to Candana Kanishtha or Kanita, the writer says : " 我昔曾聞旃檀罽呢吒 *Wo hsi ch'ang wên, chan-t'an chi-ni-chá wang*," i. e., "I heard of old that King Candana Kanishtha," etc. (in *fas.* 6., chia-ni ch'a), etc., etc. The Chinese character *hsi* usually means "of yore" or "in olden times," but it also signifies the past indefinitely, near as well as distant. If we thus understand the term in the sense of "some time ago," or simply "once," there will be no difficulty in demonstrating that Açvaghosha was an elder contemporary of Kanishka, though we cannot apparently accept the Chinese tradition which says they were intimately known to each other. Because in that case Açvaghosha would not refer to the king in such a hearsay manner as stated in the book above mentioned. Taking all in all, this does not prevent us asserting that they were contemporaneous.</small>

<small>[1] Cf. A. Schiefner's German translation of Târanâtha's *History of Buddhism*, p. 89: "Nachdem König Çritschandra die Herrschaft ausgeübt hatte, waren viele Jahre vergangen, als im Westen im Lande Tili und Mâlava ein an Jahren junger König Kanika in die Herrschaft gewählt wurde."</small>

<small>[2] Târanâtha's statement differs from this According to him Kanika and Kanishka are not the same king; the former being that of Tili and Málava, while the latter that of Jâlamdhara. *Vide* pp. 58 and 96. Târanâtha might have confused them.</small>

inent position in northern countries was called Açvaghosha. His influence in the spiritual world was as incomparable as the temporal power of Kanishka who conquered Kashmir and Jâlamdhara. **The king sent a message to Açvaghosha to come to his kingdom, who, however, owing to his old age, could not accept the invitation, but sent him a leading disciple of his called Jñânayaça, accompanied with a letter treating the essential points of Buddhism."**[1]

Though the Tibetan tradition considerably differs in many respects from the Chinese accounts above mentioned, they both agree in this point that Açvaghosha and Kanishka had some intercourse, or that at least they were contemporaneous and known to each other. So we may take it as an established fact that Açvaghosha, the author of the 大乘起信論 *Mahâyânaçraddhotpâda-çâstra* (*Discourse on the Awakening of Faith in the Mahâyâna*), was living at the time of Kanishka.[2]

I do not think there is any need here to enumerate all different opinions about the time of Kanishka, which has been already approximately fixed by the untiring investigation of European scholars, such as Princep, Lassen, Cunningham, Wilson, Fergusson,

---

[1] Târanâtha also states this event (*Geschichte des Buddhismus*, p. 92). But the king is not Kanishka, but Kanika, and the name of the disciple is not Jñânayaça but Dschnânakriya.

[2] A further corroboration of this view will be met with when we treat later on of the conversion of Açvaghosha by Parçva or his disciple Puṅyayaças.

Max Müller, and others.[1] So long as our present aim is to assign the time of Açvaghosha more definitely than stating vaguely some three or five hundred years after the Nirvâna of Buddha, suffice it to say that he lived at the time extending from the latter half of the first century before Christ to about 50 or 80 A. D. If we fix the date of Buddha's death in the fifth century before Christ, Açvaghosha must be said to have lived during the six hundredth year after the Nirvâna. At the very most his time cannot be placed later than the first century of the Christian era.

I have spared no pains, even at the risk of tediousness, in gathering all the information obtainable from Chinese sources relative to the date of Açvaghosha, because this date is of paramount importance when we enter into the discussion of the development of the Mahâyâna Buddhism, which is commonly and erroneously considered to be the sole work of Nâgârjuna.

NATIVITY AND PEREGRINATIONS.

There is not so much discordance in the traditions about the wanderings of Açvaghosha as about his date, though indeed we do not have as yet any mean of ascertaining his birth-place, other than the statements

[1] Max Müller's opinion, as stated before, is that Kanishka lived A. D. 85–106; Lassen thinks the Gondopharean dynasty was succeeded by Kanishka, king of the Yüeh chih, about one hundred years before Christ ; Princep places his reign during the first century A. D ; Cunningham thinks his consecration was 58 A. D.; Fergusson, 79 A. D ; Rhys Davids, about 10 A. D., etc.

of discordant authorities. According to Târanâtha,[1] he was a son of a rich Brahman called Samghaguhya who married the tenth and youngest daughter of a merchant in Khorta. As a youth, when thoroughly familiar with every department of knowledge, he went to Odiviça, Gaura, Tîrahuti, Kâmarûpa, and some other places, defeating everywhere his Buddhist opponents by his ingenious logic.

All these places are situated in Eastern India, and among the Chinese traditions the *Record of the Triratna* (*Li tai san pao chi*) as well as the *Accounts of Buddha and the Patriarchs* (*Fo tsu tung chi*) agree with Târanâtha in placing Açvaghosha's native land in the East; but the *Life of Vasubandhu* makes Açvaghosha a native of Bhâshita in Çrâvastî, while in Nâgârjuna's work, *the Mahdyânaçdstravydkhyd* 釋摩訶衍論 (*Shih mo ho yen lun*), he is mentioned as having been born in Western India, Loka being the father and Ghoṇâ the mother. The *Record of Buddha and the Patriarchs Under Successive Dynasties* (*Fo tsu li tai t'ung tsai*) agrees with neither of the above statements, for it says (*fasciculi* 5): "The twelfth patriarch, Açvaghosha Mahâsattva was a native of Vârâṇasî." A further contradicting tradition is pointed out by Prof. S. Murakami in one of his articles on the history of Buddhism,[2] quoting the *Shittanzô* 悉曇藏 (*fas.* 1), which makes Açvaghosha a man of South India.

[1] *Geschichte des Buddhismus*, p. 90
[2] The *Bukkyô Shirin*, Vol. I., No. 6. 1894. Tokyo, Japan.

A majority of the traditions place his native country in East India; but there is no means of confirming these. One thing, however, seems to be certain, namely, that Açvaghosha was not born in the northern part of India, which place is supposed by most Western Buddhist scholars to be the cradle of the Mahâyâna school.

Wherever the native country of Açvaghosha may have been, both the Chinese and Tibetan records agree that he made a journey to Central India, or Magadha. It seems that every intellectual man in India, the people of which, living in affluence, were not occupied with the cares of making a living, sought to gain renown by dialectics and subtle reasonings, and Açvaghosha, as a Brahman whose "intellectual acquirements were wonderfully deep," and whose "penetrating insight was matchless,"[1] could not resist the temptation. Not satisfied with his intellectual campaign against commonplace Buddhists in his neighborhood, who were crushed down as "rotten wood before a raging hurricane,"[2] he went, according to a Chinese tradition, to Pâtaliputra, and according to the Tibetan, to Nâlanda. The *Life of Açvaghosha* evidently refers to this fact when it states that Pârçva, the eleventh patriarch and eventual teacher of Açvaghosha, on being informed of the paramount influence of the Brah-

---

[1] The *Transmission of the Dharmapitaka* (*Fu fa tsang ch'uan, fas.* 5).

[2] The same as above.

man tîrthaka (i. e., Açvaghosha) in Central India and of the fact that his conquest over Buddhists had silenced the bell (*ghanta*) in some monastery (*vihára*), journeyed from Northern India to convert the bitterest opponent into a faithful follower of Buddha. He adds that Açvaghosha left his home and lived henceforth in Central India. But according to the *Transmission of the Dharmapitaka* (*Fu fa tsang ch'uan, fas.* 5) we find Açvaghosha even after his conversion still in Pâtaliputra, from which he was taken by King Kanishka to the latter's own capital, Gandhâra, in the Northwest of India.

Thus all that we can say about the birth-place and wanderings of Açvaghosha is: (1) he was a Brahman by birth either of South, or of West, or of East, but not of North India; (2) he acquired in Central India his highest reputation as a Brahman disputant, and, after his conversion, as the greatest Buddha follower of the time, intellectually as well as morally; (3) his later life was spent according to the Chinese authority in the North where he wrote probably the *Mahâlamkâra-sûtraçdstra* (*Book of Great Glory*) which describes matters mostly relating to Western India.

APPELLATIONS.

The author of the *Mahâyânaçraddhotpâdaçâstra* (*Discourse on the Awakening of Faith in the Mahâyâna*) is most commonly known in the Chinese Buddhist literature by the name of Açvaghosha. But according to his *Life* he was also called Kung-tê-jih 功德日 (i. e., merit-sun; in Sanskrit, Puṇyaditya?). For he was not only a philosopher, but a preacher and an organiser, for "while in North India he widely propagated the doctrine of Buddha, led and benefited the masses, and through good and excellent [missionary] methods perfected the merits of the people." The *Record of Buddha and the Patriarchs* (*Fo tsou t'ung tsai*), where it is stated that his other name was Kung-chang 功勝 (Puṇyaçrîka?), can be said almost to agree with the above. While thus no other name or appellation of his is known in China, Târanâtha mentions nine more names: Kâla (Time), Durdarsha (Hard-to-be-seen), Durdarshakâla (Hard-to-be-seen-time), Mâtrceta (Mother-child), Pitrceta (Father-child), Çûra (Hero), Dharmika-Subhûti (Virtuous-mighty), and Maticitra (Intelligence-bright).[1]

In I-tsing's *Correspondence from the South Sea* (*Nan hai chi kuei ch'uan*,[2] Chap. 32, "On chanting"), the name Mâtrceta is mentioned, but I-tsing does not identify him with Açvaghosha, though the legend attached to the former closely resembles that of the latter told in Târanâtha. Târanâtha states that when Açvaghosha became a sthavira and advocate of the

[1] *Geschichte des Buddhismus*, p. 90.

[2] 南海寄歸傳 by I-tsing 義淨 who left China A. D. 671 for a pilgrimage to India and came back A. D. 695. The book is a work on the vinaya as observed by the Sarvastivâdin, which the pilgrim witnessed in India as well as in Ceylon. An English translation by J. Takakusu, London.

Tripitaka, he had a dream one night in which the venerable Târâ gave him the instruction to write hymns on Buddha for the expiation of his former sinful deeds; that according to this admonition he wrote many hymns praising the virtues of Buddha, amongst which one containing one hundred and fifty çlokas[1] is the best of all; that the hymns composed by him are full of benediction like the very words of Buddha, because he was predicted by the Blessed One to be a hymnist.[2]

Compare the above with this from I-tsing:

"The venerable Mâtrceta (Mother-child) was a man of great intellect, of excellent virtue, eminently standing above all sages in India. A tradition says that when Buddha was taking a walk one time with his kinsmen, disciples, and many other people, a nightingale (?), observing his personal feature as elegant and majestic as a gold mountain, uttered in the wood some pleasant, harmonious notes that sounded like praising the virtues of Buddha. Buddha then turning towards the disciples said: 'The bird overcome by the joy of seeing me utters a pitiful cry. By this merit it will after my death obtain a human form,-Mâtrceta 摩底哩制吒 by name, and praise and adore my intrinsic virtues with a number of hymns.' This man first followed the doctrine of a tîrthaka worshipping Maheç-

---

[1] Schiefner notes: Çatapantschâçatika nâma stotra, Tandjur B. I, unter den Stotra's.
[2] *Geschichte des Buddhismus*, p. 91.

vara[1] and composed many hymns to adore him. But in the meantime he came across his own name recorded [in a Buddhist writing]; inspired by this, he took refuge in Buddha, changed his garb, abandoned his laymanship, and in many ways praised, honored and adored Buddha. Regretting his misbehavior in the past and desiring to perform good deeds in the future and also lamenting the unfortunate fate that prevented him from having a personal interview with the Great Teacher rather than bowing before his bequeathed image, he at last decided with all his rhetorical talent and in solemn fulfilment of the Lord's prophecy, to praise his virtues and merits [in hymns]. He first composed four hundred çlokas and then one hundred and fifty çlokas;[2] all of which describe the six Pâramitâs [Perfections] and state the excellent virtues possessed by the World-Honored-One," etc.

At the end of the same Chapter (i. e., Chap. 32) in I-tsing's *Correspondence* he refers to Açvaghosha and Nagârjuna both of whom composed some beautiful and popular hymns that were sung by Buddhists throughout India at the time of his pilgrimage. But if the Tibetan statement is reliable, I-tsing may have

---

[1] Cf. the following statement in Târanâtha, p. 90 "Als er (Açvaghosha) in den Mantra- und Tantra-Formeln und in der Dialektik sehr bewandert wurde, gab ihm Maheçvara selbst Anleitung."

[2] "Hymn of One Hundred and Fifty Çlokas" (Çatapancashad buddhastotra), translated into Chinese by I-tsing during his stay in the Nâlanda-vihâra, Central India. At the time of the compilation of the *Cheng yüan catalogue* the original is said to have existed.

been mistaken in recording Açvaghosha and Mâtrceṭa as different characters. The Tibetan and Chinese version of the one hundred and fifty çloka hymn being still existent, the comparison of which, however, I have not yet been able to make, will furnish an interesting testimony for the identification.

Many legendary explanations have been invented about the name of Açvaghosha, as might be expected of the imaginative Indian mind, but not being worth while quoting from the materials at my command, no reference will be made to them here.

CONVERSIONS.

A consensus of traditions both Tibetan and Chinese maintains that Açvaghosha was in his earlier life a most powerful adherent of Brahmanism, though we are tempted to discredit it on the ground that later Buddhist writers may have wished to exaggerate the superiority of Buddhism to all other Indian philosophical and religious doctrines, by chronicling the conversion of one of its strongest opponents to their side. Whatever the origin of the legend may be, how did his conversion take place? By whom was he converted? About these points the Tibetan and the Chinese tradition by no means agree, the one standing in a direct contradiction to the other. While the Tibetan account is full of mystery and irrationality, the Chinese is natural enough to convince us of its probable occurrence.

THE AWAKENING OF FAITH. 25

According to Târanâtha[1] Âryadeva, the most eminent disciple of Nâgârjuna, defeated and proselyted Açvaghosha,[2] not by his usual subtlety in dialectics, but by the superiority of his magical arts. Açvaghosha made use of every tantric formula he could command, in order to free himself from the enchantment in which he was held by his enemy, but all to no purpose whatever. Thus when he was in an utterly desperate condition, he happened to read the Buddhist Sûtra which was kept in his place of confinement and in which he found his destiny prophesied by Buddha,[3] he was seized with deep regret for his former hostile attitude toward the Dharma, and immediately renouncing his tîrthakism, professed the doctrine of Çâkyamuni.

The Tibetan tradition presents some unmistakable indications of a later invention: the use of tantric formulæ, the so-called prophecy of the Tathâgata, and the anachronism of Âryadeva. On the other hand, the Chinese records are worth crediting, though they are not unanimous as to how the conversion took place and who was the proselytist.

According to the *Life of Açvaghosha*, Parçva[4] was

---

[1] *Geschichte des Buddhismus*, German translation by Schiefner, pp. 84-85.

[2] He is mentioned there by the name of Durdarshakâla.

[3] Cf. this with the accounts of Mâtrceṭa-Açvaghosha told in I-tsing.

[4] The conversion of Açvaghosha by Parçva as here stated may be considered an addition to the proof already demonstrated for the contemporaneousness of Açvaghosha and King Kanishka; for

the man who converted him. They agreed at their first meeting that on the seventh day thence they should have the king, ministers, çrâmanas, tîrthakas and all great teachers of the Dharma gathered in the Vihâra and have their discussion there before all those people. "In the sixth night the sthavira entered into a samâdhi and meditated on what he had to do [in the morning]. When the seventh day dawned, a great crowd was gathered like clouds. The Sthavira Parçva arrived first and ascended a high platform with an unusually pleasant countenance. The tîrthaka [i. e., Açvaghosha] came later and took a seat opposite him. When he observed the çrâmana with a pleasant countenance and in good spirits, and when he also observed his whole attitude showing the manner of an able opponent, he thought: 'May he not be Bhikshu Chin? His mind is calm and pleasant, and besides he bears the manner of an able antagonist. We shall indeed have an excellent discussion to-day.'

"They then proposed the question how the defeated one should be punished. The tîrthaka [Açvaghosha] said: 'The defeated one shall have his tongue cut out.' The sthavira replied: 'No, he shall become a disciple [of the winner] as the acknowledgement of defeat.' The tîrthaka then replied: 'Let it be so,' and asked, 'Who will begin the discussion?' The

---

Parçva, according to the Tibetan as well as the Chinese authority, was a co-operator at least, if not the president, of the third Buddhist convocation promoted by the King of Kashmir.

Sthavira Parçva said: 'I am more advanced in age; I came from afar for the purpose [of challenging you]; and moreover I was here this morning earlier than you. So it will be most natural for me to speak first.' The tîrthaka said: 'Let it be so. Following the subject of your argument, I shall completely baffle you.'

"The Sthavira Parçva then said: 'What shall we have to do, in order to keep the kingdom in perfect peace, to have the king live long, to let the people enjoy abundance and prosperity, all free from evils and catastrophies?' The tîrthaka was silent, not knowing what to reply. As now according to the rule of discussion one who could not make a response is defeated, Açvaghosha was obliged to bow [before the opponent] as a disciple of his. He had his head shaved, was converted to a çrâmana, and instructed in the perfection-precepts.

"When he [Açvaghosha] was alone in his room, he was absorbed in gloomy, unpleasant reflexion as to why he, possessing a bright intellect and far-sighted discretion, and having his reputation widely spread all over the world, could be defeated with a single question and be made a disciple of another. Parçva well knew his mind and ordered him to come to his room where the master manifested himself in several supernatural transformations. Açvaghosha now fully recognised that his master was not a man of ordinary type, and thus feeling happy and contented, thought it his duty to become one of his disciples.

"The master told him: 'Your intellect is bright enough, hard to find its equal; but it wants a final touch. If you study the doctrine I have mastered, attend to my capability and insight into the Bodhi, and if you become thoroughly versed in the method of discussion and clearly understand the principle of things, there will be no one who can match you in the whole world.'

"The master returned to his own country [North India]; the disciple remained in Central India, making an extensive study of the Sûtras, seeking a clear comprehension of the doctrine, Buddhistic as well as non-Buddhistic. His oratorical genius swept everything before him, and he was reverentially honored by the four classes of the people, including the king of [Central] India who treated him as a man of distinction."

According to the *Transmission of the Dharmapitaka* (*Fu fa tsang chuan*), however, Açvaghosha was not converted by Parçva, but by his disciple and patriarchal successor, Punyayaças. Though the two works, *Life of Açvaghosha* and the book just mentioned, differ in some other points, they are evidently two different versions of the one original legend. As the book is not as yet accessible to English readers, I here produce the whole matter translated from the Chinese version. The comparison will prove interesting.

"Full of a proud and arrogant spirit that speedily grew like a wild plant, he [Açvaghosha] firmly believed in the existence of an ego-entity and cherished the ultra-egotistic idea. Being informed that an Âcarya called Puṇyayaças, who, deep in knowledge and wide in learning, proclaimed that all things are relative [=çûnya, lit. empty], there is no âtman, no pudgala; Açvaghosha's arrogant spirit asserted itself, and presenting himself to Puṇyayaças challenged him saying: 'I confute all [false] opinions and doctrines in the world, as hailstones strike tender grass. If my declaration prove false and not true, I will have my own tongue cut out in acknowledgment of defeat.' Thereupon Puṇyayaças explained to him that Buddhism distinguishes two kinds of truth, that while 'practical truth' hypothetically admits the existence of an âtman, there is nothing conditional in 'pure [or absolute] truth,' all being calm and tranquil, and that therefore we cannot prove the ego as an absolute entity.

"Açvaghosha would not yet surrender himself, because being over-confident of his own intellectual power he considered himself to have gained the point. Puṇyayaças said: 'Carefully think of yourself; tell not a lie. We will see which of us has really won.'

"Açvaghosha meanwhile came to think that while 'practical truth' being only conditional has no reality at all, 'pure truth' is calm and tranquil in its nature, and that therefore these two forms of truth are all unobtainable, and that if they have thus no actuality [or existence], how could they be refuted [as false]? So feeling now the superiority of his opponent, he tried to cut out his tongue in acknowledgement of the defeat. But Puṇyayaças stopped him, saying: 'We teach a doctrine of love and compassion, and do not demand that you cut out your tongue. Have your head shaved instead and be my disciple.' Açvaghosha thus converted was made a çrâmana by Punyayaças.

"But Açvaghosha who felt extremely ashamed of his [former] self-assumption was thinking of attempting his own life. Puṇyayaças, however, attaining arhatship, entered into a samâdhi and divined what was going on in the mind of Açvaghosha. He ordered him to go and bring some books out of the library. Açvaghosha said to the Âcarya: 'The room is perfectly dark; how can I get in there?' To this Punyayaças answered: 'Just go in, and I shall let you have light.' Then the Âcarya through his supernatural power stretched far into the room his right hand whose five fingers each radiating with light illuminated everything inside of the walls. Açvaghosha thought it a mental hallucination, and knowing the fact that a hallucination as a rule disappears when one is conscious of it, he was surprised to see the

---

[1] The reasoning is somewhat unintelligible. The passages must be defective, and although I might venture to supply the necessary words to make them more logical and intelligible to the general reader who is not acquainted with the çûnyatâ philosophy, I have not tried to do so, thinking that it is enough here if we see in what the subject of the discussion consisted.

light glowing more and more. He tried his magical arts to extinguish it till he felt utterly exhausted, for the mysterious light suffered no change whatever. Finally coming to realise that it was the work of no other person than his teacher, his spirit was filled with remorse, and he thenceforth applied himself diligently to religious discipline and never relapsed."[1]

The *Record of Buddha and the Patriarchs* (*Fo tsou tung tsai*) agrees with the *Transmission of the Dharmapitaka* (*Fu fa tsang chuan*) in making Puṇyayaças, instead of Parçva, the master of the conversion. But the former does not state how Açvaghosha was converted.

Though so far it remains an open question who was the real master of Açvaghosha, we can be sure of this, that he had intimate spiritual communication with both Parçva and Puṇyayaças. Parçva, who was an older contemporary of Puṇyayaças, was probably already advanced in age when Acvaghosha came to be personally acquainted with him, and so he did not have time enough to lead the young promising disciple to a consummate understanding of the doctrine of Buddha. After the demise of this venerable old patriarch, Açvaghosha therefore had to go to Punyayaças for a further study of his religion, till he was capable of forming his own original thoughts, which are set forth in his principal work, the *Discourse of*

[1] The *Transmission of the Dharmapitaka* (*Fu fa tsang chuan*) *fas.* 5.

the *Awakening of Faith* (*Çraddhotpâda-çastra*). This assumption is justified when we notice that Açvaghosha in the *Book of Great Glory* pays his homage to Parçva as well as to Puṇyayaças.

Now by way of a supplementary note to the above, let us say a word about Wassiljew's observation,[1] which states that while Hînayânists or Çrâvakas ascribe the conversion of Açvaghosha to Parçva, the Mahâyânistic record says that Âryadeva converted him. This assertion is evidently incorrect, for the *Life of Açvaghosha* as well as the *Transmission of the Dharmapitaka* (*Fu fa tsang chuan*) in which the honor of his conversion is given to the successor of Parçva as aforesaid, do not certainly belong to the work of the Hînayâna school. It is the Tibetan tradition only, and not the general Mahâyânist statement, that Âryadeva converted Açvaghosha, and there is no ground at all for the assertion of Wassiljew, which practically leads us to take everything Tibetan for Mahâyânistic and everything Chinese for Hînayânistic.

LISTS OF PATRIARCHS

The incorrectness of the Tibetan story, as to the conversion of Açvaghosha by Âryadeva above referred to, is further shown by a list of the Buddhist patriarchs in India appearing in various Buddhist books either translated from Sanskrit into Chinese or com-

[1] *Buddhismus*, German edition, p. 222, and also see Târanâtha, translated by Schiefner, p. 311.

piled in China from sundry sources. In every one of them Açvaghosha is placed after Parçva or Puṇya-

	THE PO TSU T'UNG TSAI	THE PO TSU T'UNG CHI	THE FU FA TSANG CHUAN	BUDDHABHADRA[1]	SARVÂSTI-VÂDIN
1	Mahâkâçyapa	Mahâkâçyapa	Mahâkâçyapa	Ânanda	Mahâkâçyapa
2	Ânanda	Ânanda	Ânanda	Madhyântika	Ânanda
3	Çaṇavâsa	Çaṇavâsa	Çaṇavâsa	Çaṇavâsa	Madhyântika
4	Upagupta	Upagupta	Upagupta	Upagupta	Çaṇavâsa
5	Dṛtaka	Dṛtaka	Dṛtaka	Kâtyâyana	Upagupta
6	Micchaka	Micchaka	Micchaka	Vasumitra	Maitreya
7	Vasumitra	Buddhanandi	Buddhanandi	Kṛshṇa	Kâtyâyana
8	Buddhânandi	Buddhamitra	Buddhamitra	Parçva	Vasumitra
9	Buddhamitra	Parçva	Parçva	Açvaghosha	Kṛshṇa
10	Parçva	Puṇyayaças	Puṇyayaças	Ghosha	Parçva
11	Puṇyayaças	Açvaghosha	Açvaghosha		Açvaghosha
12	Açvaghosha	Kapi	Kapimala		Kumârata
13	Kapimala	Nâgârjuna	Nâgârjuna		
14	Nâgârjuna	Kanadeva			
15	Kanadeva (Âryadeva)				
...					
34					Nâgârjuna
35					Deva

[1] He was a native of Kapilavastu and came to China A D. 406. A translator of many Sanskrit works. His list belongs to the Sarvâstivâdin, though it is a little different from the succeeding one. The former contains fifty-four and the latter fifty-three patriarchs. See the *Ch'u san tsang chi chi* 出三藏記集 by 僧祐 (Nanjo's Catalogue, No. 1476).

yaças, and before both Nâgârjuna and Âryadeva, the most brilliant disciple of the former. The list on the opposite page, therefore, as noticed elsewhere, will furnish good material for fixing the time of Açvaghosha. It does not make any practical difference whether he was converted by Parçva himself or his immediate successor and disciple Puṇyayaças, because it is most probable they all were contemporaneous. The list generally gives twenty-three or twenty-eight patriarchs beginning with Mahâkâçyapa, but not deeming it necessary to give a complete list, I have cut it short at Deva.

Chieh-sung[1] refutes in his *Chuan fa chang tsung lun* 傳法正宗論 (*A Treatise on the Right Transmission of the Dharma*) the authority of the *Transmission of the Dharmapitaka* (*Fu fa tsang chuan*), but he agrees with it down to the seventeenth patriarch. The principal point of his refutation is simply that Bodhidharma, the founder of the Chinese Dhyâna school, should be included in the list.

AS AN ARTIST.

We cannot conclude the accounts concerning Açvaghosha without mentioning an anecdote from a Chinese source.[2] The *Çraddhotpâdaçâstra* (*The Awak-*

---

[1] 晉昇, a priest of the Dhyâna school who died A. D. 1071 or 1072. He wrote among other works one on the fundamental identicalness of Confucianism and Buddhism.

[2] The *Transmission of the Dharmapitaka* (*Fu fa tsang chuan, fas.* 5).

THE AWAKENING OF FAITH. 35

ening of Faith,) proves he was a philosopher of a high grade; the *Buddhacaritakâvya* (*The Life of Buddha*) and the *Mahâlamkâraçâstra* (*The Book of Great Glory*) reveal his poetical genius; and the following story indicates that he was a musician :[1]

"He [Açvaghosha] then went to Pâtaliputra for his propaganda-tour, where he composed an excellent tune called Lai cha huo lo (賴吒和羅 *Râstavara?*), that he might by this means convert the people of the city. Its melody was classical, mournful, and melodious, inducing the audience to ponder on the misery, emptiness, and non-âtman-ness of life. That is to say, the music roused in the mind of the hearer the thought that all aggregates are visionary and subject to transformation; that the triple world is a jail and a bondage, with nothing enjoyable in it; that since royalty, nobility, and the exercise of supreme power, are all characterised with transitoriness, nothing can prevent their decline, which will be as sure as the dispersion of the clouds in the sky; that this corporeal existence is a sham, is as hollow as a plantain tree, is an enemy, a foe, one not to be intimately related with; and again that like a box in which a cobra is kept, it should

---

[1] The fact agrees well with Târanâtha's statement which in its German translation reads as follows: "Die von ihm verfassten Loblieder sind auch in allen Ländern verbreitet; da zuletzt Sänger und Possenreisser dieselben vortrugen und bei allen Menschen des Landes mit Macht Glauben an den Buddha entstand, erwuchs durch die Loblieder grösserer Nutzen zur Verbreitung der Lehre." *Geschichte des Buddhismus*, German translation, p. 91.

never be cherished by anybody; that therefore all Buddhas denounce persons clinging to a corporeal existence. Thus explaining in detail the doctrine of the none-âtman and the *çûnyatâ*, Açvaghosha had the melody played by musicians, who, however, not being able to grasp the significance of the piece, failed to produce the intended tune and harmony. He then donned a white woolen dress, joined the band of musicians, beating the drum, ringing the bell, and tuning the lyre, and this done, the melody in full perfection gave a note at once mournful and soothing, so as to arouse in the mind of the audience the idea of the misery, emptiness, and non-âtman-ness of all things. The five hundred royal princes in the city thus moved all at once were fully awakened, and abhorring the curse of the five evil passions abandoned their worldly life and took refuge in the Bodhi. The king of Pâtaliputra was very much terrified by the event, thinking that if the people who listen to this music would abandon their homes [like the princes], his country would be depopulated and his royal business ruined. So he warned the people never to play this music hereafter.

WORKS IN CHINESE TRANSLATIONS.

The works ascribed to Açvaghosha and still existing in Chinese translations are eight in number. They are: (1) The 大乘起信論 *Tai shêng ch'i hsin lun* (*Mahâyânaçraddhotpâdaçâstra*): *discourse on the awakening of faith in the Mahâyâna.* It is the principal work of Açvaghosha, and through this we are able to recognise what an important position he occupies in the development of the Mahâyânistic world-conception and theory of final emancipation. Its outlines and the accounts of its Chinese translation will be given below. (2) The 大宗地玄文本論 *Ta sung ti hsüan wên pên lun, a fundamental treatise on the spiritual stages for reaching final deliverance.* The book has a decided tendency to mysticism, explaining a gradual development of religious consciousness through fifty-one different spiritual stages. It may be considered a precursory work out of which Vajrabodhi's Mantrism finally made a full manifestation. It was translated by Paramârtha between A. D. 557 569. Twenty *fasciculi*, forty chapters. (3) The 大莊嚴論經 *Ta chuang yen lun ching* (*Mahâlamkârasûtraçâstra*), the *Book of Great Glory*, or a compilation of stories illustrating the retribution of karma. The stories relate mostly to the events that occurred in Western India. Beal translated some of them in his *Buddhist Literature in China*. The Chinese translator is Kumârajîva, *circa* A. D. 405. Fifteen *fasciculi*. (4) The 佛所行讚 *Fo shu hing tsan* (*Buddhacaritakâvya*), a well known poem on the life of Buddha. The Chinese translation is by Dharmaraksha between A. D. 414-421. Five *fasciculi*, twenty eight chapters, Beal's English translation forms Vol. XIX. of *The Sacred Books of the East;* and Cowell's translation from Sanskrit, Vol. XLIX of the same. (5) The 尼乾子

問無我義經 *Ni kan tzŭ wên wu wu i ching*, a sûtra on a Nirgrantha's asking about the theory of non-ego. The book foreshadows the Mâdhyamika philosophy of Nâgârjuna, for the two forms of truth are distinguished there, Pure Truth (*Parmârtha-satya*) and Practical Truth (*Samvrtti-satya*),[1] and the Çûnyatâ theory also is proclaimed. (6) The 十不善業道經 *Shih pu shan yeh tao ching*, a sûtra on the ten no-good deeds. (7) The 事師法五十頌 *Shih shih fa wu shih sung*, fifty verses on the rules of serving a master or teacher. (8) The 六趣輪廻經 *Lu tao lun 'hui ching*, a sûtra on transmigration through the six states of existence. These last four works are very short, all translated by Jih-ch'êng (Divayaças?), between A. D. 1004–1058.

CHINESE TRANSLATIONS OF THE "DISCOURSE ON THE AWAKENING OF FAITH."

Let us give here some remarks on the Chinese translations of Açvaghosha's principal and best known work *The Awakening of Faith*. The Sanskrit original is long lost, probably owing to the repeated persecutions of Buddhism by Chinese emperors at different times. According to the *Chêng yüan catalogue* 貞元錄 (compiled between A. D. 785–804) the Sanskrit text is said to have existed at that time. It is a great pity that such an important Buddhist philosophical work

---

[1] Notice Açvaghosha's discussion with Punyayaças as above mentioned.

as the present çāstra can be studied only through translations.[1]

There are two Chinese translations still existing in the Tripiṭaka collection. The first translation was made by Paramârtha (波羅末陀), otherwise called Kulanâtha (狗羅那陀), of Ujjayana (or Ujjayini, modern Oujein) in Western India. He came to China A. D. 546 and died A. D. 569 when he was 71 years old. Among many other translations, the present one came from his pen on the tenth day of September, A. D. 554.

The second one is by Çikshânanda (實叉難陀), of Kusutana (Khoten), who began his work on the eighth of October, A. D. 700. He died in China A. D. 710 at the age of 59.

As to the problem whether the original of the two Chinese translations is the same or different, my impression is that they were not the same text, the one having been brought from Ujjayana and the other from Khoten. But the difference, as far as we can judge from the comparison of the two versions, is not fundamental.

In the preface to the second translation of the Kao

---

[1]An inquiry has been made by the present English translator as to whether the original Sanskrit copy could be found either in India or in Nepal; but Prof. Satis Chandra Âchâryya, of the Buddhist Text Society, Calcutta, with whom he has been communicating on the subject, informs him that as far as India is concerned there is almost no hope of securing it, and also that his friend in Nepal has been unable so far to discover the original.

li edition, the unknown writer states to the following effect: "The present Çâstra has two translations. The first one is by Paramârtha and the second one is from the Sanskrit text brought by Çikshânanda who found also the older Sanskrit original in the Tz'u an tower. As soon as he had finished the rendering of the Avatamsakasûtra into Chinese, he began a translation of his own text with the assistance of several native Buddhist priests. The new translation occasionally deviates from the older one, partly because each translator had his own views and partly because the texts themselves were not the same."

Though the *Chéng yüan* 貞元錄 as well as the *K'ai yüan*[1] 開元錄 catalogue affirm that the two translations were from the same text, this can only mean that they were not radically divergent. For if any two editions differ so slightly as not to affect the essential points, they can be said to be practically the same text.

Which of the two translations then is the more correct? To this question we cannot give any definite answer as the originals are missing. The first translation has found a more popular acceptance in Japan as well as in China, not because it is more faithful to the original, but because a most learned and illustrious Buddhist scholar called Fa tsang 法藏 (A. D.

---

[1] A catalogue of Buddhist books collected in the K'ai yüan period (A. D. 713-741) of the Tung Dynasty, by 契嵩 Chih-shang, A. D. 730. Its full name *K'ai yüan shih chiao lu*. Twenty *fasciculi*.

643-712) wrote a commentary on it. And on that account the commentary is more studied than the text itself. Fa tsang assisted Çikshânanda in preparing the second translation, but he preferred the first one for his commentary work, partly because the first one had already found a wide circulation and some commentators before his time, and partly because both translations agreeing in all their important points, he did not like to show his "partiality," as a commentator on Fa tsang says, to the one in the preparation of which he himself took part.

The present English translation is made from the second Chinese version by Çikshânanda, but the first version has been carefully compared with it, and wherever disagreements occur between them they have been noticed in footnotes.

OUTLINES OF THE "DISCOURSE ON THE AWAKENING OF FAITH."

I cannot help saying a few words here about the importance of Açvaghosha's main work which is scarcely known in the West, and if so, wrongly. Even Samuel Beal who is considered one of the best authorities on Chinese Buddhism, makes a misleading reference to our author in his *Buddhism in China*. The following quotation from the same apparently shows that at least when he wrote it, in 1884, he had a very insufficient knowledge of the subject. He says (page 138):

"His (Açvaghosha's) writings still survive in a Chinese form, and when examined will probably be found to be much tinged by a pseudo-Christian element.... But there is one book, the *K'i-sin-lun*, or 'Treatise for Awakening Faith,' which has never yet been properly examined, but, so far as is known, is based on doctrines foreign to Buddhism and allied to a perverted form of Christian dogma." The incorrectness of this statement will readily be seen by the reader when we proceed further on.

Wassiljew, another of the highest Western authorities on the subject, seems to be entirely ignorant of the existence of the present work. It is very strange that those who are considered to be quite well acquainted with the development of the Mahâyânistic thought, do not place in the right light a prominent, if not the principal, actor, who, so far as is known to us, practically initiated this great spiritual and intellectual movement in India. Wassiljew says in his *Buddhismus* (pp. 83-84):

"Zu welcher besonderen Schule Açvaghosha gehörte, wird nicht mit Bestimmtheit überliefert: aus der Legende, nach welcher er sich bei der Abfassung der Vibhâshâ betheiligte, dürfen wir jedoch den Schluss ziehen, dass er zu den Repräsentanten der Vaibhâschika's gerechnet ward."

It is true that in the *Life of Vasubandhu* Açvaghosha is said to have taken part in the compilation of the Vibhâshâ, but it is of no account whatever in the face of the present book in which we can clearly trace almost all elements of the thought fully developed afterwards by Nâgârjuna and other later Mahâyâna representatives.

I wish here, in order to show the significance of Açvaghosha, to call the attention of the reader to the three most salient points in his doctrine which will distinguish him from all Hînayâna schools. The three points constituting the gist of this Çâstra then are: (1) the conception of suchness (*Bhûtatathatâ*); (2) the theory of the triple personality; (3) the salvation by faith or the Sukhâvati doctrine.

The conception of suchness assumes other names, namely, The Womb of the Tathâgata (*Thatâgatagarbha*), when considered from its embracing all possible merits, and the All-Conserving Mind (*Âlayavijñâna*), when it becomes the principle of evolution and is said to have developed from the teaching of Buddha as expounded in the old canonical sûtras, such as the *Lankâvatara* and the *Çrîmâlâ*. Whatever the origin of the idea of suchness might have been, its "absolute aspect" evidently foreshadows the *Çûnyatâ* philosophy of the Mâdhyamika school. It is very doubtful whether Nâgârjuna, as told in a Chinese tradition, was a personal disciple of Açvaghosha, but it is highly probable that he was much influenced by him in forming his system.

The second thesis, the theory of the triple personality, that is one of the most distinctive characteristics of the Mahâyâna Buddhism, seems to have been first established by Açvaghosha. The pantheistic idea of suchness (*Bhûtatathatâ*), and the religious consciousness which always tends to demand something embodied in infinite love (*karuna*) and infinite wisdom (*jñâna*), and the scientific conception of the law of causation regulating our ethical as well as physical world, or in short the doctrine of karma,—these three factors working together in the mind of Açvaghosha, culminated in his theory of the triple personality.

The doctrine of salvation by faith whereon the Japanese Shin Shyû (True Sect) and Jôdô Shyû (Pure Land Sect) laid down their foundation also, appears first in the present çastra. If the quotation in the *Mahâyânaçraddhotpâda* actually refers to the Sukhhâvatî Sûtras, as we may fairly assume, there is a great probability in the statement that during the first four centuries after the Nirvâna there was already a variety of free interpretations about the teaching of the Master, which, commingled with the other religio philosophical thoughts in India, eventually made a full development under the generel names of the Mahâyâna and the Hînayâna schools.

A supplementary point to be noticed in Açvaghosha is the abundance of similar thoughts and passages with those in the *Bhagavadgîta*. The coincidence between the latter and the *Saddharmapundarîka* has been pointed out by Kern in his *Buddhismus und seine Geschichte* (Vol. II., p. 500, footnote). While it is an open question which of the two has an earlier date, the Mahâyâna Buddhism as a whole must be permitted to have some common points with the canonical book of Çivaism.

In conclusion I wish to state that as this book, the *Awakening of Faith*, is of paramount importance in its being the first attempt of systematising the fundamental thoughts of the Mahâyâna Buddhism, as well as in its forming a main authority of all the Mahâyânistic schools, those who study the doctrinal history of Buddhism cannot dispense with it; and that, in spite of its highest importance, no attempt has yet been made to make it accessible to the reader who is not familiar with the Chinese language, and so I here offer to the public an English translation of the entire text.

DISCOURSE.

FOR the purpose of awakening in all beings a pure faith in the Mahâyâna,[1] of destroying their doubts and attachment to false doctrines, and of affording them an uninterrupted inheritance of Buddha-seeds, I write this Discourse.

There is a principle whereby the root of faith in the Mahâyâna can be produced, and I shall explain it.

The explanation consists of five parts:

[1] The term Mahâyâna here seems not to have been used as it usually is in contrast to the Hînayâna. Açvaghosha adopts it simply to denote the greatness of suchness (*bhûtatathatâ*) as well as to prove its being the safest and surest means of salvation. It is therefore the name given to the first principle itself, and not to any philosophical system or religious dogmatics. But the term used in this wise by Açvaghosha and perhaps in earlier Mahâyâna texts gradually lost its original sense in the course of the development of this progressive religious view. It was then transferred to distinguish the system at large from that of the so-called Çrâvakas, to which the followers of the former gave in contrast to their own the rather humiliating name Hînayâna. At the time of Açvaghosha the controversy between them was probably not as vehement as it proved later on. And this fact may be seen from the tolerant spirit shown in the third convocation under the reign of King Kanishka. By the Mahâyâna followers Açvaghosha is unanimously recognised as the forerunner of Nâgârjuna by whose marvellous genius the system was brought to maturity

attributes are like the ocean, revealing to us the principle of anâtman and forming the storage of infinite merits.

[Adoration] to the congregation (*samgha*) of those who assiduously aspire after perfect knowledge (*samvaksambodhi*).

That all beings (*sarvasattva*) may rid themselves of doubt, become free from evil attachment, and, by the awakening of faith (*çraddha*), inherit Buddha-seeds, I write this Discourse.[1]

verse; while dharma in the second sense may safely be rendered by "law" or "doctrine" as generally understood by Western Buddhist scholars, to most of whom, however, the first significance of the term is strangely unknown. Max Müller fitly remarks in his introduction to the English translation of the *Vajracchedîkâ*, p. xiv: "Dharma in its ordinary Buddhist phraseology may be correctly rendered by law. Thus the whole teaching of Buddha is called the good law, Saddharma. But in our treatise dharma is generally used in a different sense. It means form ($\epsilon l\delta o\varsigma$) and likewise what is possessed of form, what is therefore different from other things, what is individual, in fact, what we mean by a thing or an object. This meaning has escaped most of the translators, both Oriental and Western, but if we were always to translate dharma by law, it seems to me that the whole drift of our treatise would become unintelligible." In this translation dharma is rendered sometimes by "thing," sometimes by "law," sometimes by "truth" or "doctrine," according to the context. But when it is synonymous with suchness (*bhûtatathatâ*), I have retained its original Sanskrit form, capitalised.

[1] An almost similar passage is repeated in the succeeding paragraph, while it does not occur in the older translation It may be a mistake on the part of the new translation, but I have left it as it stands in the text.

ADORATION.

ADORATION to the World-honored Ones (*Bhagavat*)[1] in all the ten quarters, who universally produce great benefits, whose wisdom is infinite and transcendent, and who save and guard [all beings].

[Adoration] to the Dharma[2] whose essence and

[1] There are ten appellations most commonly given to a Buddha: (1) *Tathâgata* (the one who thus comes, or he who has been expected and fulfils all expectations, the perfect one); (2) *Arhat* (the worthy one, but according to Nâgârjuna's *Mahâprajnâpâramitâçâstra*, Chinese translation by Kumârajîva, Vol. III., p. 17, one who has destroyed all enemies of evil passions, or one who is revered by gods and men, or one who will not be reborn; see also Vol. II., p. 20); (3) *Samyaksambuddha* (one who is perfect by enlightenment); (4) *Vidyâcaranasampanna* (one who is perfect in knowledge and conduct); (5) *Sugata* (one who goes well); (6) *Lokavid* (one who knows the world); (7) *Anuttara* (one who has no superior); (8) *Purushadamyasârathi* (the tamer of all beings); (9) *Câstâdevâmanushyânâm* (the teacher of gods and men); (10) *Buddha* (the enlightened one). When *Lokavid* and *Anuttara* are considered to be one title, as in the *Sutra on the Ten Apellations*, *Bhagavat* is added to make the tenth.

[2] According to a general interpretation of Mahâyâna Buddhists dharma means: (1) that which exists; (2) the object of understanding. Dharma may therefore be rendered in the first sense by "object," or "thing," or "substance," or "being," including everything mental as well as physical in its broadest sense, and so sarvadharma will designate all possible existences in the uni-

I. Introductory.
II. General Statement of Principles.
III. The Explanation Itself.
IV. The Practice of Faith.
V. Benefits [derived therefrom].

I. INTRODUCTORY.

There are eight inducements [to write this Discourse]:—

1. A general object, i. e., that the author might induce all beings to liberate themselves from misery and to enjoy blessing, and not that he might gain thereby some worldly advantages, etc.

2. That he might unfold the fundamental truth of the Tathâgata and let all beings have a right comprehension of it.

3. That he might enable those who have brought their root of merit (*kuçalamûla*) to maturity and obtained immovable faith, to have a philosophical grasp of the doctrine of the Mahâyâna.

4. That he might enable those whose root of merit is weak and insignificant, to acquire faith and to advance to the stage of immovable firmness (*avaivartikatva*).[1]

5. That he might induce all beings to obliterate

[1] *Avaivartikatva* means literally "never retreat." Faith is said to become immovably firm when one enters into the group of those who cannot be shaken in the possession of absolute truth (*samyaktvaniyataraçi*). For a further explanation see the reference in the Index to *samyaktvaniyataraçi*.

the previously acquired evils (*durgati* or *karmâvarana*), to restrain their own thoughts, and to free themselves from the three venomous passions.[1]

6. That he might induce all beings to practise the orthodox method of cessation [or tranquilisation *çamatha*] and of intellectual insight (*vidarçana*),[2] to be fortified against the commission of mental trespasses due to inferiority of minu.

7. That he might induce all beings in the right way to ponder on the doctrine of the Mahâyâna, foi thus they will be born in the presence of Buddhas,[3] and acquire the absolutely immovable Mahâyâna-faith.

8. That he might, by disclosing those benefits which are produced by joyfully believing in the Mahâyâna, let sentient beings become acquainted with the final aim of their efforts.

Though all these doctrines are sufficiently set forth

---

[1] They are: (1) covetousness (*lobha*); (2) malice (*dvesha*); (3) ignorance (*moha*).

[2] *Camatha* and *Vidarçana* or *Viparyana* constitute one of the five methods of discipline, for whose full explanation see the reference in the Index to these terms.

[3] This passage, which is considered to be a reference to the Sukhâvatî Sûtras, such as the Larger and the Smaller *Sukhâvatî-vyûha*, or the *Amitâyur-dhyâna*, seems to prove that some of the Mahâyâna texts of the Pure Land Sect had been in existence before the time of Açvaghosha who gives towards the end of his Discourse a quotation apparently taken from one of the above-mentioned Sûtras. The Sûtras therefore must be at least one or two hundred years older than Açvaghosha, in order that they might be quoted as an authentic teaching of Buddha.

THE AWAKENING OF FAITH. 51

in the Mahâyâna Sûtras,[1] yet as the predispositions and inclinations of the people[2] are not the same, and the conditions for obtaining enlightenment vary, I now write this Discourse.

There is another reason for doing so. At the time of the Tathâgata the people were unusually gifted, and the Buddha's presence, majestic both in mind and body, served to unfold the infinite significances of the Dharma with simplicity and yet in perfection. Accordingly there was no need for a philosophical discourse (*çâstra*).

After the Nirvâna of the Buddha there were men who possessed in themselves the intellectual power to understand the many-sided meanings of the Sûtras,[3]

---

[1] The view here proposed by Açvaghosha, which is called by Chinese Buddhists the theory of the evolution of the Tathâgatagarbha, is considered to be an elucidation of the doctrine taught by Buddha in such Mahâyâna Sûtras as the *Lankâvatâra, Ghanavyûha, Crîmâlâ*, etc.

[2] Literally, those who are to be converted.

[3] There are twelve divisions called *Angas* in the Mahâyânist writings, while in the Pâli only nine are counted. The twelve *angas* are: (1) *sûtra* (aphorisms); (2) *geya* (verses in which the same thing is repeated as in the prose part); (3) *vyâkarana* (Buddha's prophecy about Bodhisattva's attainment of Buddhahood in the future); (4) *gâthâ* (independent verses); (5) *udâna* (sermons on Buddha's own account); (6) *nidâna* (sermons as the occasion required); (7) *avadâna* (legends, but according to Chinese interpretation parables); (8) *ityukta* (speeches relating to the former deeds of Bodhisattvas); (9) *jâtaka* (accounts of Buddha's own former lives); (10) *vaipulya* (doctrines of deep significance); (11) *adbhutadharma* (extraordinary phenomena); (12) *upadeça* (expositions).

even if they read only a few of them. There were others who by their own intellectual powers could understand the meanings of the Sûtras only after an extensive reading of many of them. Still others lacking in intellectual powers of their own could understand the meanings of the Sûtras only through the assistance of elaborate commentaries. But there are some who, lacking in intellectual powers of their own, shun the perusal of elaborate commentaries and take delight in studying and cultivating enquiries which present the many-sidedness and universality of the doctrine in a concise form.

For the sake of the people of the last class I write this Discourse, in which the most excellent, the deepest, and the most inexhaustible Doctrine of the Tathâgata will be treated in comprehensive brevity.

II. GENERAL STATEMENT.

In what does the general statement consist?

The Mahâyâna can be briefly treated as to two aspects, namely, What it is, and What it signifies.[1]

[1] "What is" and "What signifies" are respectively in Chinese *yu fa* 有法 and *fa* 法, but in the older translation *fa* 体 and *i* 義 This is a little puzzling, but if we bear in mind that in Chinese as well as in Sanskrit *fa* or *dharma* means both the substance itself and its attribute or significance, or law that regulates its movements, we will understand that Paramârtha, the first translator, used *fa* here in the sense of substance or "what is," while Çikshânanda, the second translator, used the word in the sense of significance or that by which a thing is conceived, the ordinary meaning of *i*.

THE AWAKENING OF FAITH.   53

What is the Mahâyâna? It is the soul[1] of all sentient beings (*sarvasattva*), that constitutes all things in the world, phenomenal and supra-phenomenal;[2] and through this soul we can disclose what the Mahâyâna signifies.

Because the soul in itself, involving the quintessence of the Mahâyâna, is suchness (*bhûtatathatâ*), but it becomes [in its relative or transitory aspect, through the law of causation] birth-and-death (*samsâra*) in which are revealed the quintessence, the attributes, and the activity of the Mahâyâna.

The Mahâyâna has a triple significance.[3]

The first is the greatness of quintessence. Because the quintessence of the Mahâyâna as suchness

---

[1] "Soul" is not used here in a dualistic sense, but as Dr. Paul Carus defines it in the last chapter of *The Soul of Man*. Speaking of the soul of the universe he defines the term as "the formative principle which gave and still gives shape to the world" (*loc. cit.*, first edition, p. 437). The literal translation of the Chinese character 心 *hsin* is kernel, or heart, or essence of all things. The Chinese *hsin*, however, is rather indiscriminately used in our text for both Sanskrit terms, *Hrdaya* (kernel or heart) and *Citta* (mind, the thinking faculty). These terms are more or less synonymous, especially from Açvaghosha's standpoint, that does not allow the transcendental existence of a metaphysical soul-entity. In this translation soul denotes the absolute aspect of suchness, and mind its relative aspect, wherever this distinction is noticeable.

[2] This is a literal translation of the Chinese *chu shi chien* 出世間. It signifies anything transcending conditionality or worldliness.

[3] This triad which has a striking similarity to Spinoza's conception of substance, attributes and modes, also reminds us of the first principles (*padârtha*) of the Vaiçeshika philosophy, that is, substance (*dravya*), qualities (*guna*), and action (*karma*).

exists in all things, remains unchanged in the pure as well as in the defiled, is always one and the same (*samatâ*), neither increases nor decreases, and is void of distinction.

The second is the greatness of attributes. Here we have the Tathâgata's[1] womb[2] (*tathâgatagarbha*) which in exuberance contains immeasurable and innumerable merits (*punya*) as its characteristics.

The third is the greatness of activity, for it [i. e., Mahâyâna] produces all kinds of good work in the world, phenomenal and supra-phenomenal. [Hence the name *Mahâ*yâna (great vehicle).]

[Again this Dharma is called the Mahâ*yâna* ;] because it is the vehicle[3] (*yâna*) in which all Buddhas

---

[1] Tathâgata literally means one who thus or truly comes. That the omnipresent principle of suchness could come or go appeared contradictory and seemed to render an explanation necessary. The *Vajracchedikâ-Sûtra*, Max Müller's English translation, Chap. XXIX: "And again, O Subhûti, if anybody were to say that the Tathâgata goes, or comes, or stands, or sits, or lies down, he, O Subhûti, does not understand the meaning of my preaching. And why? Because the word Tathâgata means one who does not go anywhere, and does not come from anywhere; and therefore he is called the Tathâgata (truly come), holy and fully enlightened."

[2] Cf. the *Bhavadgîtâ* (*Sacred Books of the East*, Vol. VIII., Chap. XIV., p. 107): "The great Brahman is a womb for me, in which I cast the seed. From that, O descendant of Bharata! is the birth of all things. Of the bodies, O son of Kuntî! which are born from all wombs, the main womb is the great Brahman, and I am the father, the giver of the seed."

[3] Cf. the *Saddharma-pundarîka*, Chap. II. (*Sacred Books of the East*, Vol. XXI., p. 40): "By means of one sole vehicle, to wit, the Buddha-vehicle, Çâriputra, do I teach creatures the law; there is no second, nor a third."

from the beginning have been riding, and Bodhisattvas[1] when riding in it will enter into the state of Buddhahood.

III. THE EXPLANATION.

In what does the explanation of the general statement consist?

This part consists of three subdivisions:
1. The Revelation of the True Doctrine.
2. The Refutation of False Doctrines.
3. The Practice of the Right Path.

1. The Revelation of the True Doctrine.

In the one soul we may distinguish two aspects. The one is the Soul as suchness (*bhûtatathatâ*), the other is the soul as birth-and-death (*samsâra*). Each in itself constitutes all things, and both are so closely interrelated that one cannot be separated from the other.

A. The Soul as Suchness.

What is meant by the soul as suchness (*bhûtatathatâ*), is the oneness of the totality of things (*dharmadhâtu*),[2] the great all-including whole, the quintes-

---

[1] Literally, one who seeks perfect enlightenment, or one who is full of wisdom and compassion.

[2] S. Beal in his English translation of Açvaghosha's *Buddhacarita* (*Sacred Books of the East*, Vol. XIX., p. 324, footnote) considers *dharmadhâtu* to be "the mystic or ideal world of the Northern Buddhists" and says it means literally the "limit of dharma." The interpretation is evidently wrong, not only because *dhâtu* according to the *Madhyanta-vibhâga-çâstra* by Vasubandhu

sence of the Doctrine. For the essential nature of the soul is uncreate and eternal.

All things, simply on account of our confused subjectivity (*smrti*),[1] appear under the forms of individuation. If we could overcome our confused subjectivity, the signs of individuation would disappear, and there would be no trace of a world of [individual and isolated] objects.[2]

Therefore all things in their fundamental nature are not namable or explicable. They cannot be adequately expressed in any form of language. They are

---

(two Chinese translations : one by Paramârtha A. D. 557-569, and the other by Hsüan-tsang A. D. 691) means root, base, cause, or principle ; but because *Dharmadhâtu, fa kai* 法界 in Chinese, is not used by the Northern Buddhists in the sense that Beal gives. It means on the other hand this actual world considered from the point of its forming the basis of the law ; or, to use modern scientific terminology, it is existence in its organised totality. Açvaghosha uses the term here in this sense.

[1] The term is usually rendered by recollection or memory, but Açvaghosha uses it apparently in a different sense. It must mean subjectivity, or the perception of particularity, or that mental activity which is not in accordance with the suchness of things ; if otherwise, the whole drift of the present Discourse becomes totally unintelligible. *Smṛtî* is in some degree obviously synonymous with *Avidya* (ignorance) which is more general and more primordial than the former. Ignorance appears first and when it starts the world-process, "subjectivity" is evolved, which in its turn causes particularisation to take place. Particularisation does not annihilate suchness, but it overshadows the light of its perfect spiritual wisdom.

[2] Schopenhauer who says, "no subject without object," seems to express a similar idea that without subjectivity, "the objective world," i. e., "the world as *Vorstellung*, as representation of objects" would vanish.

without the range of apperception. [They are universals.] They [things in their fundamental nature] have no signs of distinction. [They are not particulars.] They possess absolute sameness (*samatâ*). [They are universals.] They are subject neither to transformation, nor to destruction. They are nothing but the one soul, for which suchness is another designation. Therefore they cannot be [fully] explained by words or exhausted by reasoning.

While all words and expressions are nothing but representations and not realities, and their existence depends simply on our confused subjectivity, suchness has no attribute [of particularity] to speak of. But the term suchness is all that can be expressed in language, and through this term all other terms may be disposed of.

In the essence of suchness, there is neither anything which has to be excluded, nor anything which has to be added.[2]

[1] If I understand Açvaghosha correctly, he intends to say that to the sentient subject the world consists of a number of isolated objects. The nature of subjectivity is sense-apperception ; and in sense-apperception the particular things are represented in the particularity only, not in their suchness as momentarily materialised universals. We must overcome subjectivity in order to discover suchness ; but when suchness is recognised, it is at once understood to constitute the essence and only true reality of things.

[2] The older translation has : "In the essence of suchness, there is nothing to be excluded, for all things are true ; nor is there nything to be added, for all things are such as they are. Be it nown therefore that as thus all things are undemonstrable and

Now the question arises : If that be so, how can all beings conform to and have an insight into [suchness]?

The answer is : As soon as you understand that when the totality of existence is spoken of, or thought of, there is neither that which speaks nor that which is spoken of, there is neither that which thinks nor that which is thought of ; then you conform to suchness ; and when your subjectivity is thus completely obliterated, it is said to have the insight.

Again there is a twofold aspect in suchness if viewed from the point of its explicability The first is trueness as negation (*çûnyatâ*),[1] in the sense that

unrepresentable [by our confused understanding], they are called suchness."

[1] The term *çûnyatâ* which means literally void or emptiness, has suffered a great deal of misunderstanding by those who are not well acquainted with Buddhist phraseology. If Mahâyânists used the term, as imagined by some critics, in the sense of absolute nothingness, denying the existence of everything conditional as well as unconditional, relative as well as independent, how could they speak about the highest truth (*paramârthasatya*) or the most excellent perfect enlightenment (*anuttarasamyaksambodhi*) which all conveys the sense of affirmation ? What the Çûnyatâ doctrine positively insists on, is the denial of sensationalism, and the annihilation of the imagination that weaves a dualistic world-conception. If this could be called a nihilism, every intellectual attempt to reach a unitary view of the universe would be nihilistic, for it declares the untenability of a separate existence of matter and thought, me and not-me, etc. It is odd enough that such a self-evident truth should have escaped the keen observance of Christian critics. Açvaghosha here states that the bhûtatathatâ is at once çûnya and açûnya. It is çûnya because it transcends all forms of separation and individuation ; it is açûnya because all possible things in the world emanate from it. Even Nâgârjuna

it is completely set apart from the attributes of all things unreal, that it is the real reality. The second is trueness as affirmation (açûnyatâ), in the sense that it contains infinite merits, that it is self-existent.

And again by trueness as negation we mean that in its [metaphysical] origin it has nothing to do with things defiled [i. e., conditional], that it is free from all signs of distinction existing among phenomenal objects, that it is independent of unreal, particularising consciousness.

Thus we understand that suchness (bhûtatathatâ) is neither that which is existence, nor that which is non-existence, nor that which is at once existence and non-existence, nor that which is not at once existence and non-existence; that it is neither that which is unity, nor that which is plurality, nor that which is at once unity and plurality, nor that which is not at once unity and plurality.[1]

who is supposed to be the founder of the nihilistic Prajñâpâramitâ system by Christian students of Buddhism, says in his *Mâdhyamika-çâstra*, Chap. XXII., that the idea of çûnyatâ and that of açûnyatâ are both wrong, but that from the deficiency of language to denote the exact state of things he has made use of these terms. (Observe that Açvaghosha says the very same thing in the preceding passages.) Nâgârjuna therefore apparently had something in his mind to define, but that something having nothing in common with things we daily encounter in our sense-world, he designated it çûnya, empty, and he hoped by thus abnegating all phenomenal existences, we could reach the highest reality, for ignorant minds are deeply saturated with wrong affirmations and false judgements.

[1] Cf. Nâgârjuna's "Eight No's" doctrine which says: "There is no production (*utpâda*), no destruction (*uccheda*), no annihilation (*nirodha*), no persistence (*çâçvata*), no unity (*ekârtha*), no

In a word, as suchness cannot be comprehended by the particularising consciousness of all beings, we call it the negation [or nothingness, çûnyatâ].

The truth is that subjectivity does not exist by itself, that the negation (çûnjatâ) is also void (çûnya) in its nature, that neither that which is negated [viz., the external world] nor that which negates [viz., the mind] is an independent entity.[1]

By the so-called trueness as affirmation, we mean that [as soon as we understand] subjectivity is empty and unreal, we perceive the pure soul manifesting itself as eternal, permanent, immutable and completely comprising all things that are pure. On that account we call it affirmation [or reality, or non-emptiness, açunyatâ]. Nevertheless, there is no trace of affirmation in it, because it is not the product of a confused subjectivity, because only by transcending subjectivity (smŗti) can it be grasped.

b. *The Soul as Birth-and-Death.*

The soul as birth-and-death (samsâra) comes forth [as the law of causation] from the Tathâgata's womb (Tathâgatagarbha). But the immortal [i. e., such-

---

plurality (nânârtha), no coming in (âgamana), no going out (nirgama)." The statement means that pure truth (paramârtha) transcends all modes of relativity. (See the first chapter of the Mâdhyamika-çâstra.)

[1] In the Kantian sense of "things in themselves." The Mâdhyamika school would say they are all Atyanta-çûnyatâ, complete void, meaning that things are subject to transformation and have no absolute existence.

ness] and the mortal [i. e., birth-and-death] coincide with each other.[1] Though they are not identical, they are not a duality. [Thus when the absolute soul assumes a relative aspect by its self-affirmation] it is called the all conserving mind (*âlaya-vijnâna*).[2]

The same mind has a twofold significance as the organiser and the producer of all things.

Again it embraces two principles: (1) Enlightenment; (2) Non-enlightenment.

Enlightenment is the highest quality of the mind; it is free from all [the limiting] attributes of subjectivity (*smrti*). As it is free from all [limiting] attri-

---

[1] Cf. the *Bhagavadgîtâ*, Chap. IX., p. 84 : "I am immortality and also death; and I, O Arjuna! am that which is and that which is not." See also Chap. X., p. 90.

[2] *Âlaya* or *Alaya* comes from the root *lî*, which means: adhere; melt, dissolve; sit upon, dwell in, stay in, etc.; while its nominal form *laya* means: act of clinging; melting, fusion, solution, dissolution; rest, repose; place of rest, residence, house, dwelling. According to Paramârtha, who belongs to the so-called "Older Translators," the original Sanskrit equivalent of the "all-conserving mind" seems to be *alaya* or *aliya*, for he translates it by *Wu mo shih*, not-disappearing mind, in the sense that this mind retains everything in it. But Hsüan-tsang, the leader of the "New Translators," renders it by *tsang shih*, that is, the mind that hoards or preserves, or dwelling-mind or receptacle-mind, according to which the original seems to be *âlaya*, or *laya* with the prefix *â*-instead of its negative form with the particle *a*. The ultimate significance of the term in question, however, does not materially differ, whether it is *wu mo*, not-disappearing, or *tsang*, house, place of keeping things. My translation of the same is rather liberal, in order to make it more intelligible to the general reader. Some other names given to the *âlaya-vijnâna* are *citta*, mind; *âdâna*, the supporting; *âçraya*, foundation or seeds.

butes of subjectivity, it is like unto space (âkâça), penetrating everywhere, as the unity of all (dharmadhâtu). That is to say, it is the universal Dharmakâya[1] of all Tathâgatas.

On account of this Dharmakâya, all Tathâgatas are spoken of as abiding in enlightenment *a priori*.

Enlightenment *a priori* is contrasted with enlightenment *a posteriori*. Through enlightenment *a posteriori* is gained no more than enlightenment *a priori*.

Now we speak of enlightenment *a posteriori*; because there is enlightenment *a priori*, there is non-

---

[1] There seems to be a general misconception about the exact significance of the term *Dharmakâya* which constitutes the central point of the Mahâyâna system. Most Western Buddhist scholars render it the Body or Personality of the Law, understanding by law the doctrine of Buddha. This may be correct in the Southern Buddhism as well as in its historical sense, because after the Nirvâna of Buddha it was quite natural for his disciples to personify the doctrine of their teacher, as their now only living spiritual leader. But in the course of time it acquired entirely different significance and ceased to mean the personification of the Doctrine. Now *dharma*, as aforesaid, does not only mean law or doctrine, but also it means an individual object, an idea, a substance, or, when it is used in its broadest sense, existence in general. *Kâya* means a body or person, but not in the sense of an animated, sentient being; it denotes a system in which parts are connected, a unified whole, that which forms a basis, etc. Dharmakâya therefore signifies that which constitutes the ultimate foundation of existence, one great whole in which all forms of individuation are obliterated, in a word, the Absolute. This objective absolute being meanwhile has been idealised by Mahâyânists so that that which knows is now identical with that which is known, because they say that the essence of existence is nothing but intelligence pure, perfect, and free from all possible worries and evils.

enlightenment, and because there is non-enlightenment we can speak of enlightenment *a posteriori*.

Again, when the mind is enlightened as to its own ultimate nature, it is called perfect enlightenment; when it is not enlightened as to its ultimate nature, it is not perfect enlightenment.

Common people[1] (*prthagjana*), who, becoming conscious of errors that occur in a succession of their mental states, abstain from making conclusions, may be spoken of as enlightened; but in reality theirs is non-enlightenment.

Çrâvakas,[2] Pratyekabuddhas, and those Bodhi-

---

[1] *Prthagjana* has a technical sense in Buddhism, for any one that is ignorant of the doctrine of non-âtman and commits all those actions which lead one to a constant transmigration, is counted among the *profanum vulgus*, to distinguish him from the Çrâvaka, Pratyekabuddha, and Bodhisattva.

[2] The *Saddharmapundarîka-Sûtra* contains an explanation of these terms generally adopted by Mahâyânists, which read as follows (see Kern's English translation of the same, Chap. III., p. 80): "Now, Çâriputra, the beings who have become wise have faith in the Tathâgata, the father of the world, and consequently apply themselves to his commandments. Amongst them there are some who, wishing to follow the dictates of an authoritative voice, apply themselves to the commandment of the Tathâgata to acquire the knowledge of the *four great truths*, for the sake of *their own* complete Nirvâna. These one may say to be those who, coveting the vehicle of the disciple (Çrâvaka), fly from the triple world." ... This is the definition given to the Çrâvakayâna. We proceed next to that of the Pratyekabuddhayâna: "Other beings, desirous of the science without a master, of self-restraint and tranquillity, apply themselves to the commandment of the Tathâgata to learn to understand *causes and effects* (*i. e., the twelve chains of relation*) for the sake of *their own* complete Nirvâna. These one may say to be those who, coveting the vehicle of the Pratyekabuddha,

sattvas who have just entered their course, recognising the difference between subjectivity and the transcending of subjectivity both in essence and attributes, have become emancipated from the coarse form of particularisation. This is called enlightenment in appearance.

Bodhisattvas of the Dharmakâya,[1] having recognised that subjectivity and the transcending of subjectivity have no reality of their own [i. e., are relative], have become emancipated from the intermediate form of particularisation. This is called approximate enlightenment.

Those who have transcended the stage of Bodhisattvahood and attained the ultimate goal, possess a consciousness which is consistent and harmonious;

---

fly from the triple world." . . . Those who belong to these two classes desire to achieve only the salvation of their own, and not that of all mankind, in which respect Bodhisattvas stand far superior to them. We read in the same Sûtra to the following effect: "Others again, desirous of the knowledge of the all-knowing, the knowledge of Buddha, the knowledge of the self-born one, the science without a master, apply themselves to the commandment of the Tathâgata to learn to understand the knowledge, powers, and freedom from hesitation, of the Tathâgata, for the sake of the *common weal and happiness, out of compassion to the world, for the benefit, weal, and happiness of the world at large, both gods and men, for the sake of the complete Nirvâna of all beings.* These one may say to be those who, coveting the great vehicle (mahâyâna), fly from the triple world. Therefore they are called Bodhisattva Mahâsattva." (The italics are mine.)

[1] Those who have recognised the all-prevailing Dharmakâya, but who have not as yet been able to perfectly identify themselves with it.

they have recognised the origin from which consciousness [or mentation] starts.[1] This will truly be called enlightenment.

Having transcended the attributes of enlightenment and the subtlest form of particularisation, they [i. e., Buddhas] have gained a perfect and eternal insight into the very nature of the soul [i. e., suchness], because the latter now presents itself to them in its absolute and immutable form.[2] Therefore they are called Tathâgatas, and theirs is perfect enlightenment; and therefore it is said in the Sûtra[3] that those who have an insight into the non-reality of all subjectivity, attain to the wisdom of the Tathâgata.

In the preceding statement we referred to the origin from which consciousness [or mentation] starts according to the popular expression. In truth there is no such thing as the origin of consciousness [or mentation]; for consciousness [being purely subjective] has no absolute [but only a phenomenal] existence. How can we then speak of its origin?

The multitude of people (*bahujana*) are said to be

[1] Consciousness, i. e., mentation or mental activity, is transient, it takes place in time, and must not be confused with soul, or suchness, or eternal wisdom.

[2] In the older translation these passages are somewhat simplified.

[3] The *Lankâvatâra Sûtra*. There are three Chinese translations of the same still extant among the Japanese Tripitaka collection: (1) by Gunabhadra, A. D. 443, four fasciculi; (2) by Bodhiruci, A. D. 513, ten fasciculi; (3) by Çikshânanda, A. D. 700–704, seven fasciculi

lacking in enlightenment, because ignorance (*avidya*) prevails there from all eternity, because there is a constant succession of confused subjective states (*smrti*) from which they have never been emancipated.

But when they transcend their subjectivity, they can then recognise that all states of mentation, viz., their appearance, presence, change, and disappearance [in the field of consciousness] have no [genuine] reality.[1] They are neither in a temporal nor in a spatial relation with the one soul,[2] for they are not self-existent.

When you understand this, you also understand that enlightenment *a posteriori* cannot be manufactured, for it is no other thing than enlightenment *a priori* [which is uncreate and must be discovered].[3]

And again enlightenment *a priori*, when implicated in the domain of defilement [i. e , relativity], is differentiated into two kinds of attributes :

(1) Pure wisdom (*prajñâ?*); (2) Incomprehensible activity (*karma?*).[4]

---

[1] The older translation differs a little, but agrees in the main.

[2] The older translation reads : "The four states of mentation are simultaneous [they belong together in time, i. e:, they are in uninterrupted succession], but have no self-existence, because enlightenment *a priori* always remains in its sameness."

[3] This passage is wanting in the older translation.

[4] The differentiation of enlightenment into two distinct qualities, wisdom and action, or, according to the terminology of later Mahâyânists, wisdom and love, constitutes one of the principal thoughts of the Mahâyâna Buddhism and shows a striking similarity to the Christian conception of God who is considered to be full of infinite love and wisdom.

By pure wisdom we understand that when one, by virtue of the perfuming[1] power of the Dharma, disciplines himself truthfully [i. e., according to the Dharma], and accomplishes meritorious deeds, the mind [i. e., âlaya-vijñâna] which implicates itself with birth-and-death will be broken down, and the modes of the evolving-consciousness[2] will be annulled; while the pure and genuine wisdom of the Dharmakâya manifests itself.[3]

Though all modes of consciousness and mentation are mere products of ignorance, ignorance in its ultimate nature is identical and not-identical[4] with enlightenment *a priori;* and therefore ignorance in one sense is destructible, while in the other sense it is indestructible.

This may be illustrated by [the simile of] the water and the waves which are stirred up in the ocean. Here the water can be said to be identical [in one sense] and not-identical [in the other sense][5] with the waves. The waves are stirred up by the wind, but the water remains the same. When the wind ceases, the motion of the waves subsides; but the water remains the same.

[1] This term will be explained later on. See p. 84.
[2] For the explanation see below, p. 76.
[3] Note that the Dharmakâya is not the "Body of the Law," but suchness (*bhûtatathatâ*) itself, which transcends the limits of time and space as well as the law of causation.
[4] Literally, "neither identical nor not-identical."
[5] Literally, "neither identical nor not-identical."

Likewise, when the mind of all creatures which in its own nature is pure and clean, is stirred up by the wind of ignorance (*avidya*), the waves of mentality (*vijñâna*) make their appearance. These three [i. e., the mind, ignorance, and mentality], however, have no [absolute] existence, and they are neither unity nor plurality.[1]

But the mind though pure in its essence is the source of the awakened [or disturbed] mentality. When ignorance is annihilated, the awakened mentality is tranquilised, whilst the essence of the wisdom remains unmolested.[2]

Incomprehensible activity which we know proceeds from pure wisdom, uninterruptedly produces all excellent spiritual states. That is to say, the personality (*kâya*) of the Tathâgata,[3] which in exuberance contains immeasurable and ever-growing merits, reveals itself to all beings according to their various predispositions [or characters], and accomplishes for them innumerable [spiritual] benefits.

Further there is a fourfold significance in the na-

[1] That is, they are one in one sense, but different in the other sense.

[2] In the older translation the last two paragraphs read:
"Likewise the mind of all beings though clean and pure in its own nature is disturbed [or awakened] through the wind of ignorance. Neither the mind nor ignorance has any form and attribute [of its own]. They condition each other. But the mind itself not being the principle of disturbance its movability will cease when ignorance is gone, though its essence, wisdom, remains unmolested."

[3] Or the *Tathâgatagarbha*.

ture of enlightenment whose purity may be likened unto space or a bright mirror.

The first great significance which may be likened unto space and a bright mirror, is trueness as negation (çûnyatâ), in the sense that enlightenment is absolutely unobtainable by any modes of relativity or by any outward signs of enlightenment.

The second great significance which may be likened unto space and a bright mirror, is trueness as affirmation (açûnyatâ), in the sense that all things [in their ultimate nature] are perfect and complete, and not subject to destruction; in the sense that all events in the phenomenal world are reflected in enlightenment, so that they neither pass out of it, nor enter into it, and that they neither disappear nor are destroyed; that they are in one eternal and immutable soul which by none of the defiled things can be defiled and whose wisdom-essence enveloping immeasurable and innumerable merits, becomes the cause of perfuming the minds of all beings.

The third great significance which may be likened unto space and a bright mirror, is the affirmation as free from the hindrances (âvarana), in the sense that enlightenment is forever cut off from the hindrances both affectional (kleçâvarana) and intellectual (jñeyâvarana), as well as from the mind [i. e., âlaya-vijñâna] which implicates itself with birth-and-death, since it is in its true nature clean, pure, eternal, calm, and immutable.

The fourth great significance which may be likened unto space and a bright mirror, is the affirmation as unfolding itself, in the sense that on account of a liberation from the hindrances, it transforms and unfolds itself, wherever conditions are favorable, in the form of a Tathâgata or in some other forms, in order that all beings might be induced thereby to bring their root[1] of merit (*kuçalamûla*) to maturity.[2]

By the so-called non-enlightenment, we mean that as the true Dharma [i. e., suchness] is from all eternity not truthfully recognised in its oneness, there issues forth an unenlightened mind and then subjectivity (*smrti*). But this subjectivity has no self-existence independent of enlightenment *a priori.*

To illustrate: a man who is lost goes astray because he is bent on pursuing a certain direction; and his confusion has no valid foundation other than that he is bent on a certain direction.

It is even the same with all beings. They become

---

[1] Max Müller renders the term by "stock of merit," but I think "stock" is not very fitly adopted to denote the sense usually attached to it by Buddhists. According to them, karma, be it meritorious or not-meritorious, has an efficient power to bear the fruit; therefore every act done by us like the root of a plant has a regenerative force potentially reserved within itself, and does not, like a stock of things which are not necessarily alive, remain dormant lacking productive powers in it.

[2] According to the older translation, the first significance is called the "mirror of transcendental (or empty) trueness"; the second, the "mirror of the perfuming principle"; the third, the "mirror of the dharma of liberation"; and the fourth, the "mirror of the perfuming cause."

unenlightened, foster their subjectivity and go astray, because they are bent on enlightenment. But non-enlightenment has no existence of its own, aside from its relation with enlightenment *a priori*. And as enlightenment *a priori* is spoken of only in contrast to non-enlightenment, and as non-enlightenment is a non-entity, true enlightenment in turn loses its significance too. [That is to say, they are simply relative.]

In blindness[1] there arose non-enlightenment of which three aspects are to be noted. These three are not independent.

The first aspect is ignorant action (*avidyakarma?*).[2] A disturbance[3] of the mind [i. e., *âlaya-vijñâna*] caused by non-enlightenment characterises the beginning of karma. When enlightened, the mind is no more dis-

[1] Rather "carelessness." This is missing in the older translation.

[2] The term "ignorant action" reminds us of Schopenhauer's "blind will" and we might translate the Chinese terms *pu chiao* 不覺 ignorant or unconscious, by "blind." On the other hand, the expression reminds one of Goethe's words in Faust: "Im Anfang war die That," i. e., in the beginning there was karma; and this karma starting in an unenlightened condition was blind or ignorant, it was as yet unconscious of its goal which is the attainment of the eternal truth, the discovery of enlightenment *a priori*. Cf. also the *Chândogya Upanisad*, VI, 2.

[3] By "disturbance" is meant that the mind or soul, awaking from a state of perfect sameness and tranquillity, discriminates the subject and the object, me and not-me. The "disturbance" itself, however, is neither good nor bad; the fault lies in clinging to this dual aspect of existence as absolute, utterly ignoring their fundamental identity. Efface the clinging from your mind, and you are purified and saved.

turbed. But by its disturbance misery (*duhkha*) is produced according to the law of causation.

The second aspect is that which perceives [i. e., the ego or subject]. In consequence of the disturbance of the mind there originates that which perceives an external world. When the mind is not disturbed, perception does not take place.

The third aspect is the external world. Through perception an unreal external world originates. Independent of that which perceives [i. e., the ego or subject], there is no surrounding world [or the object].[1]

Conditioned by the unreal external world, six kinds of phenomena arise in succession.

The first phenomenon is intelligence [i. e., sensation]. Being affected by the external world the mind becomes conscious of the difference between the agreeable and the disagreeable.

The second phenomenon is succession [i. e., memory]. Following upon intelligence, memory retains the sensations agreeable as well as disagreeable in a continuous succession of subjective states.

The third phenomenon is clinging. Through the retention and succession of sensations agreeable as well as disagreeable, there arises the desire of clinging.

The fourth phenomenon is an attachment to names

---

[1] This is the idealistic phase of the Mahâyâna Buddhism. Berkeley says: "Take away the perceiving mind and you take away the objective world."

[or ideas, *samjñā*], etc.[1] By clinging the mind hypostasises all names whereby to give definitions to all things.

The fifth phenomenon is the performance of deeds (*karma*). On account of attachment to names, etc., there arise all the variations of deeds, productive of individuality.

The sixth phenomenon is the suffering due to the fetter of deeds. Through deeds suffering arises in which the mind finds itself entangled and curtailed of its freedom.

Be it therefore known that all defiled things do not exist by themselves, for all of them have arisen from ignorance.

Now there is a twofold relation between enlightenment and non-enlightenment: (1) identity; (2) non-identity.

The relation of identity may be illustrated by the

[1] Here is again a strange agreement with Western philosophy. The nominalists speak of names as mere *flatus vocis* and the things-in-themselves (i. e., what is conceived by names) are declared to be unknowable by Kant. Dr. Paul Carus goes one step further by declaring that there are no things-in-themselves, but forms-in-themselves, viz., the eternal types of beings or Plato's ideas. The clinging to names is based on the metaphysical error of interpreting names as entities or things-in-themselves, which exhibits the nominalistic phase of Buddhism. On the other hand, the strong emphasis laid on the reality of suchness, or what Dr. Carus calls the purely formal, shows the realistic phase of Buddhism. The word "hypostasises" used in the next passage means literally in the younger translation "firmly builds a basis for," in the older one we read literally "one sets separately forth what is unreal, i. e., names and words."

simile of all kinds of pottery which though different are all made of the same clay. Likewise the undefiled (*anâçrava*)[1] and ignorance (*avidya*) and their various transcient forms come all from one and the same entity. Therefore Buddha teaches[2] that all beings are from all eternity ever abiding in Nirvâna.[3] In truth enlightenment cannot be manufactured, nor can it be created; it is absolutely intangible; it is no material existence that is an object of sensation.

The reason why enlightenment nevertheless assumes tangible material form is that it suffers defilement[4] which is the source of all transient forms of manifestation. Wisdom itself has nothing to do with material phenomena whose characteristic feature is

[1] A dharma not subject to the transformation of birth and death is called 無漏 *wu lou* in Chinese and *anâçrava* in Sanskrit. It is commonly used in contrast to 有漏 *yu lou* and *sâçrava*, which means "defiled" or "conditional."

[2] This teaching is set forth in the fourth chapter of the *Vimalakîrtinirdeça Sûtra*, one of the most popular Mahâyâna texts in China as well as in Japan. There are several Chinese translations still extant, the earliest of which was produced during the first half of the third century of the Christian era.

[3] Observe that Nirvâna is here used as a synonym of suchness (*bhûtatathatâ*).

[4] That is to say, being mixed up in the material world. "Defilement" does not necessarily mean evil or immorality. Anything that does not come directly from the fountain-head of suchness, but is in some way or other "perfumed" by ignorance, the principle of individuation, is called defiled or impure. From the ethical point of view it may be good or bad, according to our subjective attitude towards it. All that should be avoided is a clinging to the phenomenal existence.

extension in space, and there are no attributes there by which wisdom can become tangible. This is the meaning of Buddha's brief statement just referred to.

The relation of non-identity may be illustrated by the difference that obtains among the various kinds of pottery. The relation among the undefiled and ignorance and their various transient forms of manifestation is similar to it.

And again, by the law of causation (*hetupratyaya*) in the domain of birth-and-death (*samsâra*) we mean that depending on the mind [i. e., *âlaya-vijñana*] an evolution of the ego (*manas*) and consciousness (*vijñâna*)[1] takes place in all beings.

What is meant by this?

In the all-conserving mind (*âlaya-vijñâna*) ignorance obtains; and from the non-enlightenment starts that which sees, that which represents, that which apprehends an objective world, and that which constantly particularises. This is called the ego (*manas*).

[1] *Manovijñâna* in the older translation. Now *vijñâna* (or *manovijñâna*), *manas* and *citta* are to a certain extent synonymous and interchangeable, as al> designating that which feels, thinks and wills, or what is commonly called mind. According to a general interpretation of Mahâyânists, the following distinction is made among them: *citta*, mind, is more fundamental, somehow corresponding to the conception of the soul, for it has the inherent capacity for ideation as well as for the power of storing up within itself the results of experience; the most characteristic feature of the *manas*, the ego, is to constantly reflect on itself and to unconsciously assert the existence of the ego; the *vijñâna*, consciousness, is principally the faculty of feeling, perceiving, discriminating, judging, etc., in short, general mental activity or consciousness.

Five different names are given to the ego [according to its different modes of operation].

The first name is activity-consciousness (*Karma-vijñâna?*) in the sense that through the agency of ignorance an unenlightened mind begins to be disturbed [or awakened].

The second name is evolving-consciousness [*pravṛtti-vijñâna*, i. e., the subject], in the sense that when the mind is disturbed, there evolves that which sees an external world.

The third name is representation-consciousness, in the sense that the ego (*manas*) represents [or reflects] an external world. As a clean mirror reflects the images of all description, it is even so with the representation-consciousness. When it is confronted, for instance, with the five objects of sense, it represents them at once, instantaneously, and without any effort.

The fourth name is particularisation-consciousness, in the sense that it discriminates between different things defiled as well as pure.

The fifth name is succession-consciousness [i. e., memory], in the sense that continuously directed by the awakening consciousness [or attention, *manaskara*] it [*manas*] retains and never loses or suffers the destruction of any karma, good as well as evil, which had been sown in the past, and whose retribution, painful as well as agreeable, it never fails to mature, be it in the present or in the future; and also in the sense that it unconsciously recollects things gone by, and in imagination anticipates things to come.

Therefore the three domains[1] (*triloka*) are nothing but the self-manifestation of the mind [i. e., *âlaya-vijñâna* which is practically identical with suchness, *bhûtatathatâ*].[2] Separated from the mind, there would be no such things as the six objects of sense.

Why?

Since all things, owing the principle of their existence to the mind (*âlaya-vijñâna*), are produced by subjectivity (*smrti*), all the modes of particularisation are the self-particularisation of the mind. The mind in itself [or the soul] being, however, free from all attributes, is not differentiated. Therefore we come to the conclusion that all things and conditions in the phenomenal world, hypostasised and established only through ignorance (*avidya*) and subjectivity (*smrti*) on the part of all beings, have no more reality than the images in a mirror.[3] They evolve simply from

---

[1] They are: (1) Domain of feeling (*kâmaloka*); (2) Domain of bodily existence (*rûpaloka*); (3) Domain of incorporeality (*arûpaloka*).

[2] The mind or *âlaya-vijñâna* is suchness (or, as Dr. Carus would say, "purely formal thought,") in its operation, where it may be called the rational principle in nature or the *Gesetzmässigkeit* of the cosmos. It manifests itself not only in human reason, but appears also as the principle of individuation, determining all particular forms of existence, as will be explained in the following lines.

[3] Compare Schopenhauer's conception of the world as *Vorstellung*.

the ideality of a particularising mind. When the mind is disturbed, the multiplicity of things is produced; but when the mind is quieted, the multiplicity of things disappears.

By ego-consciousness (*manovijñâna*) we mean that all ignorant minds through their succession-consciousness cling to the conception of *I* and *not-I* [i. e., a separate objective world] and misapprehend the nature of the six objects of sense. The ego-consciousness is also called separation-consciousness, or phenomena-particularising-consciousness, because it is nourished by the perfuming[1] influence of the prejudices (*âçrava*), intellectual as well as affectional.

The mind [or consciousness, *vijñâna*] that starts from the perfuming influence of ignorance which has no beginning cannot be comprehended by the intellect of common people (*prîhagjana*), Crâvakas and Pratyekabuddhas.

It is partially comprehended by those Bodhisattvas at the stage of knowledge-and-practice, who discipline themselves, practise contemplation and become the Bodhisattvas of the Dharmakâya; while even those who have reached the highest stage of Bodhisattvahood cannot thoroughly comprehend it.

The only one who can have a clear and consummate knowledge of it is the Tathâgata.[2]

---

[1] The term will be explained later.

[2] The same idea is expressed in the *Crîmâlâ Sûtra* as well as in the *Lankâvatara Sûtra* where Buddha preaches the unfathom-

Why?

While the essence of the mind is eternally clean and pure, the influence of ignorance makes possible the existence of a defiled mind. But in spite of the defiled mind, the mind [itself] is eternal, clear, pure, and not subject to transformation.

Further as its original nature is free from particularisation, it knows in itself no change whatever, though it produces everywhere the various modes of existence.

ⅹ When the oneness of the totality of things (*dharmadhâtu*) is not recognised, then ignorance as well as particularisation arises, and all phases of the defiled mind are thus developed.* But the significance of this doctrine is so extremely deep and unfathomable that

---

ableness of the nature of suchness which, though pure in its essence, is yet subject to defilement or conditionality,—the mystery that can be comprehended only by a fully enlightened mind. Referring to this incomprehensibility of the relation of suchness and ignorance, let me quote what Herbert Spencer says in his *First Principles* (American ed., p. 45): "For every religion, setting out though it does with tacit assertion of a mystery, forthwith proceeds to give some solution of this mystery ; and so asserts that it is not a mystery passing human comprehension. But an examination of the solutions they severally propose, shows them to be uniformly invalid. The analysis of every possible hypothesis proves, not simply that no hypothesis is sufficient, but that no hypothesis is even thinkable. And thus the mystery which all religions recognise, turns out to be a far more transcendent mystery than any of them suppose—not a relative, but an absolute mystery." Is not the relation of suchness and ignorance the very mystery to which Spencer makes the allusion here? Açvaghosha's solution is that only Buddha can grasp it.

it can be fully comprehended by Buddhas and by no others. Now there are six different phases of the defiled[1] mind thus developed :

1. Interrelated [or secondary] defilement by attachment, from which Çrâvakas, Pratyekabuddhas and those Bodhisattvas at the stage of faith-adaptation can be freed.

2. Interrelated [or secondary] defilement by succession, from which Bodhisattvas with strenuous efforts at the stage of faith, can partially be freed, and at the stage of pure-heartedness, completely.

3. Interrelated [or secondary] defilement by the particularising intelligence, from which Bodhisattvas are gradually freed during their advancement from the stage of morality to the stage of wisdom, while upon reaching the stage of spirituality, they are eternally freed from it.

4. Non-interrelated [or primary] defilement by be-

---

[1] The defilement which is the product of the evolution of the *âlaya-vijnâna*, is of two kinds, primary and secondary. The primary defilement is *a priori*, originating with the birth of the mind. There is as yet no distinct consciousness in it of the duality of the subject and the object, though this is of course tacitly asserted. Açvaghosha calls the primary defilement "non-interrelated," meaning that there is no deliberate reflexion in the ego to assert itself. The secondary defilement called "interrelated" on the other hand explicitly assumes the ego in contradistinction to the non-ego and firmly clings to this conception, which brings forth all selfish desires and actions on the part of the defiled mind. The former being more fundamental than the latter is completely effaced from the mind only after going through all different stages of religious discipline.

lief in an external world, which can be exterminated at the stage of matter-emancipation.

5. Non-interrelated [or primary] defilement by belief in a perceiving mind, which can be exterminated at the stage of mind-emancipation.

6. Non-interrelated [or primary] defilement by the fundamental activity, which can be exterminated in entering upon the stage of Tathâgatahood, passing through the highest stage of Bodhisattvahood.

From not recognising the oneness of the totality of things (*dharmadhâtu*), Bodhisattvas can partially be liberated by passing first from the stage of faith and the stage of contemplation to the stage of pureheartedness; while when they enter upon the stage of Tathâgatahood, they can once for all put an end [to the illusion].

By "interrelated" we mean that there is [in this case] a distinction [or consciousness of a duality] between the mind in itself and particularisation, that there is [here] a distinction [or consciousness of a duality] between the defiled and the pure, [and therefore] that there is [here] an interrelation between that which perceives and that which determines.

By "non-interrelated" we mean that the mind [in this case] is perfectly identified with non-enlightenment, so that there is no distinction [or consciousness of a duality] between these two, [and therefore] that there is no consciousness of interrelation between that which perceives and that which determines.

The defiled mind is called affectional hindrance (*kleçâvarana*), because it obscures the fundamental wisdom of suchness (*bhûtatathatâ*). Ignorance is called intellectual hindrance (*jñeyâvarana*), because it obscures the spontaneous exercise of wisdom from which evolve all modes of activity in the world.

What is meant by this?

On account of the defiled mind attachment affirms itself in innumerable ways; and there arises a distinction [or consciousness] between that which apprehends and that which is apprehended. Thus believing in the external world produced by subjectivity, the mind becomes oblivious of the principle of sameness (*samatâ*) that underlies all things.

The essence of all things is one and the same, perfectly calm and tranquil, and shows no sign of becoming; ignorance, however, is in its blindness and delusion oblivious of enlightenment, and, on that account, cannot recognise truthfully all those conditions, differences, and activities which characterise the phenomena of the universe.

Further we distinguish two phases of the self-manifestation of the mind [i. e., *âlaya-vijñâna*, under the law of causation] as birth-and-death (*samsâra*). The first is the cruder phase, being the state of an interrelated mind; the second is the more refined phase, being the state of a non-interrelated mind. The crudest phase is the subjective condition of common people (*prthagjana*); the more refined of the crude or the cruder of the refined is the subjective state of a Bodhisattva.[1] These two phases [of the *âlaya-vijñâna* as the principle of birth-and-death] originate through the perfuming power of ignorance.

The birth-and-death (*samsâra*) has its *raison d'être* (*hetu*) and its cause [or condition, *pratyaya*]. Non-enlightenment is the *raison d'être*, and the external world as produced by subjectivity is the condition. When the *raison d'être* is annihilated, the condition is annihilated [i. e., loses its conditioning power]. When the condition is annihilated, the state of an interrelated mind is annihilated. When the *raison d'être* is annihilated, the state of a non-interrelated mind [too] is annihilated.

It may be asked: If the mind be annihilated, how can there be mentation? If mentation really occurs, how can there be annihilation?

In reply we say that while the objection is well founded, we understand by the annihilation, not that of the mind itself, but of its modes [only].

To illustrate: the water shows the symptoms of disturbance when stirred up by the wind. Have the wind annihilated, and the symptoms of disturbance on the water will also be annihilated, the water itself remaining the same. Let the water itself, however, be annihilated, the symptoms of disturbance would no more be perceptible; because there is nothing

---

[1] The older translation adds: The most refined of the refined is the spiritual state of a Buddha.

there through which it can show itself. Only so long as the water is not annihilated, the symptoms of disturbance may continue.

It is even the same with all beings. Through ignorance their minds become disturbed. Let ignorance be annihilated, and the symptom of disturbance will also be annihilated, while the essence of the mind [i. e., suchness] remains the same. Only if the mind itself were annihilated, then all beings would cease to exist, because there would be nothing there by which they could manifest themselves. But so long as the mind be not annihilated, its disturbance may continue.

A constant production of things defiled and pure is taking place on account of the inter-perfuming of the four different powers which are as follows: the first is the pure dharma, that is, suchness (*bhûtatathatâ*); the second is the principle of defilement, that is, ignorance (*avidya*); the third is the subjective mind, that is, activity-consciousness (*karmavijñâna?*); the fourth is the external world (*vishaya*) of subjectivity, that is, the six objects of sense.

By "perfuming" we mean that while our worldly clothes [viz., those which we wear] have no odor of their own, neither offensive nor agreeable, they acquire one or the other according to the nature of the substance with which they are perfumed.

Now suchness is a pure dharma free from defilement. It acquires, however, a quality of defilement owing to the perfuming power of ignorance. On the other hand, ignorance has nothing to do with purity. Nevertheless, we speak of its being able to do the work of purity, because it in its turn is perfumed by suchness.

How are defiled things continually produced by perfuming?

Determined by suchness [in its relative aspect], ignorance becomes the *raison d'être* of all forms of defilement. And this ignorance perfumes suchness, and, by perfuming suchness, it produces subjectivity (*smrti*). This subjectivity in its turn perfumes ignorance. On account of this [reciprocal] perfuming, the truth is misunderstood. On account of its being misunderstood, an external world of subjectivity appears [viz., a conception of particulars as particulars]. Further, on account of the perfuming power of subjectivity, various modes of individuation are produced. And by clinging to them, various deeds are done, and we suffer as the result miseries, mentally as well as bodily.

There are two senses in what we call "the perfuming power of the external world of subjectivity": (1) that which strengthens particularisation;[1] (2) that which strengthens attachment.

There are again two senses in what we call "the perfuming power of the subjective mind": (1) that

---

[1] The older translation has "subjectivity" instead of "particularisation." These two terms are synonymous and frequently interchanged in the later translation as well as in the older one.

which strengthens the fundamental activity-consciousness, whereby Arhats, Pratyekabuddhas and Bodhisattvas are subject to the miseries of birth and death; (2) that which strengthens the phenomena-particularising-consciousness, whereby all common people (*prihagjana*) are subject to the miseries of being fettered by prior deeds (*karma*).

There are also two senses in what we call "the perfuming power of ignorance": (1) a fundamental perfuming, in the sense that the activity-consciousness is thereby actualised; (2) a perfuming of intellect and affection, in the sense that the phenomena-particularising-consciousness is thereby actualised.

How are pure things constantly produced by perfuming?

Suchness perfumes ignorance, and in consequence of this perfuming the mind involved in subjectivity is caused to loathe the misery of birth and death[1] and to seek after the blessing of Nirvâna. This longing and loathing on the part of the subjective mind in turn perfumes suchness. On account of this perfuming influence we are enabled to believe that we are in possession within ourselves of suchness whose essential nature is pure and immaculate; and we also recognise that all phenomena in the world are nothing but the illusory manifestation of the mind (*âlaya-vijñâna*) and have no reality of their own. Since we

---

[1] Birth and death do not necessarily refer to our life only, but in their widest sense to the phenomenal world.

thus rightly understand the truth, we can practise the means of liberation, can perform those actions which are in accordance [with the Dharma]. Neither do we particularise, nor cling to. By virtue of this discipline and habituation during the lapse of innumerable asamkhyeyakalpas,[1] we have ignorance annihilated.

As ignorance is thus annihilated, the mind [i. e., âlaya-vijñâna] is no more disturbed so as to be subject to individuation. As the mind is no more disturbed, the particularisation of the surrounding world is annihilated. When in this wise the principle and the condition of defilement, their products, and the mental disturbances are all annihilated, it is said that we attain to Nirvâna and that various spontaneous displays of activity are accomplished.[2]

[1] Literally, countless ages, but it has a technical meaning. Childer's Pali Dictionary, *sub voce*: "The term *kalpa* is given to certain vast periods or cycles of time, of which there are three, *Mahâkalpa*, *Asamkhyeyakalpa* and *Antarakalpa*. All the *Cakravâtas* are subject to an alternate process of destruction and renovation, and a *Mahâkalpa* is a period which elapses from the commencement of a *cakravâta* to its complete destruction. Each *Mahâkalpa* is subdivided into four *Asamkhyeyakalpâs*. . . . Each *Asamkhyeyakalpa* contains twenty *Antarakalpâs*, an *Antarakalpa* being the interval that elapses while the age of man increases from ten years to an *asamkhyeya*, and then decreases again to ten years; this period is of immense duration." See also the third *Koçathâna* (chapter) of the *Abhidharmakoça* by Vasubandhu.

[2] Notice that Nirvâna is not inactivity or nothingness as commonly supposed. It is, according to Açvaghosha, the annihilation

There are two senses in what we call "the perfuming of the subjective mind": (1) the perfuming of the phenomena-particularising-consciousness, whereby all common people (*prthagjana*), Çrâvakas, and Pratyekabuddhas are induced to loathe the misery of birth and death, and, each according to his own capacity, to step towards the most excellent knowledge (*bodhiparinishpatti*); (2) the perfuming of the ego (*manas*), whereby courageously making up their minds, Bodhisattvas unhesitatingly step towards and enter into Nirvâna, that has no fixed abode.

There are also two senses in what we call "the perfuming of suchness": (1) essence-perfuming, and (2) activity-perfuming.

The Essence-Perfuming.—Embracing in full from all eternity infinite spotless virtues (*anâçrava*) and incomprehensibly excellent spiritual states that can efficiently exercise an eternal and incessant influence upon all beings, suchness thereby perfumes the minds of all beings.[1]

In consequence of this perfuming power, they are caused to loathe the misery of birth and death, and to long for the blessing of Nirvâna, and believing that they are in possession within themselves of the true,

of the ego-conception, freedom from subjectivity, insight into the essence of suchness, or the recognition of the oneness of existence.

[1] The older translation: "(1) Embracing from all eternity things spotless and possessing in full some inconceivable activity and (2) being capable to objectify itself, suchness through these two attributes constantly and eternally exercises its perfuming power."

valid Dharma, to call forth their aspiration (*cittotpâda*)[1] and to discipline themselves.

Here a question arises: If all beings are uniformly in possession of suchness and are therefore equally perfumed by it, how is it that there are some who do not believe in it, while others do; and that there are such immeasurable stages and inequalities among them, which divide the path from the first stage of aspiration up to the last stage of Nirvâna, while according to the Doctrine all these differences should be equalised?

In reply we say this: Though all beings are uniformly in possession of suchness, the intensity [of the influence] of ignorance, the principle of individuation, that works from all eternity, varies in such manifold grades as to outnumber the sands of the Ganges. And it is even so with such entangling prejudices (*kleça* or *âçrava*) as the ego-conception, intellectual and affectional prejudices, etc. [whose perfuming efficiency varies according to the karma previously accumulated by each individual],—all these things being comprehended only by the Tathâgata. Hence such immeasurable degrees of difference as regards belief, etc.[2]

[1] This has a technical sense and is explained below.

[2] The view here set forth is illustrated in the fifth chapter of the *Saddharma-pundarîka Sûtra* by the relation of the rain and plants. "Then, Kâçyapa, the grasses, shrubs, herbs, and wild trees in this universe, such as have young and tender stalks, twigs, leaves, and foliage, and such as have middle-sized stalks, twigs, leaves, and foliage, and such as have the same fully developed, all those grasses, shrubs, herbs, and wild trees, smaller and greater

Further, there is made in the doctrine of all Buddhas a distinction between *raison d'être* (*hetu*) and cause (*pratyaya*). When both are fully satisfied, the final goal [of Buddhism] is attained and actualised.

To illustrate: the combustible nature of the wood is the *raison d'être* of a fire. But if a man is not acquainted with the fact, or, though acquainted with it, does not apply any method [whereby the potential principle can be actualised], how could he produce a fire and burn the wood?

It is even so with all beings. Although they are in possession of suchness as the perfuming *raison d'être*, yet how could they attain to Nirvâna, if they do not happen, as the cause, to see Buddhas or Bodhisattvas, or good sages, or even if they see them, do not practise good deeds (*carya*), do not exercise wisdom (*prajñâ*), do not destroy prejudices (*kleça*)?

Conversely, by the cause alone, i. e., by their mere happening to see all good sages, it is not sure for them that they will be induced to loathe the misery

---

(other) trees will each, according to its faculty and power, suck the humid element from the water emitted by that great cloud, and by that water which, *all of one essence*, has been abundantly poured down by the cloud, they will each, according to its germ [i. e., **karma**], acquire a regular development, growth, shooting up, and bigness; and they will produce blossoms and fruits, and will receive, *each severally*, their names. Rooted in *one and the same* soil, *all those* [*atfferent*] *families* of plants and germs are drenched and vivified by water *of one essence throughout*.' (Kern's English Translation, p. 119. The italics and words in brackets are by the present translator.)

of birth and death and to long for the blessing of Nirvâna, unless indeed they were in possession within themselves of the intrinsic perfuming principle as the *raison d'être*. It is, therefore, only when both the *raison d'être* and the cause are fully actualised that they can do so.

How are the *raison d'être* and the cause to be fully actualised?

Now, there is an inherent perfuming principle in one's own being, which, embraced and protected by the love (*maitri*) and compassion (*karunâ*) of all Buddhas and Bodhisattvas, is caused to loathe the misery of birth and death, to believe in Nirvâna, to cultivate their root of merit (*kuçalamûla*), to habituate oneself to it, and to bring it to maturity.

In consequence of this, one is enabled to see all Buddhas and Bodhisattvas, and, receiving instructions from them, is benefited, gladdened, induced to practise good deeds, etc., till one attain to Buddhahood and enter into Nirvâna.

The Activity-Perfuming.—By this is meant nothing else than the perfuming influence of the external cause over all beings. It asserts itself in innumerable ways. Briefly speaking we may distinguish two kinds of it : (1) individual; and (2) universal.

The Individual Cause.—All beings since their first aspiration (*cittotpâda*) till the attainment of Buddhahood are sheltered under the guardianship of all Buddhas and Bodhisattvas who, responding to the requirements of the occasion, transform themselves and assume the actual forms of personality.

Thus for the sake of all beings Buddhas and Bodhisattvas become sometimes their parents, sometimes their wives and children, sometimes their kinsmen, sometimes their servants, sometimes their friends, sometimes their enemies, sometimes reveal themselves as devas or in some other forms.

Again Buddhas and Bodhisattvas treat all beings sometimes with the four methods of entertainment,[1] sometimes with the six pâramitâs,[2] or with some other deeds, all of which are the inducement for them to make their knowledge (*bodhi*) perfect.

Thus embracing all beings with their deep compassion (*mahâkarunâ*), with their meek and tender heart, as well as their immense treasure of blissful wisdom, Buddhas convert them in such a way as to suit their [all beings'] needs and conditions; while all beings thereby are enabled to hear or to see Buddhas, and, thinking of Tathâgatas or some other personages, to increase their root of merit (*kuçalamûla*).

This individual cause is divided into two kinds: (1) that which takes effect immediately, enabling one without delay to attain to Buddhahood; (2) that which takes effect gradually, enabling one to attain to Buddhahood only after a long interval.

[1] *Catvâri-sangrahavastûni* in Sanskrit. They are (1) *dâna*, charity; (2) *priyavacana*, endearing speech; (3) *arthacaryâ*, beneficial action; (4) *samânârthâ*, co-operation.

[2] This is explained below.

Each of these two is further divided into two kinds: (1) that which increases one's root of merit; (2) that which induces one to enter into the path (*mârga*).

The Universal Cause. — With universal wisdom (*samatâjñâna?*) and universal wishes (*samatâpranidhâna?*) all Buddhas and Bodhisattvas desire to achieve a universal emancipation of all beings. This desire is eternal and spontaneous on their part. And now as this wisdom and these wishes have the perfuming power over all beings, the latter are caused to think of or to recollect all Buddhas and Bodhisattvas, so that sometimes hearing them, sometimes seeing them, all beings thereby acquire [spiritual] benefits (*hitatâ*). That is, entering into the samâdhi of purity, they destroy hindrances wherever they are met with, and obtain all-penetrating insight,[1] that enables one to become conscious of the absolute oneness (*samatâ*) of the universe (*sarvaloka*) and to see innumerable Buddhas and Bodhisattvas.[2]

Again, this perfuming of the essence and the activity may be divided into two categories: (1) that which is not yet in unison [with suchness]; (2) that which is already in unison [with suchness].

By that perfuming which is not yet in unison [with suchness] we understand the religious discipline of

---

[1] Literally, an unimpeded eye.
[2] The older translation differs a little, but without any considerable change in the meaning.

common people (*prthagjana*), Çrâvakas, Pratyeka-buddhas, and novice Bodhisattvas. While their strength of faith (*çraddhâbala*) perfumed by the ego (*manas*) and the ego-consciousness (*manovijñâna*) enables them to continue their religious discipline, they have not yet attained to the state of non-particularisation, because their discipline is not yet in unison with the essence of suchness; nor have they yet attained to the spontaneity of action (*svayamkarma?*)[1], because their discipline is not yet in unison with the activity of suchness.

By that perfuming which is already in unison [with suchness], we understand the religious discipline of Bodhisattvas of the Dharmakâya. They have attended to the state of non-particularisation, because their discipline is in unison with the self-essence of all Tathâgatas; they have attained to the spontaneity of action, because their discipline is in unison with the wisdom and activity of all Tathâgatas. Allowing them-

---

[1] The spontaneity of action means action without attachment or free from the ego-conception. It is somewhat similar to Lao-Tze's idea of *wu wei*, non-assertion. Cf. also the following passages from the *Bhagavadgîtâ*, Chap. IV., p. 59: "Actions defile me not. I have no attachment to the fruit of actions." P. 60: "He is wise among men, he is possessed of devotion, who sees inaction in action and action in inaction." . . . "Forsaking all attachment to the fruit of action, always contented, dependent on none, he does nothing at all, though he engages in action." P. 64: "He . . . who identifies his self with every being, is not tainted though he performs (action)." "Action in inaction and inaction in action" exactly coincides with the practical side of Açvaghosha's doctrine of suchness (*bhûtatathatâ*).

selves to be influenced only by the power of the Dharma, their discipline acquires a nature of spontaneity and thereby perfumes suchness and destroys ignorance.

Again the incessant perfuming of the defiled dharma [i. e., ignorance] from all eternity works on; but when one attains to Buddhahood, one at once puts an end to it.

The perfuming of the pure dharma [i. e., suchness] works on to eternity, and there is no interruption of it. Because by virtue of the perfuming of the Dharma, that is, suchness, subjectivity is on the one hand annihilated, and the Dharmakâya is on the other hand revealed, and the perfuming process of the activity [of suchness] thus originated forever goes on.

c. The Threefold Significance of the Mahâyâna Explained.

Again the quintessence and the attributes of suchness (*bhutatathatâ*) know no diminution or addition, but remain the same in common people (*prthagjana*), Crâvakas, Pratyekabuddhas, Bodhisattvas, and Buddhas. It was not created in the past, nor is it to be annihilated in the future; it is eternal, permanent, absolute; and from all eternity it sufficingly embraces in its essence all possible merits (*punya*).

That is to say, suchness has such characteristics as follows: the effulgence of great wisdom; the universal illumination of the dharmadhâtu [universe]; the true and adequate knowledge; the mind pure and clean in its self-nature; the eternal, the blessed, the self-regulating and the pure;[1] the tranquil, the immutable, and the free. And there is no heterogeneity in all those Buddha-dharmas which, outnumbering the sands of the Ganges, can be neither identical (*ekârtha*) nor not-identical (*nânârtha*) [with the essence of suchness], and which therefore are out of the range of our comprehension. Accordingly suchness is called the Tathâgata's womb (*tathagatagarbha*) or the Dharmakâya.[2]

It may be questioned: While it was stated before that suchness is devoid of all characteristics (*lakshana*), how can it now be said without contradiction that it embraces in full all such merits?

In reply it would be said that though suchness in truth abundantly embraces all merits, yet it is free in its nature from all forms of distinction; because all objects in the world are of one and the same taste, are of one reality, have nothing to do with the modes of particularisation, and are not of dualistic character. Depending on the principle of birth-and-death, such as the activity-consciousness (*karmavijñâna?*), etc., however, all signs of difference and individuation appear.

---

[1] These four qualities are usually considered by Mahâyânists to be those of Nirvâna as well.

[2] Observe here again that Dharmakâya is used in a sense quite different from its ordinary interpretation as the "Body of the Law.

How are those qualifications to be assigned to suchness?

Though all things in their [metaphysical] origin come from the soul alone and in truth free from particularisation, yet on account of non-enlightenment there originates a subjective mind [i. e., *âlaya-vijnâna*] that becomes conscious of an external world (*vishaya*). This we call ignorance (*avidya*). Nevertheless the essence of the mind [or the soul] is perfectly pure, and there is no awakening of ignorance in it. Thence we assign to suchness this quality, the effulgence of great wisdom.

If the mind being awakened perceive an external world, then there will be something that cannot be perceived by it. But the essence of the mind has nothing to do with perception [which presupposes the dual existence of a perceiving subject and an object perceived]; so there is nothing that cannot be perceived by it, [that is, the world of relativity is submerged in the oneness of suchness]. Thence we assign to suchness this quality, the universal illumination of the universe (*dharmadhâtu*).

When the mind is disturbed, it fails to be a true and adequate knowledge; it fails to be a pure, clean essence; it fails to be eternal, blissful, self-regulating, and pure; it fails to be tranquil, etc. On the contrary, it will become transient, changeable, unfree, and therefore the source of falsity and defilement, while its modifications outnumber the sands of the

Ganges. But when there is no disturbance in the essence of the mind, we speak of suchness as being the true, adequate knowledge, etc., and as possessing pure and clean merits that outnumber the sands of the Ganges.

When the mind is disturbed it will strive to become conscious of the existence of an external world and will thus betray the imperfection of its inner condition. But as all infinite merits in fact constitute the one mind which, perfect in itself, has no need of seeking after any external things other than itself, so suchness never fails to actualise all those Buddha-dharmas, that, outnumbering the sands of the Ganges, can be said to be neither identical nor non-identical with the essence of the mind, and that therefore are utterly out of the range of our comprehension. On that account suchness is designated the Tathâgata's womb (*tathâgatâgarbha*) or the Tathâgata's Dharma-kâya.

What is meant by the activity of suchness is this: all Buddhas, while at the stage of discipline, feel a deep compassion (*mahâkaruṇâ*) [for all beings], practise all pâramitâs, the four methods of entertainment (*catvâri-sangrahavastûni*), and many other meritorious deeds; treat others as their own self, wish to work out a universal salvation of mankind in ages to come, through limitless numbers of kalpas; recognise truthfully and adequately the principle of equality (*samatâ*) among people; and do not cling to the individual existence of a sentient being.[1]

By virtue of such a great wisdom that works means of emancipation (*upâyajñâ?*),[2] they annihilate ignorance that knows no beginning; recognise the Dharmakâya in its original purity; spontaneously perform incomprehensible karma[3] as well as various unfettered moral activities; manifest themselves throughout the universe (*dharmadhâtu*), identify themselves with suchness, and leave no traces of compulsion.[4]

And how is this?

Because all Tathâgatas are the Dharmakâya itself,[5] are the highest truth (*paramârthasatya*) itself,

[1] The older translation reads: "For they consider all sentient beings as their own self and do not cling to their individual forms. How is this? Because they know truthfully that all sentient beings as well as their own self come from one and the same suchness, and no distinction can be established among them."

[2] Cf. the second, third, fourth, fifth, and seventh chapter of the *Saddharma-pundarîka Sûtra*, in which Buddha preaches about the means of salvation.

[3] That is, "action in inaction and inaction in action."

[4] Açvaghosha's conception of religious life as identical in its essence with poetry or fine art, I think, closely resembles that of Kant who says in his *Critique of Judgment* that the production of fine art should appear as if the work of nature. To quote his own words: "Als Natur aber erscheint ein Produkt der Kunst dadurch, dass zwar alle Pünktlichkeit in der Uebereinkunft mit Regeln, nach denen allein das Produkt das werden kann, was es sein soll, angetroffen wird, aber ohne Peinlichkeit, d. i., ohne eine Spur zu zeigen, dass die Regel dem Künstler vor Augen geschwebt und seinen Gemüthskräften Fesseln angelegt habe." (*Kritik der Urtheilskraft*, Kirchmann's edition, p. 169.)

[5] Cf. *Vajracchedikâ*, Chap. XVII: "And why, O Subhûti, the

and have nothing to do with conditionality (*samvrtti-satya*) and compulsory actions; whereas the seeing, hearing, etc. [i. e., the particularising senses] of the sentient being diversify [on its own account] the activity of Tathâgatas.

Now this activity [in another word, the Dharmakâya] has a twofold aspect. The first one depends on the phenomena-particularising-consciousness, by means of which the activity is conceived by the minds of common people (*prthagjana*), Çrâvakas, and Pratyekabuddhas. This aspect is called the Body of Transformation (*nirmânakâya*).

But as the beings of this class do not know that the Body of Transformation is merely the shadow [or reflection] of their own evolving-consciousness (*pravrtti-vijñâna*), they imagine that it comes from some external sources, and so they give it a corporeal limitation. But the Body of Transformation [or what amounts to the same thing, the Dharmakâya] has nothing to do with limitation and measurement.[1]

The second aspect [of the Dharmakâya] depends on the activity-consciousness (*karmavijñâna*) by means of which the activity is conceived by the minds of

---

name of Tathâgata ? It expresses true suchness (*bhûtatathatâ*).
... It expresses that he had no origin. ... It expresses the destruction of all qualities (*dharma*). .. It expresses one who had no origin whatever. ... Because, O Subhûti, no-origin is the highest goal."

[1] The older translation reads simply: "They cannot thoroughly understand it [i. e., the true nature of the *Nirmânakâya*]"

Bodhisattvas while passing from their first aspiration (*cittotpâda*) stage up to the height of Bodhisattvahood. This is called the Body of Bliss (*sambhogakâya*).

The body has infinite forms. The form has infinite attributes. The attribute has infinite excellencies. And the accompanying rewards[1] of Bodhisattvas, that is, the region where they are predestined to be born [by their previous karma], also has infinite merits and ornamentations. Manifesting itself everywhere, the Body of Bliss is infinite, boundless, limitless, unintermittent [in its action], directly coming forth from the mind.[2]

All these merits being actualised through the perfuming of such spotless deeds as the pâramitâs[3], etc., as well as through the incomprehensible perfuming power [of enlightenment *a priori*], the Sambhogakâya

---

[1] Buddhists distinguish two kinds of the retribution which we receive as the fruit of karma previously accumulated by ourselves: the first one called "principal" is our bodily existence; the second called "accompanying" is the region where we are destined to be born.

[2] The older translation has: "It is boundless, cannot be exhausted, is free from the signs of limitation. Manifesting itself wherever it should manifest itself, it always exists by itself and is never destroyed or lost."

[3] The six Pâramitâs are commonly enumerated: (1) charity (*dâna*); (2) morality (*çîla*); (3) patience (*ksânti*); (4) energy (*vîrya*); (5) meditation (*dhyâna*); (6) wisdom (*prajnâ*). When we speak of the ten Pâramitâs, the following four are to be added: expediency (*upâya*); prayer or vow (*pranidhâna*); strength (*bala*); knowledge (*jnâna*). An explanation of the six Pâramitâs is given below.

embraces infinite attributes of bliss and merit. Therefore it is also called the Body of Reward.

What is recognised by common people (*prthagjana*), etc., is the coarsest form of the activity of the Dharmakâya. There is a variety of it according to the six different states of creation.[1] It has no attributes of infinite merits and blessings.

What is recognised by Bodhisattvas at the first stage is a finer form of the activity of the Dharmakâya. As they firmly believe in suchness, they can have a partial insight into it, and understand that the Body of the Tathâgata is not departing, is not coming, is free from arrest[2] [i. e., the Tathâgata's work is eternal and constant], that every thing is but a reflected shadow of the mind, not independent of suchness. But these Bodhisattvas have not yet freed themselves from the finest form of particularisation, because they have not yet entered into the order of the Dharmakâya.

Bodhisattvas at the stage of pure-heartedness are able to recognise the finer form of the activity [of the Dharmakâya]. Their insight is more penetrating than the former. When they reach the height of Bodhisattvahood their insight becomes perfect.

By the finer form of the activity we understand

[1] The six states of creation (*gati*) are: (1) *Deva* (gods); (2) *Manushya* (men); (3) *Asura* (demons); (4) *Preta* (ghosts); (5) *Tiryagyoni* (animals); (6) *Nâraka* (inhabitants of hell).

[2] Cf. the *Vajracchedikâ Sûtra*, Chap. XXIX (*Sacred Books of the East*, Vol. XLIX., p. 142).

the Body of Bliss (*sambhogakâya*). As long as they are possessed by the activity-consciousness, they would conceive the Body of Bliss.[1] But when they are liberated from it, all traces of individuation would become obliterated. Because all Tathâgatas come from [one and the same] Dharmakâya, have no distinction of this-ness and that-ness, have no corporeal forms that are characterised by reciprocal limitation.

A question arises here: If the Dharmakâya of Buddhas is devoid of variously differentiated corporeal forms, how is it that it can manifest itself in various corporeal forms at all?

In reply we say: The Dharmakâya can manifest itself in various corporeal forms just because it is the real essence of them. Matter (*rûpa*) and mind (*citta*) from the very beginning are not a duality. So we speak of [the universe as] a system of rationality (*prajñakâya*), seeing that the real nature of matter just constitutes the norm of mind. Again we speak of [the universe as] a system of materiality (*dharmakâya*), seeing that the true nature of mind just constitutes the norm of matter.[2]

Now depending on the Dharmakâya, all Tathâgatas manifest themselves in bodily forms and are inces-

[1] The last two sentences are missing in the older translation.

[2] Cf. the following passages from the *Prajñâ-pâramitâ-hrdaya Sûtra*: "Form (*rûpa*) is emptiness (*çûnyatâ*), and emptiness is indeed form. Emptiness is not different from form, form is not different from emptiness. What is form that is emptiness, what is emptiness that is form."

santly present at all points of space.[1] And Bodhisattvas in the ten quarters, according to their capabilities and wishes, are able to manifest infinite Bodies of Bliss and infinite lands of ornamentation, each one of which, though stamped with the marks of individuality, does not hinder the others from being fused into it, and this [mutual fusion] has no interruption.

But the manifestation of the Dharmakâya in [infinite] bodily forms is not comprehensible to the thought and understanding of common people; because it is the free and subtlest activity of suchness.[2]

Again, in order that all beings might be induced to step forward from the gate of birth-and-death to that of suchness, we endeavor to let them understand that those modes of existence such as matter (*rûpa*), etc. [i. e., the five skandhas][3] are imperfect.

Why are they imperfect?

When we divide some gross [or composite] matter, we can reduce it to atoms (*anu*). But as the atom will also be subject to further division, all forms of material existence, whether gross or fine, are nothing but the shadow of particularisation produced by a subjective mind, and we cannot ascribe any degree of [absolute, or independent] reality to them.

[1] The older translation: "Therefore it is preached that the Dharmakâya is omnipresent. The corporeal forms by which it manifests itself have no limitation.

[2] This passage is missing in the older translation.

[3] They are matter (*rûpa*); sensation (*vedanâ*); idea (*samjnâ*); action (*samskâra*); and consciousness (*vijnâna*).

Let us next go over to and examine the other skandhas [that have temporal existence]. We find there too that we can gradually reduce them to kshanas [i. e., infinitesimal divisions of time], whose nature, however closely scrutinised, does not give any sign of [indivisible] oneness.

It is even the same with the objects of non-aggregate (*asamskrta-dharma*).[1] They cannot have their own existence independent of the universe (*dharmadhâtu*). Be it therefore understood that the same may be said in regard to all objects without exception in the ten quarters of space.[2]

As a lost man who takes the east for the west,

---

[1] All phenomena in the world, physical as well as mental, are divided into two great classes : (1) *Samskrtadharma*, i. e., that which consists of parts temporal or spatial; (2) *Asamskrtadharma*, i. e., that which does not consist of parts. The first class is subdivided into four principal departments which are also subject to a further subdivision, seventy-two in the Hînayâna system (according to the *Abhidharmakoça-çâstra*), and ninety-four in the Mahâyâna (according to the *Vijndnamâtrasiddhi-çâstra*). The four principal departments are (1) *Rûpa* (physical phenomena); (2) *Citta* (thought or understanding); (3) *Caittadharma* or *Cittasamprayuktasamskâra* (mental phenomena); (4) *Cittaviprayuktasamskâra* (that which does not belong to the former, namely, relation that obtains among things). As for the second class, *Asamskrtadharma*, Mahâyânists subdivide it into six while Hinayânists subdivide it into three. For details see the two Çâstras above mentioned.

[2] The last five paragraphs are missing in the older translation which has simply this instead: "The external world which consists in the six objects of sense does not exist independently of our mind, and the mind having no forms and attributes cannot be grasped even if we search for it throughout the ten quarters."

while the quarter is not changed on account of his confusion, so all beings, because of their misleading ignorance, imagine that the mind is being disturbed, while in reality it is not.

But when they understand that the disturbance of the mind [i. e., birth-and-death] is [at the same time] immortality [viz., suchness], they would then enter into the gate of suchness.

2. *The Refutation of False Doctrines.*

All false doctrines invariably come out of the âtman-conception. If we were liberated from it, the existence of false doctrines would be impossible.

There are two kinds of the âtman-conception: (1) Belief in the existence of a personal âtman [or ego-soul]; (2) Belief in the existence of âtman in things [or things-in-themselves].[1]

a. Five False Views Held by Those Who Believe in a Personal Atman.

There are five different views springing from it [belief in the ego], which are held by common people (*prthagjana*).

First, hearing that it is said in the Sûtra[2] that the

---

[1] This denial of the existence of things-in-themselves is one of the principal features of the Mahâyâna as distinguished from the Hînayâna Buddhism.

[2] It is not exactly known to what Sûtra or Sûtras this refers, but the analogy of this kind is frequently met with in most of the Mahâyâna texts.

Dharmakâya of the Tathâgata is perfectly tranquil and may be likened unto space (*âkâsa*), yet not understanding its purport, ignorant people cling to the view that the nature of the Tathâgata is eternal and omnipresent in the same sense as space is.

In order that this clinging to the false doctrine may be eliminated, be it clearly understood that space is nothing but a mode of particularisation and that it has no real existence of its own. Where there is a perception of space, there is side by side a perception of a variety of things, in contradistinction to which space is spoken of as if existing independently. Space therefore exists only in relation to our particularising consciousness.

Further since matter (*rûpa*) as stated before, is merely a particularisation of the confused mind, it is clear enough that space cannot have any independent existence. In a word all modes of relative existence, our phenomenal world as a whole, are created simply by the particularisation of the confused mind. If we become dissociated from the latter, then all modes of relative existence vanish away by themselves; while the soul alone, in its truth and suchness, pervades the whole universe. The soul, therefore, that constitutes the essential nature of the Tathâgata, cannot be compared with space, though the latter may be said to be in a certain limited sense eternal and real.

Secondly, hearing that it is said in the Sûtras that all things in the world without exception are perfect emptiness (*atyantaçûnyatâ*, that even Nirvâna[1] or suchness is also perfect emptiness, is devoid in its true nature of all characteristics (*lakshanâ*), yet not understanding its purport, ignorant people cling to the view that Nirvâna or suchness is a nothing, devoid of contents.

In order that this clinging may be eliminated, be it clearly understood that suchness or Dharmakâya in its self-nature (*svabhâva*) is not a nothing (*çûnyatâ*) but envelopes in full immeasurable merits (*guna*) which make up its true nature.

Thirdly, hearing that it is said in the Sûtras[2] that the Tathâgata's womb (*tathâgatagarbha*) envelopes in full all kinds of merits which constituting its true nature do neither suffer augmentation nor diminution, yet not understanding its purport, ignorant people cling to the view that there is in the Tathâgata's womb itself an inherent and fundamental distinction between the two objects, matter (*rûpa*) and mind (*citta*).

In order that this clinging may be eliminated, be

[1] Fa-tsang, a commentator of the present Discourse, quotes the *Mahâprajnâ-pâramitâ-Sûtra* as here referred to. The Sûtra says: "Even Nirvâna is like a mirage, like a dream. Nay, if there be something superior to Nirvâna, I declare it is also like a mirage, like a dream."

[2] For instance, we read in the second volume of the *Lankâvatara Sûtra* (translated into Chinese by Çiksânanda): "The Tathâgatagarbha is in its intrinsic nature pure, clean, eternal, permanent, unintermittent, and immutable; it embraces the thirty-two excellent qualities, and abides within the body of all sentient beings," etc.

it clearly understood that suchness (*bhûtatathatâ*) has nothing to do with any form of distinction produced by defilement, and that even in case we speak of its possessing innumerable meritorious characteristics, they are free from the traces of defilement.

Fourthly, hearing that it is said in the Sûtras[1] that even all impure and defiled things in the world are produced through the Tathâgata's womb (*tathâgata-garbha*), and that all things in the world are not at variance with suchness, yet not understanding its purport, ignorant people imagine that the Tathâgata's womb all-containingly envelopes all objects of defilement in the world.

In order that this clinging may be eliminated, be it clearly understood that the Tathâgata's womb all-containingly envelopes pure and spotless merits (*guna*) which, outnumbering the sands of the Ganges, are not at variance with suchness; that the prejudices (*âçrava* or *kleça*) and defiled objects, which also outnumber the sands of the Ganges, are nothing but non-entity, have from the first no self-existence (*svabhâva*), have never been in correspondence with the Tathâgata's womb; that there is no reason to suppose that the Tathâgata's womb had been corresponding with defiled objects, but has now by virtue of intellectual intuition been freed from falsity and defilement.

---

[1] Though not exactly known to what Sûtra or Sûtras the reference is made here, we can easily find similar passages in the Mahâyâna texts, such as the *Lankâvatara*, the *Crîmâlâ*, etc.

Fifthly, hearing that it is said in the Sûtras[1] that depending on the Tathâgata's womb, there is birth-and-death (*samsâra*) as well as the attainment of Nirvâna, yet not understanding its purport, ignorant people imagine that depending on the Tathâgata's womb there is a beginning for birth-and-death, and that since there is the beginning, Nirvâna is in turn subject to extinction.

In order that this clinging may be eliminated, be it clearly understood that as the Tathâgata's womb has no beginning, ignorance and birth-and-death depending on it have also no beginning; that it is a view held by the tîrthaka[2] [i. e., the followers of the Vaiçe-

---

[1] These are not also exactly known.

[2] It is not precisely known how many philosophical schools, called tîrthakas by Buddhists, were flourishing just at the time of Açvaghosha. The *Nirvâna Sûtra* and the *Vimalakîrttinirdeça Sûtra* mention six of them which were existing at the time of Buddha: (1) Pûrana Kâçyapa; (2) Maskarin Goçâliputra; (3) Sañjayin Vairattîputra; (4) Ajita Keçakambala; (5) Kakuda Kâtyâyana; (6) Nirgrantha Jñâtiputra. In a commentary on the *Vijñânamâtrâ-çâstra*, however, which is a later production than this Discourse, twelve different tîrthaka schools are enumerated. They are: (1) the Samkhya school; (2) the Vaiçesika school; (3) the school which believes in Maheçvara as the creator; (4) the school which believes in Mahâbrahma as the creator; (5) the school which maintains that Time is the creator; (6) the school which maintains that Space is the creator; (7) the school which maintains that Water is the creator; (8) the school which says that the world exists by itself; (9) the school which says that the creation comes from Quarters; (10) the school which maintains that the Ego is the principle of existence; (11) the school which maintains the immortality of articulate sounds, i. e., the Mîmamsâ school; (12) the Lokâyatika school, an Indian materialism. For further references

sika] and not taught by the Buddha, to say that there are outside of the three worlds[1] (*triloka*) some other beings coming into existence; that the Tathâgata's womb has no future [i. e., time of extinction]; and that those who have an insight into it, will eternally destroy the seeds of birth-and-death and attain to Nirvâna which has also no future [i. e., time of extinction].

These four[2] erroneous views have thus arisen from the conception of a personal âtman, and so we have laid down the four refutations as above mentioned.[3]

b. *Belief in the Existence of Atman in Things.*

As the World-honored One (*Bhagavat*), considering the inferior intellectual calibre of Çrâvakas and Pratyekabuddhas, taught them only the doctrine of non-personal âtman, [and did not make any further

---

see Dr. Enryô Inouye's *Gedô Tetsugaku* (*Philosophical Systems of the Tîrthakas*), 1897, Tokyo, Japan.

[1] They are the world of desire (*kâmaloka*), the world of form (*rûpaloka*), the world of formlessness (*arûpaloka*). (See also p. 77). The *kâmaloka* is divided into hells (*naraka*), region of ghosts (*preta*), animal life (*tiryagyoni*), human life (*manushyaloka*), and region of gods (*deva*); the *rûpaloka* into 17 heavenly abodes corre‑
\̇ding to the three stages of Dhyâna; the *arûpaloka* into four
⁀ly abodes. For details see the second chapter of the *Abhi‑
ıkoça-Çâstra*, by Vasnbandhu.

e number "four" in this paragraph should be "five," for or enumerates five misunderstandings and their refuta‑ we have seen.

⁀ whole passage is missing in the older translation.

demonstration of the doctrine], the people have in the meantime formed a fixed idea on the transitoriness of the five skandhas,[1] and, being terrified at the thought of birth and death, have fanatically craved for Nirvâna.

In order that this clinging may be eliminated, be it clearly understood that the essence of the five skandhas is uncreate, there is no annihilation of them; that since there is no annihilation of them, they are in their [metaphysical] origin Nirvâna itself; that if one be absolutely freed from particularisation and attachment, one will understand that all things both pure and defiled have only relative existence.

Be it therefore known that all things in the world from the beginning are neither matter (*rûpa*), nor mind (*citta*), nor intelligence (*prajñâ*), nor consciousness (*vijñâna*), nor non-being (*abhâva*), nor being (*bhâva*); they are after all inexplicable. The reason why the Tathâgata nevertheless endeavors to instruct by means of words and definitions is through his good and excellent skilfulness [or expediency, *upâya-kauçalya*].[2] He only provisionally makes use of words and definitions to lead all beings, while his real object is to make them abandon symbolism and directly enter

[1] See p. 104, footnote.
[2] See the second chapter of the *Saddarmapundarîka Sûtra*, in which Buddha teaches how the only one yâna (vehicle) is split through his transcendental upâya (skilfulness or expediency) into three yânas: Çrâvakayâna, Pratyekabuddhayâna, and Bodhisattvayâna.

into the real reality (*tattva*). Because if they indulge themselves in reasonings, attach themselves to sophistry, and thus foster their subjective particularisation, how could they have the true wisdom (*tattvajñâna*) and attain to Nirvâna?

3. Ways of Practising the Right Path.

By this we mean that all Bodhisattvas, by their aspiration (*cittotpâda*)[1] and discipline (*caryâcarana*), will be able to attain to the reason that made all Tathâgatas perceive the path (*mârga*).

Briefly stated, there are three kinds of aspiration: (1) Aspiration through the perfection of faith; (2) Aspiration through knowledge and practice; (3) Aspiration through intellectual intuition.

By whom, and by which deeds, can faith (*çraddhâ*) be perfected and can the aspiration be awakened?

Now the people who belong to the group of incon-

[1] Aspiration which does not exactly correspond to the Chinese *fah hsin* and Sanskrit *cittotpâda*, has been retained for lack of a fitter term. It has a technical sense in Buddhism. Literally, *fah* or *utpâda* means producing, raising, or awakening, while *hsin* or *citta* as noticed elsewhere is mind, thought, or consciousness. *Cittopâda*, however, is more than the raising of one's thought to a higher religious life; it means the recognition of the truth that one is in possession within oneself of the highest perfect knowledge (*samyaksambodhi*); it is the birth within oneself of a higher ethical impulse constituting the essence of religion. A fuller form of *fah hsin* is *fah bodhi hsin* or *fah anuttarasamyaksambodhi hsin*. See the Mahâyâna Sûtras such as the *Saddharma Pundarîka*, *Vajracchedikâ*, *Sukhâvatî Vyuha*, *Lankâvatara*, *Avatamsaka*, etc.

stancy (*aniyatarâçi*),[1] by virtue of their root of merit (*kuçalamûla*), which has a perfuming power, firmly believe in the retribution of karma, practise the ten virtues (*daçakuçalâni*),[2] loathe the sufferings of birth and death, seek after the most excellent enlightenment (*Samyaksambodhi*), and seeing Buddhas and Bodhisattvas they wait on them, make offerings to them, discipline themselves in many [meritorious] deeds; and after the lapse of ten thousand kalpas (eons), their faith will finally be perfected.

Since then either by virtue of the instruction received from Buddhas and Bodhisattvas, or on account of their deep compassion (*mahâkarunâ*), or from their desire to preserve the right doctrine (*saddharma*) against its corruption, their aspiration [to the highest truth] will be awakened.

After having awakened the aspiration they will

---

[1] There are three groups of people: (1) Those who are constantly abiding in absolute truth (*samyaktvaniyata-râçi*); (2) Those who are constantly abiding in falsehood (*mithyâtvaniyata-râçi*); (3) Those who are inconstant (*aniyata-râçi*).

[2] The ten virtues (*daçakuçalâni*) consist in not committing the ten evils (*daçâkuçalâni*) which are as follows: (1) Killing a living being (*prânâtipâda*); (2) Stealing (*adattâdâna*); (3) Committing adultery (*kâmamithyâcâra*); (4) Lying (*mrshâvâda*); (5) Slander (*paiçunya*); (6) Insulting speech (*pârushya*); (7) Frivolous talk (*sambhinnapralâpa*); (8) Avarice (*abhidhya*); (9) Evil intent (*vyâpâda*); (10) False view (*mithyâdrshthi*). The ten evils here enumerated should be avoided by the lay members of Buddhism. For the Çramaneras there is a different set of precepts specially intended for them, called the *Daçaçikshapada*, with which the ten virtues must not be confused as they are by some.

enter into the group of constant truth (*samyaktvaniyata-râçi*) and never relapse, always abiding in the essence of the Buddha-seed and identifying themselves with its excellent principle.

There is, however, a certain class of people whose root of merit (*kuçalamûla*) from time immemorial is poor, and whose prejudices (*kleça* or *âvrava*) are intense, deeply veiling their minds. Such people, even if they see Buddhas and Bodhisattvas, wait on them, and make offerings to them, will sow merely the seeds of men (*manushya*) and gods (*deva*) [i. e., they will be born in the future as men or gods], or the seeds of the enlightenment of Çrâvakas and Pratyekabuddhas [i. e., their attainment would not be higher than that of Crâvakas or Pratyekabuddhas].

Some of them may even aspire to seek after the Mahâbodhi,[1] but owing to the instability of their character, they will ever osciliate between progress and retrogression.

Some of them, happening to see Buddhas and Bodhisattvas, may make offerings to them, wait on them, practise many [meritorious] deeds, and, while ten thousand mahâkalpas (æons) are not yet elapsed, may meantime come into some favorable circumstances and thereby awake aspiration. What are those favorable circumstances? For instance, they may witness the personal figure of a Buddha, or may make some offerings to the congregation of priests

[1] The older translation reads "Mahâyâna."

(*samgha*), or may be instructed by Çrâvakas or Pratyekabuddhas, or may be moved by seeing others aspire [to the highest truth].

But this kind of aspiration as a rule is not constant. In case they come into unfavorable circumstances, they may happen to fall down to the stage of Çrâvakahood or Pratyekabuddhahood.

Now, briefly speaking, three faculties of the soul will be awakened by the perfection of faith: (1) rightness of comprehension [lit., right, straight mind], for it truthfully and intuitively contemplates suchness (*bhûtatathatâ*); (2) profundity of virtue [lit., deep, heavy mind], for it rejoices in accumulating all good deeds; (3) greatness of compassion (*mahâkarunâ*), for it desires to uproot the miseries (*duhkha*) of all beings.

It may be asked whether there is ever any need for one to discipline oneself in all good deeds and to try to save mankind, since all sentient beings (*sarvasattva*) as well as all things (*sarvadharma*) in the world, abiding in the oneness of the universe (*dharmadhâtu*) that has no second, will, as can be logically inferred, have nothing to do but calmly to contemplate suchness.

In reply we say, yes. Because the mind may be likened unto a precious jewel which is pure and bright in its essence but buried in a gross veinstone. Now there is no reason to suppose that one can make it clean and pure only by contemplating it, and without applying any means [of purification] or a degree of workmanship.

It is even the same with suchness. Though it is pure and bright in its essence and sufficiently envelopes all merits (*guna*), yet it is deeply buried in infinite external defilements. And there is no reason to suppose that a man can make it pure and clean only by earnest contemplation on it, and without trying any means [of emancipation] or of discipline.

It is therefore an urgent necessity that all good deeds should be accumulated, that all beings should be delivered, that those infinite external defilements and impurities should be cast off, that the true doctrine should be revealed.

With regard to "means" [or "skilfulness," *upâya*] there are, briefly stated, four kinds.

The first one is called the means of practising the fundamental [truth, *mûla*]. That is to say, by contemplating the true essence of all dharmas, which, being uncreate and free from imagination, is not concerned with the metempsychosis of birth and death, and by contemplating the truth that all things originate from the co-operation of the principle (*hetu*) and the causes (*pratyaya*), and that the retribution of karma is irrevocable, one will evoke deep compassion, discipline oneself in all good deeds, embrace and convert all beings, and not dwell in Nirvâna, since suchness [in its absolute aspect] has nothing to do with Nirvâna or with birth-and-death. As this attitude [towards all objects] is in accord [with the nature of suchness], it is called the means of practising the [fundamental] truth.

The second one is called the means of abeyance. That is, by feeling shame and remorse, one may put an end to all evils and not let them grow, since suchness is free from all marks of imperfection. Thus to be in accord with suchness and to put an end to all evils is called the means of abeyance.

The third one is called the means of strengthening the root of merits (*kuçalamúla*). By raising reverential feelings toward the Triple Treasure (*triratna*), one will revere, make offerings to, pay homage to, praise, rejoice in, and beseech the Triple Treasure; and thereupon one's orthodox faith being strengthened, one will at last awake a desire for the most excellent knowledge (*bodhiparinishpatti*). Through the protection of the majestic power of the Buddha, Dharma, and Samgha, one's karma-hindrances (*karmâvarana*) will now get purified and one's root of merit firmly established; because suchness is free from all hindrances and envelopes all merits. Thus to be in accord with suchness and to practise good deeds is called the means of strengthening the root of merits.

The fourth one is called the universal means of great vows (*mahâpranidhâna*). That is, one may make the vow that in ages to come all beings should universally be delivered and take refuge at ease in the

Anupadhiçesa Nirvâna,[1] because the true nature of all objects is free from relativity, is one and the same, making no distinction between this and that, and is absolutely calm and tranquil. Thus to be in accord with the three attributes [i. e., non-relativity, sameness, tranquillity] of suchness and to make such a great vow is called the universal means of great vows.

[Now to return to the former subject], when the Bodhisattva thus aspires to the highest truth, he is able to have a partial insight into the Dharmakâya of the Buddha; and according to the power of the vow (*pranidhânavaça*), he performs eight things, to wit, his descent from the palace in the Tushita heaven[2]

---

[1] Mahâyânists in general distinguish four aspects of Nirvâna; (1) Nirvâna that is pure and spotless in its self-nature, i. e., absolute suchness, possessed equally by all beings; (2) Nirvâna that has remnant (*upadhiçesa*), i. e., a state of relative suchness, which, though freed from the affectional hindrance (*kleçâvarana*), is still under the fetter of materiality, which causes suffering and misery; (3) Nirvâna that has no remnant (*anupadhiçesa*), i. e., a state of relative suchness which is free from the misery of birth and death, being entirely liberated from the fetter of materiality; (4) Nirvâna that has no fixed abode, i. e., a state of suchness in its spontaneous activity which is free from the intellectual hindrance (*jneyâvarana*) and full of love and wisdom, believes neither in birth-and-death nor in Nirvâna, but eternally abiding in the suchness of things benefits all sentient beings. Çrâvakas and Pratyekabuddhas can recognise the first three aspects of Nirvâna, but the last one is known only to Buddhas and Bodhisattvas. For further details see the tenth volume of the *Vijnânamâtrasiddhi Çâstra*, translated into Chinese by Hüan-tsang.

[2] One of the six heavenly abodes of the *Kâmaloka* (world of desire). The heavenly abodes are: (1) Region of the four kings of the cardinal points (*mahârâjakâyika*); (2) that of the thirty-

[to this world], his entrance into the human womb, his stay therein, his birth, his renunciation, his attainment of Buddhahood, his revolution of the Dharmawheel (*dharmaċakra*), and lastly his Parinirvâna.

He is not, however, as yet to be called absolute Dharmakâya, for he has not yet completely destroyed the impure[1] karma that has been accumulated during his numberless existences in the past; perchance by the influence of the evil karma he may suffer a little amount of misery. But he suffers it only for a short time, and this not because of his being fettered by the evil karma, but because of his own vow-power (*pranidhânavaça*) [which he made for the universal emancipation of mankind].

It is sometimes said in the Sûtra[2] that even those Bodhisattvas who aspired [to the highest truth] through the perfection of their faith might relapse and fall down to the evil creation (*apâyagati*).[3] But this was

three gods (*trâyastrinça*); (3) the *Yâmâ*; (4) the *Tushita*; (5) the *Nirmânatis*; (6) the *Paranirmita-vaçavatins*. See also the note to Triloka, p. 77.

[1] The term *impure* does not mean immoral, but relative conditional, dualistic or material, in contradistinction to pure, absolute, unconditional, spiritual, etc.

[2] For instance, it is stated in the second fasciculus of the *Bodhisattva-kusumamâlâ-pûrvakarma Sûtra* (? *P'u-sa ying-lo pên-yeh Ching* in Chinese, translated by Fo-nien towards the end of the third century) that those Bodhisattvas who have not yet entered on the eighth stage (there are ten stages) of Bodhisattvahood may happen to relapse in his religious course, if not be able to receive instruction in the Dharma from some fully enlightened teachers.

[3] Three of the six *gatis* are the *apâyagati* (evil path) : Hell

only said to encourage those novices who are apt to give themselves up to indulgence and so may fail to enter into the right order [i. e., *samyaktvaniyata*], though they may not really fall down [into the evil path].

Further the Bodhisattva has since his first aspiration disciplined himself in those deeds which are beneficial both to himself and others, and thereby his heart has become free from timidity, inasmuch as he would not shudder even at the thought of falling down to the stage of Çrâvakahood or Prayekabuddhahood, any more than to the evil creation (*apâyagati*).

If he learn that he is able to attain to Buddhahood only after an assiduous observance of various rules of austerity and mortification during immeasurable asamkheya-kalpas,[1] he will never be frightened nor will he falter. How then could he ever raise such thoughts as cherished by Çrâvakas or Pratyekabuddhas? How then could he fall down to the evil creation (*apâyagati*)? He has a firm faith in the truth that all things (*sarvadharma*) from the beginning are in their nature Nirvâna itself.[2]

(*nâraka*); ghost (*preta*); and animal life (*tiryagyoni*). Sometimes demon (*asura*) is added to make the fourth.

[1] For an explanation see. 87, footnote.

[2] The same monistic idea is expressed also in the following famous phrases: "Âçravas (desires or prejudices) are nothing but Bodhi (enlightenment), and birth-and-death (or this world of transformation) is nothing but Nirvâna." Individuation is the product of subjectivity; the universe in reality is one great whole.

This sort of aspiration (*cittotpâda*) is more excellent than the former, because the first asamkheyakalpa of Bodhisattvas of this class is approaching to an end, because they have attained a thorough knowledge of suchness, because all their acts are performed without any stain of attachment.

As they know that the nature of the Dharma, being free from the trace of covetousness, is the perfection of pure and stainless charity (*dânapâramitâ*), they in conformity to it practise charity (*dânapâramitâ*).

As they know that the nature of the Dharma, being free from the influence of the five sensual passions, and, having nothing to do with immorality, is the perfection of pure and stainless morality (*çilapâramitâ*), they in conformity to it practise morality (*çilapâramitâ*).

As they know that the nature of the Dharma, having nothing to do with grievance and being free from malice, is the perfection of pure and stainless patience (*kshântipâramitâ*), they in conformity to it practise patience (*kshântipâramitâ*).

As they know that the nature of the Dharma, being free from physical and mental limitations and having nothing to do with indolence, is the perfection of pure and stainless energy (*viryapâramitâ*), they in conformity to it practise energy (*viryapâramitâ*).

As they know that the nature of the Dharma, having nothing to do with disturbance or confusion, is the perfection of pure and stainless tranquilisation (*dhyânapâramitâ*), they in conformity to it practise tranquilisation (*dhyânapâramitâ*).

As they know that the nature of the Dharma, being free from the darkness of ignorance, is the perfection of pure and stainless wisdom (*prajñâpâramitâ*), they in conformity to it practise wisdom (*prajñâpâramitâ*).

What is the object of which the Bodhisattva from the stage of pure-heartedness up to the height of Bodhisattvahood has attained an intellectual intuition? The object is no less than suchness itself. We call it an object on account of the evolving-consciousness (*pravrtti-vijñâna*). But in truth there is no object in perfect intellectual intuition, neither is there a subject in it; because the Bodhisattva by means of his wisdom of non-particularisation intuitively perceives suchness (*bhûtatathatâ*) or Dharmakâya, which is beyond the range of demonstration and argumentation.

Thus he is able in a moment to go over all the worlds in the ten quarters and to make offerings to all Buddhas and to beseech them to revolve the Wheel of the Dharma (*darmacakrapravartana*). His sole desire being to benefit all beings, he does not care for any melodious sounds or words [which he can enjoy in his heavenly abode].[1] In order to encourage weak-hearted people, he shows great energy and

---

[1] In the older translation we read: "Having in view only the emancipation and beneficence of all beings, he [Bodhisattva] does not rely on words and characters."

attains to perfect enlightenment (*anuttarasamyaksam-bodhi*), all at once annihilating the lapse of immeasurable asamkheyakalpas. Or in order to instigate indolent people, he sometimes attains to Buddhahood only after long discipline and mortification through the period of immeasurable asamkheyakalpas. The reason why he achieves in this wise infinite methods (*upâya*) [of salvation] is that he wishes thereby to benefit all beings.[1]

But in fact the intrinsic nature, the faculties, the aspiration, and the intellectual attainment of all Bodhisattvas are equal [in value] and there is not any scale of gradation in them. Because they will all equally and assuredly attain to the most perfect enlightenment, only after the elapsing of three asamkheyakalpas. Yet as there are differences in various states of existence regarding their objects of seeing, hearing, etc., as well as regarding their faculties, their desires, and their character; so there are correspondingly many different forms of religious discipline [destined to] them.

(c) Three different operations of the mind are revealed in this aspiration by means of intellectual intuition: (1) Pure consciousness originating in the mind as it becomes free from particularisation; (2) moral consciousness [lit., *upâya-citta?*] originating in the mind

---

[1] The older translation reads: "It is out of [human] comprehension that he [Bodhisattva] can achieve such innumerable methods [of salvation]"

as it spontaneously performs those deeds which are beneficent to others; (3) unconscious activity (*karma-vijñânacitta*) originating in the mind as it achieves a most hidden mode of activity.

Again the Bodhisattva, having attained to the perfection of bliss and wisdom, which are his two marks of adornment, has in reaching the height of evolution (*akanishtha*) also obtained the most venerable and excellent body in the whole universe. By means of that knowledge which intuitively identifies itself [with enlightenment *a priori*], he has all at once uprooted ignorance; and thus obtaining omniscience (*sarvâkârajñâna*),[1] he spontaneously achieves incomprehensible [or divine] deeds (*acintyakarma*), reveals himself in immeasurable worlds in the ten quarters, and works out the universal emancipation of mankind.

A question arises here. As space is infinite, worlds are infinite. As worlds are infinite, beings are infinite. As beings are infinite, the modes of mentation are also infinitely diversified. And as all these objects and conditions (*vishaya*) have no limits, they can hardly be known or understood [in all their multitudinousness]. If, now, ignorance being destroyed, all modes

---

[1] A distinction is sometimes made between *Sarvâkârajñâna*, *Sarvajñâna* and *Mârgajñâna*: *Sarvâkârajñâna* is the knowledge by which we are enabled to know all forms and manifestations in their fundamental oneness; *Sarvajñâna* is simply the knowledge of all things, or omniscience; *Mârgajñâna* is the knowledge by which we can recognise the path leading to final emancipation. But they are practically the same.

of mentation are entirely annihilated as well, how can the Bodhisattva understand all things and complete his omniscience (*sarvākārajñāna*)?

In reply we say: All so-called illusory phenomena are in truth from the beginning what they are; and their essence is nothing but the one soul [or mind]. Though ignorant minds that cling to illusory objects cannot understand that all things are in their nature the highest reality (*paramārtha*), all Buddha-Tathāgatas being free from clinging [or particularising] are able to have an insight into the true nature of things. And by virtue of their great wisdom they illuminate all distinctions between the defiled and the pure; through their immeasurable and inexhaustible sources of expediency (*upāyakauçalya*), which is good and excellent, they benefit and gladden all beings according to the latters' various necessities and capabilities. Therefore the mind that is saturated with subjectivity is annihilated, while all things are understood and omniscience (*sarvākārajñāna*) is attained.[1]

[1] The older translation reads: "In reply we say: All phenomenal objecs (*vishaya*) are from the beginning [or in their metaphysical origin] of the one mind which is free from imagination and subjectivity. As all beings illusively perceive the existence of the phenomenal world (*vishaya*), they impose limitations on the mind. As they thus illusively cherish imagination and subjectivity, which are not in accordance with the nature of the Dharma, they cannot thoroughly understand it. All Buddha-Tathâgatas are, however, free from illusive perception, and [therefore their knowledge is] omniscient, because the mind constituting the principle of all things is true and valid. The self-essence [of all Buddhas] illuminates all illusive phenomena, possesses a great wisdom-activity and in-

Another question presents itself here: If all Buddhas who are in possession of infinite expediencies (*upâya*) can spontaneously benefit all beings in the ten quarters, why is it that the latter cannot always see Buddhas in person, or witness their divine transformations, or hear their instructions in the Doctrine?

The reply is: Tathâgatas are really in possession of those expediencies, and they are only waiting to reveal themselves to all beings as soon as the latter can purify their own minds.[1]

When a mirror is covered with dust, it cannot reflect images. It can do so only when it is free from stain. It is even the same with all beings. If their minds are not clear of stain, the Dharmakâya cannot reveal itself in them. But if they be freed from stain, then it will reveal itself.

IV. PRACTICE OF FAITH.

In what does the practice of faith (*çraddhâ*) consist?

This part of the Discourse is intended for those beings who have not yet entered into the order of constant truth (*samyaktvaniyata-râçi*).

numerable means [of salvation], whereby, according to the intellectual capacity of all beings, they can reveal to them various significances of the Doctrine. Therefore it is called the *Sarva-kârajnâna.*"

[1] In the older translation we read: "The Dharmakâya of all Buddha-Tathâgatas is universal (*samatâ*) and pervades every thing; it is free from compulsion and therefore spontaneous, manifesting itself through the minds of all beings."

What is meant by faith? How should one practise faith?

There are four aspects of faith. [As to faith in general]: (1) To believe in the fundamental [truth], that is, to think joyfully of suchness (*bhūtatathatā*). [As to particular faiths:] (2) To believe in the Buddha as sufficingly enveloping infinite merits, that is, to rejoice in worshipping him, in paying homage to him, in making offerings to him, in hearing the good doctrine (*saddharma*), in disciplining oneself according to the doctrine, and in aspiring after omniscience (*sarvajñāna*). (3) To believe in the Dharma as having great benefits, that is, to rejoice always in practising all pāramitās. (4) To believe in the Samgha as observing true morality, that is, to be ready to make offerings to the congregation of Bodhisattvas, and to practise truthfully all those deeds which are beneficial at once to oneself and others.

(C. Faith will be perfected by practising the following five deeds: (1) charity (*dāna*); (2) morality (*çīla*); (3) patience (*kshānti*); (4) energy (*vīrya*), (5) cessation [or tranquilisation, *çamatha*] and intellectual insight (*vidarçana* or *vipaçyana*)

How should people practise charity (*dāna*)?

(1) If persons come and ask them for something, they should, as far as their means allow, supply it ungrudgingly and make them rejoice in it. (2) If they see people threatened with danger, they should try every means of rescuing them and impart to them a

feeling of fearlessness (*vaiçaradya*). (3) If they have people who come to them desiring instruction in the Doctrine, they should, so far as they are acquainted with it, and, according to their own discretion, deliver speeches on religious discipline.

And when they are performing those three acts of charity, let them not cherish any desire for fame or advantages, nor covet any worldly rewards. Only thinking of those benefits and blessings that are at once for themselves and others, let them aspire to the most excellent, most perfect knowledge (*anuttarasamyaksambodhi*).

How should they practise morality (*çila*)?

Those Bodhisattvas who have families [i. e., lay members of Buddhism] should abstain from killing, stealing, adultery, lying, duplicity, slander, frivolous talk, covetousness, malice, currying favor, and false doctrines.[1]

In the case of Çramanas, they should, in order to vanquish all prejudices (*kleça* or *âçrava*), retire from the boisterousness of worldly life, and, abiding in solitude (*aranya*), should practise those deeds which lead to moderation and contentment as well as those of the Dhûtaguna.[2] Even at the violation of minor

---

[1] Açvaghosha evidently refers to the ten virtues (*daçakuçalâni*), for which see p. 114, though this list counts more than ten.

[2] There are twelve dhûtagunas or dhûtagangas to be observed by Bhikshus; *dhûta* means shaking off, that is, shaking off the dust of evil passions: (1) *Paindapâtika*, the rule to live on whatever food they can get by begging from door to door, that they

rules (*çila*) they should deeply feel fear, shame, and remorse. Strictly observing all those precepts given by the Tathâgata, they should not call forth the blame or disgust of the outsider, but they should endeavor to induce all beings to abandon the evil and to practise the good.[1]

How should they practise patience (*kshânti*)?

If they meet with the ills of life they should not

---

may become free from egotism. (2) *Traiciivarika*, the rule allowing the possession of three clothings: *Samghâti*, dress made of scraps; *Uttarasamghâti*, outer robe; *Antaravâsaka*, something like skirt. (3) *Khalupaçcâdbhaktika*, the prohibition of taking any food or beverage when the proper time is over, lest their attention should be disturbed. (4) *Naishadhyika*, to be in a sitting attitude while sleeping, that they may not become over-indolent (5) *Yathâsamstarika*, spreading a night-couch where they happen to be. (6) *Vrkshamûlika*, sitting under a tree. (7) *Ekâsanika*, taking one meal in a day, that their mental energy may not be weakened by eating too often. (8) *Abhyavakâçika*, living in an unsheltered place. (9) *Aranyaka*, leading a solitary, retired life in the wood. (10) *Cmâçânaka*, abiding in or by a cemetery, that they may constantly ponder on the transiency and uncleanliness of bodily existence. (11) *Pâmskûlika*, the wearing of the dress made of rags or remnants, that they may have no attachment to luxury. (12) *Nâmatika*, wearing cloth made of hair. There is a Sûtra named *Twelve Dhûtagunas* among the Chinese collection of the Tripitaka. The list in that book is a little different from what we have here; the fifth and twelfth are dropped and instead of them we have the rule of begging in due order, corresponding to *Sapadâna-cârikâ* in the Pâli list, and the rule of prohibiting taking too much food at one time, which overtaxing the stomach will obscure the clearness of mind.

[1] The reference is to the threefold precept (*trividhaçila*) which is (1) the precept of good behavior (*sambhâraçila*); (2) the precept of accumulating virtues (*kuçalasamgrâhaçila*); (3) the precept of being benevolent towards all beings (*sattvârthakriyâçila*).

shun them. If they suffer sufferings, they should not feel afflicted. But they should always rejoice in contemplating the deepest significance of the Dharma.[1]

How should they practise energy (*virya*)?

Practising all good deeds, they should never indulge in indolence (*kausidya*). They should think of all their great mental and physical sufferings, which they are now vainly suffering on account of their having coveted worldly objects during their existences in innumerable former ages (*kalpa*), and which do not give the least nourishment to their spiritual life. They should, therefore, in order to be emancipated from those sufferings in the future, be indefatigably energetic, and never raise the thought of indolence, but endeavor, out of deep compassion (*mahâkaruna*), to benefit all beings. Though disciplining themselves in faith, all novice Bodhisattvas, on account of the hindrances of their evil karma (*karmâvarana*) produced by the violation of many important precepts in their previous existences, may sometimes be annoyed by evil Mâras, sometimes entangled in worldly engagements, sometimes threatened by various diseases. As these things will severally disturb their religious course and make them neglect practising good deeds, they should dauntlessly, energetically, unintermittently, all

[1] The older translation reads: "Patiently bearing evils inflicted by others, they should not cherish any idea of revenge. They should also bear such [worldly vicissitudes] as prosperity and decline, reprehension and commendation, renown and defamation, worry and ease, etc."

six watches, day and night, pay homage to all Buddhas, make offerings (*pújá*) to them, praise them, repent and confess (*kshamá*) to them, aspire to the most excellent knowledge (*samyaksambodhi*), make great vows (*mahápranidhána*); and thereby annihilate the hindrances of evils and increase the root of merit (*kuçalamúla*).

How should they practise cessation [or tranquilisation, *çamatha*] and intellectual insight (*vidarçana* or *vipaçyana*)?

To bring all mental states that produce frivolous sophistries to a stand is called cessation. To understand adequately the law of causality and transformation is called intellectual insight. Each of them should be practised separately by the beginner. But when by degrees he obtains facility and finally attains to perfection, the two will naturally become harmonised.[1]

Those who practise cessation should dwell in solitude (*áranyaka*) and, sitting cross-legged,[2] rectify the

---

[1] Observe that cessation should be practised by the beginner, and for a time only, for the purpose of affording the mind an appreciation of suchness in its purity; the conception of this state of abstraction should then be harmonised with intellectual insight. Observe also that the methods of Indian recluses, such as fixing the breath and going into trances by fixing the thoughts on objects, are rejected as improper. The practice should assist a beginner to understand that suchness, though all particulars are dependent on it, is in its purity a reality.

[2] Those who practise this have to place the left leg above the right with both close to the body, so that the toes of the left foot shall rest on the right thigh, and those of the right foot on the left thigh, while the soles are turned upwards. This posture is con-

attitude and pacify the mind.[1] Do not fix the thoughts on the breath (*ánápánasmrti*)[2]; do not fix the thoughts on the forms (*samjña*)[3] and colors; do not fix the

sidered to be the best adapted for meditation or for obtaining mental equilibrium.

[1] Among the followers of the Dhyâna sect both in Japan and China, it is customary, while sitting cross-legged and meditating on religious subjects, to expand the abdomen outwards and to breathe very slowly, by which they can, in their opinion, most effectively concentrate their attention and gain perfect mental equilibrium. Prof. J. M. Baldwin in his *Mental Development* says in connexion with bashfulness and modesty, p. 205 footnote: "The only way that I, for one, can undo this distressing outgo of energy, and relieve these uncomfortable inhibitions, is to expand the abdomen by a strong muscular effort and at the same time breathe in as deeply as I can. . . . The comparative relief found in expanding the abdominal muscles is probably due to the fact that it allows the contents of the body to fall, and so relieves the heart from any artificial pressure which may be upon it from the surrounding organs. Further the increased heart-action which is itself a part of shyness requires all the space it can get."

[2] One of the eight subjects of recollection (*anusmrti*), or of the five methods of mental pacification. The eight subjects are: (1) Buddha; (2) dharma; (3) samgha; (4) *çíla*, morality; (5) *cága* or *tyága*, liberality; (6) *deva*, gods; (7) *ánápána*, regulation of inspiration and respiration; (8) *marana*, death. The five methods are: (1) *Açubhabhávaná*, contemplation on the impurity of the body; (2) *maitrîkaruná*, love and compassion; (3) *ánápánasmrti*, the regulation of inspiration and respiration; (4) *nidána*, law of transformation; (5) *buddhasmrti*, recollection on Buddha.

[3] There are nine Açbhasamjnâs, notions arising from the contemplation of the impurity of a dead body, which is intended to convince one of the fact that our body is not worth while clinging to: (1) Swelling (*vyâdhmataka*); (2) fissuring from decay (*vipáyaka*); (3) bloody (*vilohita*); (4) festering (*vipadumaka*); (5) blackish (*vinîlaka*); (6) being devoured by animals (*vikhâditaka*); (7) scattering (*vikshiptaka*); (8) bone (*asthi*); (9) burned up (*vidagdhaka*). The Pâli Açubhas count one more.

thoughts on space (*âkâṣa*) ;[1] do not fix the thoughts on earth, water, fire, and ether;[1] do not fix the thoughts on what you see, hear, learn, or memorise (*vijñânakrtsnâyatana*)[1]. All particularisations, imaginations and recollections should be excluded from consciousness, even the idea of exclusion being excluded; because [the suchness of] all things is uncreate, eternal, and devoid of all attributes (*alakṣhana*).

[Now in the constant flux of thoughts,] that which precedes [i. e., a sensation] has been awakened by an external object ; so the next [step to be taken by the practiser] is to abandon the idea of an external world. Then that which succeeds [in that constant flux or thoughts] is elaborated in hls own mind ; so he should in turn abandon reflexion [or thought]. In short, as his attention is distracted by the external world [outer *vishaya*], he is warned to turn it to inner consciousness [inner *citta*]; while as his retrospection in turn calls forth a succession of thoughts [or ideal associations], he is again warned not to attach himself to the latter ; because, independent of suchness, they [thoughts] have no existence of their own.

At all times, while moving, standing, sitting, or

---

[1] These constitute the ten *Krtsâyatanas* which are : (1) Blue (*nîla*); (2) yellow (*pîta*); (3) red (*lohita*); (4) white (*avadâta*); (5) earth (*prtivî*); (6) water (*ap*) ; (7) fire (*tejas*); (8) air (*vâyu*); (9) space (*âkâsa*) ; (10) consciousness (*vijnâna*). The term *Krtsâyâtana* means an universal object or element on which the attention of a samâdhi-practiser is to be fixed.

lying, the practiser should constantly discipline himself as above stated. Gradually entering the samâdhi of suchness,[1] he will finally vanquish all prejudices (*kleça* or *âçrava*), be strengthened in faith (*çraddhâ*), and immediately attain to the state of never-returning (*avaivartikatva*). But those who are sceptical, sacrilegious, destitute of faith, encumbered with the hindrances (*âvarana*) of karma, arrogant, or indolent, are not entitled to enter therein.

And again when the practiser by virtue of his samâdhi[2] attains an immediate insight into the nature of the universe (*dharmadhâtu*), he will recognise that the Dharmakâya of all Tathâgatas and the body of all beings are one and the same (*samatâ*), are consubstantial (*ekalakshana*). On that account it is also called the samâdhi of oneness (*ekalakshanasamâdhi*). By disciplining oneself in this samâdhi, one can obtain in-

---

[1] That is, perfect identification of oneself with suchness.

[2] *Samâdhi* is commonly rendered by ecstasy, trance, concentration, or meditation, all of which are misleading. The term means mental equilibrium, and the reasons why Buddhism recommends the practising of it are, that it helps us in keeping our minds free from disturbance, that it prepares us for a right comprehension of the nature of things, that it subjugates momentary impulses, giving us time for deliberation. Ecstasy or trance, instead of producing those benefits, will lead us to a series of hallucinations, and this is the very opposite of mental quietude. Rhys Davids thinks samâdhi corresponds to faith in Christianity (*S. B. E.*, XI., p. 145), and S. Beal agrees with him in his translation of Açvaghosha's *Buddhacarita*; but I doubt its correctness for the above-stated reasons.

finite samâdhis, because suchness is the source of all samâdhis.

Some people scantily supplied with the root of merit (*kuçalamûla*) may yield to the temptation of Mâras, tîrthakas, or evil spirits. [For instance] those evil ones sometimes assuming horrible forms may frighten the practiser; sometimes manifesting themselves in beautiful figures, they may fascinate him;[1] sometimes appearing in form of a deva, or of a Boddhisattva, or even of a Buddha with all his excellent and magnified features,[2] they may speak about dhârani[3] or the pâramitâ, or may give instructions about various means of emancipation (*mukti*), declaring that there is no hatred, no friendship, no causation, no

---

[1] The older translation has the following passage inserted here: "If he [the practiser] remembers that these are merely subjective, the phenomena will disappear by themselves and will no more trouble him."

[2] Buddha is supposed to have thirty-two general and eighty minor marks of bodily perfection. For particulars see the *Dharmasamgraha*, pp. 18, 19, 51 et seq., edited by Kasawara Kenjiu.

[3] *Dhârani*, which comes from the root *dhr*, meaning to hold, to maintain, to retain, to support, etc., is the name given to any concise statement describing Buddha's virtue, or stating some essential points of Buddhist teachings, or expressing supplication, or containing the exclamations of a vehement feeling; and it implies many significances in a few words, it is a kind of epigram. But later Buddhists came to use the term in quite a different sense; they called a dhârani any tantric expression which was considered to have some mysterious, supernatural powers to bring wealth to destroy enemies, to keep away calamities, etc., etc. Here *dhârani* means simply any epigrammatic proposition which will serve as a key to the deep significance of the Doctrine.

retribution, or declaring that all things in the world are absolute nothingness (*atyantaçûnyatâ*), that they are in their essence Nirvâna itself. Or they may reveal to the practiser his own past and future states of existence, they may teach him to read the thoughts of others,[1] may grant him incomparable power of eloquence, may induce him to crave covetously for worldly fame and advantages.

Further, through the influence of those evil ones the practiser may sometimes be inordinately susceptible to dissatisfaction or delight; he may sometimes be too misanthropic or too philanthropic; he may sometimes be inclined to enjoy drowsiness; he may sometimes not sleep for a long time; he may sometimes be affected by diseases; he may sometimes remain discouraged and indolent; he may sometimes rise all on a sudden with full energy, but only to sink down again into languor; he may sometimes, being over-sceptical, not believe in anything; he may sometimes, abandoning the excellent religious observance, enjoy himself in frivolous occupations, indulge in worldly affairs, gratify his desires and inclinations;

[1] Some of these miraculous powers here mentioned are considered to be possessed by the Arhat. Six supernatural faculties (*abhijnâ*) are commonly enumerated: (1) divine eyes (*divyacakshu*) by which the Arhat perceives all that is occurring in the world; (2) the divine hearing (*divyaçrotra*), by which he hears all sounds in the world; (3) reading the thoughts of others (*paracittajnâna*); (4) memory of his former lives (*pûrvanivâsânu-smrti*); (5) miraculous powers (*rddhi*); (6) knowledge how to destroy evil passions (*âçravakshaya*).

he may sometimes attain to the samâdhi of heretics [i. e., tîrthaka] and, remaining in a state of trance a day or two, or even seven, and being supplied imaginarily with some palatable food and drink, and feeling very comfortable mentally and physically, he may have no sensation of hunger or thirst;[1] he may sometimes be induced to enjoy female fascinations; he may sometimes be very irregular in taking meals, either too much or too little; he may sometimes look either very handsome or very ugly in appearance.

If the practiser get enraptured by those visions and prejudices (*kleça*), he will lose his root of merit (*kuçalamûla*) accumulated in his previous existences. Therefore he should exercise a deep and thorough contemplation, thinking that all those [heretical states of samâdhi] are the temptations of Mâras or evil spirits that take advantage of his deficiency in merits and his intensity of karma-hindrances (*karmâvarana*).

After this thought he should make another thought, viz., that all these are nothing but mental hallucinations. When he makes these thoughts, the visions and imaginations will instantly disappear, and, becoming free from all attributes [of limitation], he will enter into the true samâdhi. He has then not only liberated himself from all modes of subjectivity, he has also effaced the idea of suchness. Even when

---

[1] This apparently alludes to the Yoga-praxis, by which man is said to be able to perform several sorts of miracles beside those mentioned here.

he rises up from a deep meditation, no visionary images, no prejudices will take possession of in his mind, since he has destroyed the root of illusion through the power of the samâdhi. On the contrary, all the excellent and virtuous deeds which are in conformity with suchness will be constantly performed by him, while all hindrances without exception will be removed by him, who now exhibiting great spiritual energy will never become exhausted.[1]

Those who do not practise this kind of samâdhi will not be able to enter into the essence of the Tathâgata, for all other samâdhis practised in common with the tîrthakas have invariably some attributes [of imperfection] and do not enable one to come into the presence of Buddhas and Bodhisattvas. Therefore let Bodhisattvas [who aspire to the highest knowledge] assiduously apply themselves to the discipline and attain to the perfection of this samâdhi.

[1] The two preceding paragraphs read in the older translation as follows: "On this account, the practiser, always exercising intellectual insight, should save his mind from being entangled in the netting of falsity; he should, dwelling in right contemplation, not cling or attach [to any object], and thereby he will be able to liberate himself from all kinds of karma-hindrance. It should be known that all samâdhis practised by heretics [i. e., tîrthaka] are invariably the production of the [egoistic] conception and desire and self-assumption, that they are hankering after worldly renown advantages, and reverence. The samâdhi of suchness [on the other hand] has nothing to do with subjectivity and attachment. If one is free from indolence even when rising from meditation one's prejudices will by degrees get attenuated."

Those who practise this samâdhi will procure in their present life ten beneficial results:

1. They will always be remembered and guarded by all Buddhas and Bodhisattvas in all quarters.
2. They will not be molested by Mâras or evil spirits.
3. They will not be led astray by false doctrines.[1]
4. They will be free from disparaging the deepest Doctrine (*gambhiradharma*). Their serious misdemeanors as well as their karma-hindrances will be attenuated.
5. They will destroy all doubts, sinful recollections, and contemplations.
6. They will be strengthened in their belief in the spiritual state of Tathâgata.
7. They will be liberated from gloomy remorse; they will be courageous and unflinching in the face of birth and death.
8. Being free from arrogance and presumptuousness, they will be meek and patient and will be revered by all the world.
9. If not practising deep meditation, those prejudices (*âçrava*) which are now getting weaker, will not assert themselves in them.
10. While practising meditation, they will not be disturbed by any external objects, such as voices, sounds, etc.

---

[1] The older translation reads: "the ninety-five heretical doctrines."

But mind: when the practiser is trained only in cessation (çamatha), his mind will sink down into stupidity, and acquiring a habit of indolence, cannot rejoice in doing good acts, as he will estrange himself from deep compassion (mahākaruna). Accordingly he should discipline himself in intellectual insight (vidarçana) as well.

In what does this discipline consist?

The practiser should contemplate that all things in the world are subject to a constant transformation, that since they are transient they are misery, that since they are misery they are not things-in-themselves [i. e., âtman].[1]

He should contemplate that all things in the past are like a dream, those in the present are like the lightning, those in the future are like clouds that spontaneously come into existence.

He should contemplate that all that has a body is impure, being a lodging place of obnoxious vermin and the intermixture of prejudices (âçrava).

Contemplate that ignorant minds, on account of their groundless imagination, take the unreal as they see it, for reality.

Contemplate that all objects which come into existence by a combination of various causes (prat-

---

[1] The idea is: that which is transient is dependent, conditional and not self-regulating; and that which is without freedom is necessarily miserable, that is to say, it has no self-regulating âtman within itself.

yaya) are like a chimera, having [only a transitory existence and] no [genuine] realness at all.

Contemplate that the highest truth (*paramârtha-satya*) is not a production of mind [or subjectivity], cannot be [fully] illustrated by analogy, cannot be [exhaustively] treated by reasoning.[1]

Contemplate that on account of the perfuming power of ignorance (*avidya*) all beings from eternity su er great mental and physical sufferings in immeasurable ways; that those immeasurable and innumerable sufferings are suffered in the present and will be suffered in the future; that while it is extremely difficult to disentangle, to emancipate themselves from those sufferings, all beings always abiding in the midst of them are not conscious of the fact, and this makes them the more pitiable.

After these contemplations the practiser should awake positive knowledge [or unerring understanding], feel the highest and deepest compassion (*karuna*) for all suffering beings, rouse dauntless energy, and make great vows (*mahâpranidhâna*) as follows:

"May my mind be freed from all contradictions; may I abandon particularisation; may I personally attend on all Buddhas and Bodhisattvas, whom I shall pay homage to, make offerings to, revere and praise, and to whose instructions in the good Doctrine (*saddharma*) I shall listen; may I truthfully discipline myself according to their teachings, and to the end of

---

[1] The last three clauses are missing in the older translation.

the future never be negligent in self-discipline; may I with innumerable expediencies (*upâya*) [of salvation] deliver all beings who are drowned in the sea of misery, and bring them to the highest bliss of Nirvâna."

After these vows the practiser should at all times, so far as his energy permits, practise those deeds which are beneficial both to himself and others. While moving, standing, sitting, or lying, he should assiduously meditate what should be done and what should be avoided. This is called the practising of intellectual insight (*vidarçana* or *vipaçyana*).

And again when the practiser disciplines himself only in intellectual insight his mind may lack tranquilisation, and becoming too susceptible to scepticism, may not be in accord with the highest truth, may not attain to the wisdom of non-particularisation. Therefore cessation and intellectual insight should be practised side by side. He should consider that nothing is self-existent (*svabhâva*), and things [in their essence] are uncreate, eternally tranquil, and Nirvâna itself. But at the same time let him not forget to reflect that karma and its retribution, both good and evil, being produced by a co-operation of principle and conditions, will neither be lost nor destroyed. He should thus ponder on the law of causation, both in its good and evil karma and retribution, but at the same time let him not forget to perceive that all things, though in their essence uncreate, have no self-existence, etc., they are Nirvâna.

By practising cessation, common people (*prthag-jana*) will be cured of finding pleasures in worldliness, while Çrâvakas and Pratyekabuddhas will be cured of feeling intimidation at the thought of birth and death.

By practising intellectual insight common people will be cured of not cultivating their root of merit (*kuçalamûla*), while Çrâvakas and Pratyekabuddhas will be cured of narrow-mindedness whereby they cannot raise deep compassion [for mankind].

Therefore, cessation and intellectual insight are supplementary to, not independent of, each other. If one of the two is wanting, the practiser will surely be unable to attain to the most excellant knowledge (*bodhiparinishpatti*).

And again when those novice Bodhisattvas who are living in this present life [*sahâlokadhâtu*, i. e., the enduring world of actual existence], may sometimes suffer misfortunes that are caused by climate, weather, unforeseen famine, or what not; and when they witness those people who are immoral, fearful, infatuated with the three venomous passions (*akuçalamûla*), cling to false and self-contradictory doctrines, desert the good law and acquire evil habits; they [that is, novice Bodhisattvas], living in the midst of them, may feel so discouraged that they may come to doubt whether they can see Buddhas and Bodhisattvas, whether they can actualise their pure and spotless faith (*çraddhâ*).

Therefore, it is advisable for those novices to cherish this thought: All Buddhas and Bodhisattvas in the ten quarters having great, unimpeded supernatural powers (*abhijñâ*), are able to emancipate all suffering beings by means of various expediencies that are good and excellent (*upâyakauçalya*).

After this reflexion, they should make great vows (*mahâpranidhâna*), and with full concentration of spiritual powers think of Buddhas and Bodhisattvas When they have such a firm conviction, free from all doubts, they will assuredly be able to be born in the Buddha-country beyond (*buddha-kshetra*), when they pass away from this present life, and seeing there Buddhas and Bodhisattvas, to complete their faith and to eternally escape from all evil creations (*apâya*).[1]

Therefore, it is said in the Sûtra[2] that if devoted

---

[1] The same idea of salvation is expressed in the *Bhagavad-gîtâ*, Chap. VIII., p. 78: "And he who leaves this body and departs (from this world) remembering me in (his) last moment, comes into my essence. There is no doubt of that. . . . Therefore at all times remember me. . . . Fixing your mind and understanding on me you will come to me, there is no doubt He who thinks of the supreme divine being, O son of Prithâ! with the mind not (running) to other (objects), and possessed of abstraction in the shape of continuous meditation (about the Supreme) goes to him.'

[2] It is not exactly known from what Sûtra this passage is taken, but it is not difficult to discover similar passages in the Sûtras which constitute the canonical books of the Sukhâvatî sect, i. e., in the larger or smaller *Sukhâvatî-vyûha*, or in the *Amitâyur-dhyâna*. I here quote such a passage from Max Müller's English translation of the larger *Sukhâvatî-vyûha-Sûtra*, Sec. XXVII.: "And if, O Ânanda, any son or daughter of a good family should wish—What?—How then may I see that Tathâgata Amitâbha visibly, then he must raise his thought on to the highest perfect knowledge, he must direct his thought with perseverance and excessive

men and women would be filled with concentration of thought, think of Amitâbha Buddha in the world of highest happiness (*sukhâvati*) in the Western region, and direct (*parinâma*) all the root of their good work toward being born there, they would assuredly be born there.

Thus always seeing Buddhas there, their faith will be strengthened, and they will never relapse therefrom. Receiving instruction in the doctrine, and recognising the Dharmakâya of the Buddha, they will by gradual discipline be able to enter upon the state of truth [i. e., Buddhahood] (*samyaktva-râçi*).

V BENEFITS.

In what does this part [treating] of the benefits consist?

Such as above presented is the spiritual significance of the Mahâyâna, and I have finished elucidating it.

Those who, desiring to produce pure and spotless faith in, and knowledge of, the deepest spiritual con-

desire towards that Buddha country, and direct the stock of his good works towards being born there." As I noticed elsewhere, if those Mahâyâna texts had been considered at the time of Açvaghosha, that is, in the first century after or before Christ, as a genuine teaching of Buddha, then it would have to be admitted, it seems to me, that the Manâyâna system existed at an early stage of the development of Buddhism, most probably side by side with Hinayânism, which is generally supposed by Pâli scholars to be more primitive. But the history of Buddhism in India as a whole is still veiled with dark clouds of uncertainty, in spite of the fact that quite a few original Sanskrit texts have been recovered.

dition and the greatest Dharma of the Tathâgata, so that they have no hindrances in entering upon the Mahâyâna path (*mârga*), will diligently pursue this brief discourse, contemplate it, discipline themselves in it, and thus they can surely and unhesitatingly attain to the knowledge of all forms and manifestations (*sarvâkârajñâna*).

And if they do not awake a feeling of fear in hearing this Doctrine, they will surely be qualified to inherit the Buddha-seeds and immediately receive the prophecy (*vijâkarana*)[1] from the Buddha. Even if there be a person who could convert all beings in three thousand great chiliocosms (*trisâhasramahâsâhasra*),[2] and could induce them to observe the ten precepts of morality (*daçakuçalamârga*), his merits will not be su-

[1] This is not a mere prophecy of one's destiny, but Buddha's assurance for those Bodhisattvas who, having accumulated sufficient amount of merits, are qualified to attain in the future the most excellent, perfect knowledge and to achieve final salvation both for themselves and for all other beings. See how five hundred disciples received this assurance from Buddha in the *Saddharmapundarîka Sûtra*, Chap. VIII.

[2] Our earth which was supposed by ancient Indians to be flat, infinitely extending in space, is not the only region inhabited by sentient beings; but there are innumerable worlds outside of this *Manushyalokadhâtu*, which exist above as well as below us. Now according to the *Abhidharmakoça-çâstra* by Vasubandhu, a small chiliocosm (*sâhasralokadhâtu*) consists of one thousand of Rûpalokas and of the first Dhyâna heavens, and one thousand of small chiliocosms make a middling chiliocosm, a thousand of which in turn making a great chiliocosm. So we may take the great chiliocosm (*mahâsâhasralokadhâtu*) as including all possible heavenly bodies which fill up this boundless space.

perior to those of the person who will truthfully comprehend this Doctrine even for a second ; because the merits of the latter immeasurably and infinitely surpass those of the former.

If one practise this doctrine as it is instructed for one whole day and night, the merits thereby produced will be so immeasurable, infinite, inconceivable that all Buddhas in the ten quarters could not exhaust them, even if each of them continued to praise them for innumerable asamkheyakalpas.[1] As the merits of suchness have no limits, so the merits of the discipline are also without limit.

Those who slander this doctrine, on the other hand, commit immeasurable faults and suffer great sufferings for asamkheyakalpas. Accordingly all beings should cherish a firm faith in the Doctrine and never slander it, for this will lead to the destruction of oneself as well as others, nay, even to the destruction of the seeds of the Triple Treasure (*triratna*).

By practising this Doctrine all Buddhas have attained the most excellent knowledge (*anuttarajñāna*). By practising this Doctrine all Bodhisattvas have obtained an insight into the Dhamrakāya of the Tathāgata.

By practising this Doctrine Bodhisattvas in the past consummated, Bodhisattvas in the future will consummate, pure and spotless faith (*çraddhā*) in the Mahāyāna. Therefore those who desire to practise

---
[1] For an explanation see the footnote to *kalpa*, p. 87.

those excellent virtues that are beneficial at once to themselves and others should diligently study this Discourse.

> I have now finished elucidating
> The deepest and greatest significance [of the Dharma].
> May its merit be distributed among all creatures,
> And make them understand the Doctrine of Suchness.

GLOSSARY.

Activity-consciousness 業識 *yeh shih, karmavijñâna?* the assertion of the "Will to Live."

Affectional hindrance 煩惱障 *fan nao chang, kleçâvarana*, hindrance to the attainment of Nirvâna, arising from the assertion of the "Will to Live."

Affirmation, or Non-emptiness, 不空 *pu k'ung, açûnyatâ*, suchness as constituting the basis of reality ; it is equivalent to the Tathâgata's Womb.

All-conserving mind, The, 阿賴耶識 *a lai ya shih*, or *tsang shih*, or 阿梨耶 *a li ya*, 無沒識 *mu mo shih, âlaya-vijñâna*, a stage in the evolution of suchness, in which consciousness is awakened to recognise a distinction between suchness and birth-and-death.

Aspiration 發心 *fa hsin, cittotpâda*, desire to attain the most perfect knowledge.

Âtman 我 *wu*, (1) ego-soul ; (2) noumenon or thing-in-itself. Anâtman is a negative form of the same.

Birth-and-death 生滅 *shêng mieh, samsâra*, the material principle in contradistinction to the formal principle, suchness.

Consciousness 識 *shih, vijñâna*, mentation in general.

Defilement 染 *jan*, a cognisance of dual aspect of suchness ; not necessarily moral or intellectual fault.

Dharma 法 *fa*, (1) that which subsists, or substance ; (2) law, doctrine, or regulative principle.

Dharmakâya 法身 *fa shên*, absolute being, or absolute knowledge when considered from the idealistic point of view.

Ego 意 *i, manas*, the subjective mind which believes consciously or unconsciously in the existence of the ego-soul.

Ego-consciousness 意識 *i shih, manovijnâna*, egocentric thoughts in general; the mind that makes a deliberate assumption of a dualistic existence of the ego and the non-ego.

Enlightenment 覺 *chiao (buddhi?)*, another name for suchness, psychologically considered.

Evolving-consciousness 轉識 *chuan shih, pravrtti-vijnâna*, a state of suchness out of which mentation in general evolves.

Ignorance 無明 *wu ming, avidya*, a state of suchness in its evolution; practically the same as birth-and-death.

Intellectual hindrance 所知障 *so chih chang, jneyâvarana*, the hindrance to the attainment of Nirvâna, which arises from intellectual prejudices.

Interrelated defilement 相應染 *hsiang ying jan*, a conscious assertion of dualism.

Karma-hindrance, *yeh chang, karmâvarana*, the hindrance in the way to Nirvâna, that is brought forth by evil deeds done in previous lives.

Mahâyâna 大乘 *tai chang*, literally, great conveyance, another name for suchness.

Means, or expediency 方便 *fang pien, upâya*, when philosophically considered, the process of evolution, whereby the unconditional suchness becomes conditional.

Mind 心 *hsin, citta*, relative aspect of suchness. Soul, mind, and suchness are to a certain extent synonymous, but in this translation the following distinction is made: Suchness, when unqualified, signifies its absolute aspect and is practically the same with the soul, while the term mind is used to denote a state of suchness in its operation or evolution.

Negation, or emptiness 空 *k'ung, çûnyatâ*, an aspect of suchness as transcending all forms of relativitity.

Nirvâna 涅槃 *nieh p'an*, the recognition of the truth or suchness.

Non-enlightenment 不覺 *pu chiao (nirbuddhi?)*, another name for ignorance, psychologically considered. Non-enlightenment, defilement, birth-and-death, and ignorance, are more or less synonymous and interchangeable.

Non-particularisation 無分別 *wu fên pieh*, the subjective attitude that is free from a deliberate assertion of dualism; i is similar in a sense to Lao-Tze's "Non-assertion."

Not-interrelated defilement 不相應染 *pu hsiang ying jan*, an unconscious assertion of dualism.

Particularisation-consciousness 分別識 *fên pieh shih*, the consciousness that adheres to the dual aspect of existence; a synonym of phenomena-particularising-consciousness.

Prejudice 煩惱 *fan nao*, *âçrava* or *kleça*, the subjectivity that averts the due exercise of will and intellect.

Samâdhi 三昧 *san mei*, or 定 *ting*, literally equilibrium, a state of consciousness in which all modes of mental activity are in equilibrium.

Soul 心 *hsin*, *hrdaya* or *citta*, that which constitutes the kernel of things, but not in the Christian conception of the word; a synonym of absolute suchness.

Soul as birth-and-death, 心生滅 *hsin shêng mieh*, relative aspect of suchness as material principle; a synonym of ignorance.

Soul as suchness 心真如 *hsin chen ju*, absolute aspect of suchness as purely formal.

Subjectivity 妄念 *wang nien*, or 妄念心 *wang nien hsin*, or 心念 *hsin nien*, or simply 念 *nien*, *smrti*, literally, recollection or memory, or 分別 *fên pieh*, particularisation; the mentation that is not in accordance with the conception of suchness.

Suchness 真如 *chên ju*, *bhûtatathatâ*, the highest reality, or the "purely formal" aspect of existence.

Tathâgata's womb 如來藏 *ju lai tsang*, *tathâgata-garbha*, a state of suchness as containing every possible merit.

Totality of things 法界 *fah chieh*, *dharmadhâtu*, literally, the basis of things, that is, the universe as a whole.

Vow 願 *yüan*, or 誓願 *shih yüan*, *pranidhâna*, commonly translated prayer, but not in the Christian sense, for Buddhists think that a vow or vehement desire has power enough to achieve what is desired, according to their idealistic conception of the world.

CORRIGENDA.

Page 3, line 2, read *gâthâ* for *ghâtâs*.
" 5, " 8, " *Fo* for *Fa*.
" 12, " 13, " *peace* for *piece*.
" 12, " 20, " ³ for ¹.
" 18, " 22, " *fasciculus* for *fasciculi*.
" 24, " 12, " *conversion* for *conversions*.
" 36, " 4, " *non-âtman* for *none-âtman*.
" 60, " 5, " *çûnyatâ* for *çûnjatâ*.
" 60, " 10, insert *that* after *understanding*.
" 119, " 1, read *Anupadiçesha* for *Anupadhiçesa*.
" 126, " 17, " *latter's* for *latters'*.

INDEX.

Açbhasamjñas, 133.
Activity, incomprehensible, 66 et seq ; spontaneous, 87; unconscious, 125.
Activity-consciousness, i. e., the subjective mind, 76, 84, 96. 100, 103, 151 ; strengthened, 86.
Activity-perfuming, 91.
Açvaghosha, as an artist, 34 et seq ; his conversion, 24 et seq.; his date, 2 et seq.; his different names, 20 et seq.; his discussion with Parçva, 25 et seq ; his nativity and wanderings, 17 et seq.; his patriarchal order, 34 ; his works in Chinese translations, 36 et seq.; the first expounder of Mahâyânism, 1.
All-conserving mind, 43, 61, 75, 151.
Amitâbha-Buddha, 145.
Ânanda, 5.
Anâtman, 47, 151.
Âryadeva, 25, 32, 34.
Aspiration, 89, 113 et seq., 122, its three forms, 113 et seq.; through faith, 113 et seq.; through knowledge and practice, 113, 122; through intellectual insight, 113, 123 et seq.
Âtman, 29, 151; in things (or things-in-themselves), 106 ; personal (or ego-soul), 106.
Âtman-conception, 106.
Âtman-theory, the non-personal, 111.
Attachment to names, 72–73.
Awakening of Faith, The, its Chinese translations, 38 et seq., 45; its philosophy outlined, 41 et seq.

Benefits of the study of the Mahâyâna, 145 et seq.
Bhagavadgîta, 44, 61, 94, 145.
Bhagavat, 46.
Birth-and-death, 53, 75; its *raison d'être* and cause, 83.
Bliss, Body of, 101, 103, 104.
Bodhisattva, 55, 64.
Buddha, 128.
Buddha-carita-kâvya, 1, 35, 37.
Buddha-country, 145.
Buddha-dharmas, 95, 98.
Buddha-seeds, 47, 48, 145.
Buddha, thirty-two marks of perfection of, 135.

Causation, the law of, 75.
Cessation, 50, 128, 141, 144;
 how to practise, 132 et seq.
Charity, 122, 128 et seq.
Chiliocosms, 145.
Chimera, 142
Çikshânanda, 39
Clinging, 72.
Clouds, 141.
Compassion, 91, 92, 98, 114, 116, 129, 131, 141, 142.
Compulsion, 99.
Compulsory actions, 100.
Consciousness (or mentation), 65, 75.
Çraddhotpâda-çâstra. See "Mahâyâna-çraddhotpâda-çâstra."
Çrâvaka, 63.
Creation, six different states of, 102.
Cross-legged, sitting, 132.
Çûnya or Çûnyatâ, 29, 58, 60.
Çûra, another name for Açvaghosha, 21.

Deeds, the five, perfecting faith, 128.
Defiled mind, its six phases of defilement, 80 et seq., 82.
Defilement (or relativity), 66, 151; interrelated (or secondary), 80, 152; not-interrelated (or primary), 80 et seq., 153.
Dhârani, 135.
Dharma, The, 25, 46, 51, 67, 95, 122, 128, 131; greatest, 145; its perfuming power, 67; true, 70; valid, 89.
Dharmadhâtu, 55, 52, 79, 81, 105; its oneness, 116. (See also "Universe.")

Dharmakâya, 62, 67, 95, 96, 98, 99, 100, 102, 103, 104, 119, 127, 145, 148; absolute, 120; not a nothing, 108; not like space, 107.
Dharma-wheel (or wheel of), 120, 123.
Dharmika-Subhûti, another name for Açvaghosha, 21.
Dhûtaguna, the twelve, 129.
Dhyâna sect, 132.
Doctrine, the, 56, 89; the deepest, 140; the good, 142.
Dream, 141.
Durdarsha, another name for Açvaghosha, 21,
Durdarshakâla, another name for Açvaghosha, 21.

Ego, 75, 94; as an aspect of ignorance, 72. (See also Glossary, *sub voce* "Ego.")
Ego-consciousness, 78, 152.
Energy, 122; how to practise, 129.
Enlightenment, 61, 152; and ignorance, 67; *a posteriori*, 62, 63, 66; *a priori*, 62, 63, 66, 70, 71, 101; differentiated, 66 et seq.; its twofold relation to non-enlightenment, 73; likened unto space and a mirror in its four aspects, 69 et seq., perfect, 65; the most excellent, 114; why subject to defilement, 74. (See also "Knowledge" and "Wisdom").
Entertainment, four methods of, 92, 98.
Essence of things, free from limitation, 112

Essence-perfuming, 88 et seq.
Evil creation, 120, 121.
Evolving-consciousness, 67, 76, 123, 152.
Expediency (or skilfulness), or expediencies, 112, 126, 127. 143, 145. (See also "Means.")

Faith, 128 ; immovable, 49 (see also "Never-Returning"); the Mahâyâna, 50.
False doctrines, the refutation of, 106 et seq.
Fire and wood, simile of, 90.

Ganges, sands of the, 89, 95, 98, 108.

Hindrances, affectional, 69, 82, 151 ; intellectual, 69, 82, 152.
Hymn of One Hundred and Fifty Çlokas, 23.

Ignorance, 66, 67, 77, 78, 82, 97, 106, 142, 152; annihilated, 87; as the defiled dharma, 95; disturbs the mind, 84; how it is produced, 79 (see also "Non-Enlightenment") ; its perfuming power, 83, 86; purified, 85 ; the principle of defilement, 84.
Ignorant action, 71.
Inconstancy, group of, 113, 114.
Individual cause, 91 e. seq.
Intellectual insight, 50, 128, 141, 143 ; how to gain, 132 et seq.
Intelligence (or sensation), 72.
"Interrelated," explained, 81.

Jewel, simile of, 116.

Kâla, another name for Açvaghosha, 21.
Kalpa, 87
Kanishka, 12.
Kanishtha (or Kanita), Candana, 10, 11.
Karma, 76, 129 ; hindrances of 118, 135, 138; impure, 120 ; retribution of, 117.
Kâtyâyana, 3.
Knowledge, perfect, 47 ; positive, 142 ; the most excellent, 88, 118, 129, 144; of all forms 145. (See also "Omniscience.")
Krtsâyatanas, 134.
Kulanâtha, another name for Paramârtha, 38.
Kung-chang, another name for Açvaghosha, 21.
Kung-tê-jih, another name for Açvaghosha, 21.

Lightning, 141.
Love, and compassion, 91 ; and wisdom, 44.
Lu tao lun 'hui ching, 38.

Mahâbodhi, The, 115.
Mahâkâçyapa, 5.
Mahâlamkâra-çâstra (or Mahâlamkârasûtra-çâstra), 3, 20 35, 37.
Mahâyâna, The, 48, 49, 50, 146, 148; its being and significance, 52 et seq ; its literal meaning explained, 54; three significances of, 95 et seq.
Mahâyâna Buddhism, 1, 43. 44, 45.
Mahâyâna-çraddhotpâda-çâstra, 3, 4, 6, 20, 36–37.

Mahâyâna path, 145.
Maheçrava, 22.
Mâras, 129, 135.
Materiality, system of, 103.
Maticitra, another name for Açvaghosha, 21.
Mâtrceta, another name for Açvaghosha, 21, 22.
Matter, 103, 108, 112; as a particularisation of the confused mind, 107.
Means (or skilfulness, or expediency), four kinds of, 117 et seq.
Methods (upâya), 124. (See also "Means" and "Expediency.")
Mind (or âlaya-vijñâna), 53, 67, 68, 71, 75, 77, 78, 108, 112, 152; its essence not annihilated, 87; its identity with suchness, 106; its illusory manifestation, 86; its self-manifestation, 82; its three different operations, 124; like a jewel, 116, 117; perfect in itself, 68, 79, 98. (See also "Soul.")
Mirror, 76, 77; covered with dust, 27;
Morality, 122; how to practise, 129; the ten precepts of, 147.

Nâgârjuna, 6, 7, 23, 34, 38, 43.
Never-returning, the state of, 135. (See also "Immovable.")
Nirvâna, 74, 86, 87, 137, 143; anupadhiçesha, 119; attain to, 113; attainment of, 110; its pantheistic conception, 112; immortal, 111; not to dwell in, 117; that has no fixed abode, 88; the essence of all things, 121.
Non-aggregate objects, 105.
Non-enlightenment, 61, 70, 75, 97; as the *raison d'être* of birth-and-death, 83; compared to a man who is lost, 70; its three aspects, 71; its twofold relation to enlightenment, 73. (See also "Ignorance" and Glossary.)
"Not-interrelated," explained 81.
Non-particularisation, 94, 152; wisdom of, 123, 143.
Nothingness, absolute, 137.

Omniscience, 125, 126. (See also "knowledge.")
Order of constant truth, 127.

Parçva, 1, 19, 31, 32, 33; as a teacher of Açvaghosha, 25 et seq.
Pâramitâ, 23, 38, 98, 101, 128 135; the six, 92, 122 et seq.
Particularisation, 64, 65, 87, 97 102, 104, 112, 113, 124, 134 142.
Particularisation-consciousness 76, 153.
Passions, three venomous, 50, 144.
Patience, 122; how to practise 129
Patriarchs, Lists of, 33
Performance of deeds, 73.
"Perfuming," explained, 84.
Phenomenal world, as a phase of ignorance, 72.
Phenomena-particularising con-

sciousness, 78; strengthened, 86, 100.
Pitrceta, another name for Açvaghosha, 21.
Pottery, simile of, 74, 75.
Powers, supernatural, 145.
Practical truth (samvrtti-satya), 29, 38.
Pratyekabuddha, 63.
Precept, the threefold, 129.
Prejudices, 89, 90, 109, 115, 129, 140, 141; their perfuming influence, 78.
Prophecy, 145.
Prthagjana (common people), 63.
Pudgala, 29.
Punyayaças, 28, 31, 33; his discussion with Açvaghosha, 29 et seq.

Rationality, system of, 103.
Reality, the highest, 126. (See also "Truth.")
Recollection, subjects of, 132.
Representation-consciousness, 76.
Reward, Body of, 102.
Right order, 121,
Right path, the practising of, 113 et seq.
Root of merit, the, 49, 70, 91, 92, 115, 132, 135, 138, 144; its perfuming power, 114; strengthened, 118.

Samâdhi, 138; the power of, 139; of heretics, 138: of oneness, 135; of purity, 93.
Sambhogakâya, 101.
Sameness, principle of, 82.

Sense, six objects of, as constituting the external world, 84
Separation-consciousness, 78.
Shame and remorse, 118.
Skandhas, the five, 104, 112
Soul, 53, 60, 97; as birth-and death, 55, 60 et seq ; as suchness, 55, 57; its three faculties awakened by faith, 116 the essence of the Tathâgata 107.
Space, simile of, 69, 107
Spontaneity of action, 94
Subjective mind, its perfuming power, 88.
Subjectivity, 56, 57, 66, 70, 71. 77, 85, 138, 153; annihilated. 95; as the condition of birth-and-death, 83.
Succession (or memory), 72
Succession-consciousness (or memory), 76, 78.
Suchness, 43, 44, 53, 134, 139; as the inherent perfuming principle, 91; as the *raison d'être* 90; defiled, 84, faith in, 128; free from imperfection, 118 ; its absolute aspect, 59 et seq., its activity, 98 ; its characteristics described, 95; its differentiation, 89; its identity with the soul, 57; its negative aspect, 58 ; its positive aspect, 59; its perfuming powers, 88, 93 et seq.; its three attributes, 119; not a nothing, 108 ; not concerned with defilement, 108; possessed by all, 86; simple in its nature, yet subject to defilement, 96; to contemplate, 116; the doctrine

of, 149; the gate of, 106; the idea of, 138; the pure dharma, 84, 95.
Suffering, 73.
Sukhâvatî theory, 43-44, 145.
Supernatural faculties, the six, 137.
Sûtra, 51; quotation from, 106, 107, 109, 110, 120; quotation from the Lankâvatâra, 65; quotation from the Sukhâvatî, 145; quotation from the Vimala-kîrti-nirdeça, 74; the Mahâyâna, 51.

Târâ, 22.
Ta sung ti hsüan wên pên lun, 37.
Tathâgata, 49, 107, 139, 140; as a manifestation of enlightenment, 70; Body of, 102; personality of, 68; wisdom and activity of, 94.
Tathâgata's Wisdom, 65.
Tathâgata's Womb, 43, 54, 60, 96, 98, 108, 109; immortal, 111; its relation to birth-and-death, 110.
Things, defiled, 59; how produced, 85; non-entity of, 73; pure, how produced, 86.
Things-in-themselves, 141.
Tîrthaka, 2, 6, 135, 139.
Tranquilisation, 122, 123, 143.
Transformation, Body of, 100.
Trikâya. (See "Triple Personality.")

Triloka (three worlds), 111; as a manifestation of the mind, 77.
Triple Personality, 43-44.
Triple Treasure, the, 118, 148.
Truth, 99; (absolute, or pure, or highest = paramârtha-satya), 29, 38, 99, 119, 142.
Tukhâra, King of, 10, 11, 12. (See also "Yüeh chih.")
Tushita Heaven, 119.

Undefiled, the, 74.
Universal cause, 93 et seq.
Universal wisdom, 93.
Universal wishes, 93.
Universe, its oneness, 93.
Upagupta, 6.

Vaiçeshika school, the, 110.
Virtues, spotless, 88 (see also "Undefiled"); the ten, 114.
Vow-power, or the power of vow, 119, 120.
Vows, 132; great, 118, 142, 145.

Water, the wind, and the waves, simile of, 67, 83.
Wisdom, 74, 90, 123; pure, 66 et seq.; the true, 113; which works out emancipation, 99.
World of highest happiness, 145.

Yoga-praxis, 138.
Yüeh chih, King of, 9, 12, 13. (See also "Tukhâra.")

THE PRINCIPLE AND PRACTICE
OF MAHAYANA BUDDHISM

著　者：Dwight Giddard

發行所：南天書局有限公司
登記證字號：行政院新聞局局版臺業字第一四三六號

出版者：南天書局有限公司
台北市羅斯福路三段二八三巷14弄14號
電　話 (Tel)：(〇二)三六三〇一九〇
電　傳 (Fax)：(〇二)三六三三八三四
郵政劃撥帳戶：〇一〇八〇五三一八號

印刷者：國順印刷有限公司
板橋市中正路二一六巷2弄13號

中華民國七十九年一月影印

THE PRINCIPLE AND PRACTICE OF
MAHAYANA BUDDHISM

SMC PUBLISHING INC.
PO Box 13-342, Taiepi, Taiwan
Republic of China 10764

THE PRINCIPLE AND PRACTICE OF MAHAYANA BUDDHISM

AN INTERPRETATION OF
PROFESSOR SUZUKI'S TRANSLATION
OF
ASHVAGHOSHA'S AWAKENING OF FAITH

by

DWIGHT GODDARD

SMC PUBLISHING INC.
Taipei

Original Edition Published:
Thetford, Vermont
U.S.A. 1933

ISNB 957—9482—18—7

Dedicated to
PROFESSOR DAISETZ TEITARO SUZUKI

CONTENTS

PREFACE		ix
INTRODUCTION		xv
ONE.	Ashvaghosha's Introduction	1
TWO.	Ignorance as the source of personality	4
THREE.	Mind-essence as manifesting personality	17
FOUR.	Mind-essence as emancipation of personality	26
FIVE.	The Oneness of Mind-essence and personality	41
SIX.	The place of Mind-essence in the unitary principle of Tathagata	50
SEVEN.	False doctrines of egoism to be avoided	61
EIGHT.	The True Path to Buddhahood	67
NINE.	The right practice of the True Path	81
TEN.	The rewards of the Path	98

PREFACE

PROFESSOR DAISETS TEITARO SUZUKI made his translation of the *Mahayana Shraddhotpada Shastra* in 1900. It was published by the Open Court Publishing Company under the title: Ashvaghosha's Awakening of Faith, but is now long out of print. It was the first English version and has always been held in high regard for it was a very difficult translation to make as the Sanskrit text had disappeared and he was obliged to make the translation from Chinese texts.

But even with all Professor Suzuki's scholarship and care the English version is very difficult reading not alone because of certain infelicities of diction but more especially because of the profundities of the theme itself. This is to be regretted inasmuch as Ashvaghosha had clearly stated in his introduction that his purpose for writing was to explain the Principle and Practice of the Mahayana clearly and simply for the benefit of common people. The common people to whom Ashvaghosha dedicated his treatise were well acquainted with the teachings of the Mahayana—it was their familiar faith. If it was desirable to write an easily understood commentary for them, how much more is it desirable that the subject be presented to English readers of today, who know almost nothing about the Mahayana, in an easily understood form. Even for advanced students of the Mahayana this Scripture will be found no easy reading and they will generally find it advantageous to first read an interpretation of it before entering upon a serious study of the text itself.

Professor Suzuki, being an accomplished master of Sanskrit, Chinese and English, and being the present day highest authority on Mahayana metaphysics, is pre-eminently the one to make a scholarly and standard translation. It is understood that he is at work on the task in the hope that it may be published before the close of the present year. When it appears there will be less need for this interpretation, which is intended only to meet an immediate need but will soon pass out of use, while Professor Suzuki's new translation will become an enduring possession. I am glad to take advantage of this opportunity to pay a tribute of respect to Professor Suzuki for the wonderful group of translations of the Mahayana Scriptures which he has already accomplished and is further intending to complete. First, there was his Ashvaghosha's *Mahayana Shraddhotpada* in 1900; then in 1932 there was the *Lankavatara;* and now he is at work on *Prajna-paramita Hridaya* and the *Gandhavyuha* section of the tremendous *Avatamsaka* which is spoken of as "the

x

grandest religious document ever written." Professor Suzuki hopes to finish the task before he dies, or as he puts it, "I am not going to die until it is finished."

After the exchange of a number of letters, Professor Suzuki writes the author as follows: *"Dear Mr. Goddard: Although I am not in agreement with your idea of epitomising my old Ashvaghosha, I can not prevent your doing your own work in your own way, can I? Please do your best. There are some points in the old translation that I would like to discuss with you very fully; it is too bad that I have so much to do in my own way. . . . For many years I have intended to make a new translation and still intend to do so, but until that is out, the old is to be read and used by the public and I have no right nor power to prevent it. Will you kindly refer to this fact in your new book and say that your use of the old is on your own responsibility. . . ."*

The writer of this Interpretation in his eagerness to bring this noble Scripture to the attention of English readers that they may profit by it both intellectually and spiritually, and sincerely regretting that it lacks Professor Suzuki's entire approval, assumes this responsibility.

This Interpretation uses different terms from the Suzuki Translation, it is freely interpreted even to the extent in places of enlarging upon it, and the sequence of sections in places is rearranged in order to bring out more clearly the argument of the theme. Toward the end of the treatise there is a single sentence that seems to contradict the whole development of the theme and is probably a later interpolation. It seems wiser to leave it out altogether than to run the risk of confusing the reader's understanding of the treatise as a whole by a forced interpretation of it.

* * *

There are two other translations into English of this *Shraddhotpada Shastra.* One was made by Rev. Timothy Richard, a Christian Missionary, but he was so intent upon harmonising it with Christianity that he ruined its value as an understandable translation of a Buddhist text. The other translation was made by the editors of the magazine, THE SHRINE OF WISDOM, and was published in four successive issues: Vol. XI (1929), No. 42, and Vol. XI (1930), Nos. 43-45. It is an understandable translation, but by their unfamiliarity with Buddhist metaphysics they miss the esoteric significance of the Mahayana. It is for this reason that the present author bases his interpretation entirely upon Professor Suzuki's translation.

* * *

Beginners must not expect to find the Scripture easy reading, nor to expect to fully understand it by a cursory "once over." It must be studied and thought about over and over again. But if it faithfully and perseveringly studied and meditated upon, its teachings will awaken an unfolding faith and confidence in the principle of Tathagata and will encourage one to set his feet on the Path that leads to Buddahood. Once on the Path the gracious activity of Prajna-paramita will open its own channel for the more perfect understanding of the principle of Tathagata.

INTRODUCTION

THE Buddhist Scripture known as *Mahayana Shraddhotpada Shastra*, or as it is commonly known in English, The Awakening of Faith in the Mahayana, was probably written during the first century of the Christian Era, although nothing is definitely known as to the exact date. It was probably written in Sanskrit but no copy of a Sanskrit original has been found, although copies must have been in existence as late as 800 A.D. when it was listed in a Chinese catalog. Before the Sanskrit original had disappeared, however, two Chinese translations had been made: the first by Paramartha, who came to China from India in 546 and died in 569 aged 71, is the best known by Chinese and Japanese scholars probably because the greatest commentary on the Scripture was based upon it. The second Chinese translation was made by Shikshananda. He was born in Kotan in 651 and died in China in 710; the translation was made after 700. These two translations were made from different copies but there is no essential difference between them. There are at least seven commentaries upon them and, as is commonly the case, the commentaries are more studied than the text itself. There was a Sanskrit version made from these Chinese versions.

The authorship is usually credited to Ashvaghosha although there is no positive evidence to that effect. Ashvaghosha was a very notable scholar and Buddhist protagonist. The dates of his birth and death are unknown but there is very general agreement that he lived during the latter half of the first century A.D. for he was present at the Great Council gathered by the Emperor Kanishka in Kashmir either as its co-president or at least as the personal representative of the Emperor. He also lived just previous to Nargajuna.

Ashvaghosha was a native of Central or Southern India and was born a Brahmin. He was a notable poet, orator and controversialist. This brought him to Northern India where he challenged a famous Buddhist scholar to a debate on the relative merits of Vedantism and Buddhism. Ashvaghosha was defeated and as a penalty became the disciple of the victor. He studied faithfully under his new Master and became wholly convinced of the rationality and superiority of Buddhism. From that time on he devoted himself to the propagation of the Mahayana type of Buddhism, writing many philosophical works and poetical versions of the highest merit, besides doing a great deal of public speaking.

At that time Kanishka as King of a province of Northwestern India was extending his territories by conquest and, by his capture of Benares, had control of the largest Buddhist empire of history. The king of Benares being unable to pay the tremendous fine levied by Kanishka, gave among other things the Buddha's begging bowl and the person of Ashvaghosha. The latter followed his new protector to his capital in Khotan and there during the rest of his notable life continued his powerful advocacy of Mahayana doctrines. His most notable poetic work is *Buddha-carita,* an ornate life of Buddha from the traditional point of view; his outstanding prose work is *Mahalamkara,* the Book of Great Glory. Another shorter work entitled The Theory of Non-ego is looked upon as the forerunner of the great teachings of Nargajuna and Vasabandhu known as the Madyamika philosophy which is the basis of the more mystical aspect of Mahayana Buddhism.

Professor Suzuki in his Translation of the Awakening of Faith gives an exhaustive study and critique of the life and works of Ashvaghosha, from which this brief statement is taken, and to which further reference is urged.

* * *

This Scripture belongs to the very large section of early Mahayanistic Scriptures known as "The Prajna-paramita Family." It is very similar to The Lankavatara Sutra, which the editor has interpreted under the title: SELF-REALISATION OF NOBLE WISDOM, and apparently follows it.

In the list of Indian Buddhist Patriarchs, Asvaghosha is counted as the Twelfth and is followed by Nargajuna and Vasabandhu and the latter's brother, Asangha. These three great philosophers and writers are credited with nearly a thousand books. They were the founders of what is known as the Madyamika School of Mahayanistic philosophy that has had so profound an influence upon the philosophic thought of Japan, China and Tibet. This philosophy is based upon and is a systematization and elaboration of the thought of Ashvaghosha as presented in this treatise and others of the Prajna-paramita group.

One would be foolish to hazard a guess as to what will happen to the culture of Europe and America as this Oriental philosophy and metaphysic come into correspondence with European philosophy of "pure reason" and her materialistic science, but into contact with each other they are steadily approaching and each is too firmly intrenched in the world's thought to be easily dislodged. Hitherto the barriers of oceans and unknown languages have separated them, but these are fast fading away as barriers, and the adjustment of thought must be faced. The nations of the earth can not long remain "half slave and half free"; in the long last, Truth must emerge and dominate all alike.

* * *

The Sanskrit title of this Scripture is *Mahayana Shraddhotpada*. This is usually translated: THE AWAKENING OF FAITH IN THE MAHAYANA. For two reasons this is not a very good title in its English form. As translations go it is fairly close, but the background of meaning to the Sanskrit and English is quite different. The Sanskrit word is a compound of the two words *shraddha* and *utpada*. *Shraddha* means faith or confidence that is based on an unfolding experience that is verifiable by both the self or another and carries a sense of process and continuance. Whereas, faith, in its ordinary English sense carries the meaning of an acceptance of something that has not been proved, or that is difficult or impossible of proof. In English, "faith is the substance of things hoped for." *Shraddha* signifies a conviction that is based on unfolding experience that is leading on to certitude. *Utpada* also carries a meaning of continuance; it is an awakening that goes on to an ever increasing awareness; this is in contrast to the English "awakening" which suggests momentariness. The English title suggests a sudden awakening of faith in Buddhism; the Sanskrit, suggests the beginning of a confidence that passes into aspiration and realisation. This is confirmed by the Chinese title, the characters of which carry the meaning, the rising of sight until it includes the whole horizon. It is the unfolding or creating of something, in this case, the unfolding within the mind of an ever clearing conviction as to the truth of the principles of Mahayana Buddhism. This distinction is of the highest importance because it lies at the characteristic basis of the Mahayana, and indeed of all Buddhism. Buddhism teaches an actual becoming as the goal of a process that is inherent in the nature of Ultimate Reality itself. Christianity, on the contrary, teaches faith in a future state that is revealed and is controlled by another than the self. This becoming through one's own effort at following the Noble Path and its unfolding knowledge and Enlightenment, and its final self-giving in love for all animate life, is the whole aim of Buddhism.

The other reason why the title in English is not very satisfactory is this: The Sanskrit title is taken from the opening words in which Ashvaghosha states his reasons for writing; it does not cover the theme of the book at all. Ashvaghosha clearly states the theme of book at the close of the short introduction, when he says:

"For the sake of the people of this last class, I write this discourse in which the most excellent, the deepest, and the most inexhaustible doctrine of the Tathagata will be treated in comprehensive brevity."

Ashvaghosha is writing a commentary on the Principle and Practice of Mahayana Buddhism for the benefit of the common and little educated people, that he may awaken in them a faith in the True Path which, if followed, will lead them on to Buddhahood.

For this reason he makes the metaphysical discussion only a prelude to the explanation of the Path. Buddhism is not a philosophy that is to be accepted on faith; it is an unfolding experience that culminates in the identification of one's own life with all Life. There must be an awakening of faith, to be sure, but Buddhist faith is a cosmic process that goes on unfolding into aspiration, into knowledge, into realisation of Wisdom, into the self-giving of Bodhisattvas, into Buddhahood.

Ashvaghosha's treatment of his theme is unusually systematic and logical. He begins with a statement of the fundamental principle, passes on to its manifestation in the world of life and death, in the mental world, into the unitive world of spirit; after which he discusses its threefold significance as Tathagata. Then he explains the True Path which is the Noble Eightfold Path of Shakyamuni Buddha, and closes with a brief statement of the rewards that follow its Right Practice.

The kernel of the whole treatise lies in the meaning and significance of the Ultimate Principle of Tathagata which is described in its various aspects of significance. Sometimes it is described and spoken of as *Bhutatathata*, which Professor Suzuki prefers to translate as "Suchness." Literally the word means, "it is, such as it is," but as "Suchness" is an awkward English word that does not carry any definite meaning to uneducated ears, it only serves to confuse and baffle thought and understanding, instead of clarifying thought and carrying conviction. For that reason, in this Interpretation, it seems best to translate it, Essence of Mind, or simply Essence. Dharmakaya, the body or principle of Truth, means exactly the same thing. The Chinese use two characters, meaning, True-form, to cover the same meaning and conception, and all of these terms refer to the "substance" aspect of Ultimate Reality, or Tathagata. The term, Alayavijnana, or Universal Mind, is also used synonymous with Mind-essence when thinking of it as "storage" of Wisdom.

There are other terms used for the "potentiality" aspect of Tathagata, such as Sambhogakaya, the Bliss-body, or the Reward-body, or the Womb of Tathagata. Then there are still other terms used for the "activity" aspect of Tathagata, such as Nirmanakaya, Buddhahood in its many bodies of transformation, but all these terms refer to the same Ultimate Reality that in its nature is inconceivable. Ashvaghosha tries to elucidate this profound conception of Ultimate Reality as a ground for faith, but he teaches that certitude cannot come from knowledge alone. Certitude can only come from an intuitive self-realisation of Mind-essence. By following the Noble Path Bodhisattvas attain this realisation of highest perfect Wisdom and in the experience of that Wisdom they know that this threefold significance of Essence, Potentiality and Activity-balance is a perfect but inconceivable Oneness to which is given the name Tathagata. This term is a compound word which may mean either "thus truly comes," or "thus truly goes." That is, all that is possible to know of Ultimate Reality is what is seen in Radiant Wisdom or in the integrant Love of Buddhas as they yield up their selfness in love for all animate life.

★ ★ ★

Mahayana Buddhism may be considered under two heads: as a system of doctrine, and as a way of life.

As a system of doctrine, the Mahayana teaches the ultimate oneness of all things in Tathagata. This Ultimate Principle of Tathagata will be explained in five chapters: Ignorance as the source of personality; Mind-essence as manifesting personality; Mind-essence as emancipation of personality; the oneness of Mind essence and personality; and the place of Mind-essence in the unitive principle of Tathagata.

As a way of life that leads from ignorance to wisdom, from suffering to blissful peace, from selfish egoism to Buddhahood, it will be explained in three chapters: the True Path, the right way of following the True Path, and the rewards of the Path.

The Mahayana makes no dogmatic assertions that are to be accepted on authority; it merely suggests explanations to awaken faith but each must work out his own emancipation. It bases its explanation on things as they appear to the senses in this world of life and death, then it advances to a consideration of the relations of these appearances by the higher mental processes, and then it urges self-realisation of the true nature of things by an appeal to the highest intuitive faculties. It is thus by the path of intuitive concentration that each one is to become convinced as to the truthfulness of the suggestions, for it is by self-realisation alone that one is to become identified with Buddhism. It is thus, also, that the True Path and the right way of following the True Path is of more consequence than the doctrinal system, for it is not by behavior, nor knowledge, nor mere faith, that one finally attains Buddhahood, but by identifying one's life with the Principle of Tathagata.

THE PRINCIPLE AND PRACTICE
OF MAHAYANA BUDDHISM

ADORATION

ADORATION TO ALL THE BUDDHAS

in all the Buddha-lands; whose Wisdom is transcendent, whose Love is all-embracing; whose mission it is to guard and save all beings.

ADORATION TO THE DHARMA

whose Truth is like the ocean, embracing all but revealing the principle of Emptiness.

ADORATION TO THE BROTHERHOOD

the perfect fellowship of those who aspire after highest perfect Wisdom that they may help all beings to rid themselves of doubt and fear and evil attachments, and by the awakening of faith to inherit seeds of Buddhahood.

CHAPTER ONE

INTRODUCTION

THIS treatise is written to explain to ordinary minds the principle and practice of Mahayana Buddhism. The writer has no thought of gaining thereby any monetary return or any worldly advantage; his sole idea is that he might awaken in the minds of ordinary people a pure faith in the Mahayana and encourage them to enter upon the Path that leads to Buddhahood.

At the time the Blessed One lived, people were unusually gifted and the Buddha's presence, majestic both in mind and body, served to reveal the infinite significance of the Dharma. At that time there was no need for a philosophic commentary, because he himself was its perfect explanation. After the death of the Buddha there were men who possessed in themselves the intellectual power to understand the many-sided meanings of his teachings, and there were others who could understand them after reading many scriptures. There were still others who, lacking in intellectual power, must read elaborate commentaries before they could understand them. There were many others, also, and there still are, who, lacking in intellectual power of their own, are unable to follow even the elaborate commentaries and, if they are to understand the many-sidedness and universality of the Mahayana, must have it presented to them in a simple and concise form. It is for the sake of the people of this last class that this treatise is written.

The reasons for writing it are various: That he might unfold and explain the principle of Tathagata, which is the fundamental principle of the Mahayana, so that all beings having a right understanding of it might rid themselves of attachments to false doctrines, of fears and doubts and all the baffling miseries of life; and that they might gain from it a constant inheritance of Buddha-seeds which, when brought to maturity, will insure to them an immovable faith because it is based on self-realisation of highest perfect Wisdom. That he might unfold and explain the only true Path that leads to this self-realisation, and the only true practice that will insure the successful accomplishment of the Path, so that they whose root of merit is weak and insignificant may awaken faith to make a beginning toward ridding themselves of previously acquired false imaginations, wrong habits of greed, anger and infatuation, and then to encourage them to press on toward the stage of immovable firmness.

That he might induce all being to practise the orthodox method of concentration (*dhyana*) so that they, having brought their root of merit to full strength, may press on toward intellectual insight by reason of which they will be fortified against mental trespasses due to immaturity of thinking, and still to press on to intuitive self-realisation of highest perfect Wisdom by reason of which they will be received into the company of the Buddhas, which is the goal and reward of the practice of Mahayana.

Though all these things are sufficiently set forth in other Scriptures, yet as the dispositions and inclinations of people in different lands and in different times vary, and the conditions for attaining Enlightenment vary, the writer was prompted to the utterance of this treatise in which the highest and deepest and most inexhaustible principle of Tathagata is explained in comprehensive brevity. May common people of ordinary mentality benefit by its study and by meditation upon its teachings.

CHAPTER TWO

IGNORANCE AS THE SOURCE OF PERSONALITY.

ONE of the most difficult things to conceive is the nature of personality; almost all philosophies have diverged at that point. To common minds it appears to be an enduring entity that has issued from some cosmic womb, but what that womb may be, and what it is that issues, is impossible to conceive. Buddhists think of it as an imaginary synthesis of the five grasping aggregates of form, sensation, perception, discrimination and consciousness, all of which being empty of any self-substance and transient leaves personality a dreamlike, unreal and passing imagination.

The Blessed One devoted one of his earliest discourses to what is known as "the chain of origination," the first step of which was: "In dependence upon Ignorance the mental processes arise." This makes Ignorance the source of everything dependent upon the mental processes. Much depends, therefore, on the meaning of Ignorance. Common people have always held three things in fear and dread: Ignorance, personality and suffering. Over against these three conceptions, Mahayana Buddhism arrays three other conceptions: Wisdom, Buddhahood, Nirvana, as being true and final. It is the purpose of this treatise to explain these conceptions and to show how these three conceptions merge into the unitive and ultimate principle of Tathagata.

As Ignorance is used in connection with other terms, Wisdom, Enlightenment, relative enlightenment and non-enlightenment, there will be need to explain them, also, leaving it to a following chapter to explain personality more fully. In order to explain these terms it will be necessary to use two other terms, Mind-essence as being the basis of everything, and Ultimate Principle as the law of the self-nature of Mind-essence, and these terms, also, will be more fully explained in later chapters. We will begin by explaining the term Ignorance.

The Ultimate Principle of Mind-essence is the blending of two lesser principles: the principle of radiation or intellection, and the principle of integration or compassion. As the principle of intellection it is the principle of analysis; as the principle of integration it is the principle of synthesis. Under the principle of Intellection, Mind-essence manifests itself as Ignorance which is the aspect of individuation, and Wisdom which is the aspect of unification and Oneness. Ignorance issues into the distinctions of thinking and thought and thinker; Wisdom issues into Enlightenment (*bodhi*) and knowledge (*jnana*). From Ignorance there is a descending series of more and more particularised faculties of cognition: the thinking, discriminating, particularising mind (*manovijnana*), and the five sense minds (*vijnanas*). Beginning from the sense minds there is a rising series of more and more inclusive cognition: sense concepts, particularised perceptions, discriminations, consciousness, discursive thinking based on the dualisms of premise and syllogism leading up to conclusions that become the basis of knowledge but end up in Ignorance. The stages of this intellectual thinking begin in non-enlightenment based on false imaginations, lead on to the conceptions of an ego-personality and the multiplicities of an external world, all of which will be explained more in detail as we go on. But before we leave this general statement we will add a very brief statement contrasting with the foregoing intellectual thinking that ends in Ignorance, another series that, avoiding particularisation and discrimination, passes through right observations to relative enlightenment, and through mindfulness and intuitive concentration (*dhyana*) to perfect Enlightenment, the realisation of Wisdom and Buddhahood.

* * *

Perfect Wisdom is identical with Mind-essence: it is universal, undifferentiated, all-embracing; it is the self-nature of Tathagata considered as Universal Mind, and as Universal Womb, but as such is free from all the limiting attributes of subjectivity. It is like space, extending everywhere, penetrating everywhere, revealing the unity of all things. As Tathagata-womb it is the source of all intellection and so Tathagata perfumes all intellection. That is why Enlightenment is called Dharmakaya—the Body of Truth. Because Enlightenment is the "substance" of the Truth Principle, it is said that Tathagata ever abides in Enlightenment.

When we consider Enlightenment in its relation to sentient beings, we note that some are non-enlightened and some are relatively enlightened but, in reality, there is no difference between non-enlightenment and relative enlightenment, both are fleeting and unsubstantial manifestations of a common Mind-essence. We think of relative enlightenment as following non-enlightenment, as being relative states of mind; we think of one person as being more enlightened than another but, in truth, neither are truly Enlightened. So long as a person has not realised his own Mind-essence he can not truly be said to be Enlightened.

Common people becoming conscious of error in the succession of their mental states and who, because of it, abstain from drawing conclusions, may be spoken of, in a way, as being enlightened but their enlightenment is still non-enlightenment. Novices and disciples and those Bodhisattvas who have just begun the stages, recognising the difference between thinking based upon egoistic subjectivity and thinking that is free from it, may be said to be enlightened as to appearances; but this kind of enlightenment is only a coarse form of enlightenment. Bodhisattvas of the middle stages, having recognised that both subjectivity and the transcendence of subjectivity are alike unreal, may be said to be enlightened as to relations, that is, to be relatively enlightened, an intermediate form of enlightenment. Those who have ascended the stages of Bodhisattvahood to the highest and have thereby attained a consciousness that is both clear and comprehensive, are able to realise that all mentation is mind-made; theirs is a right knowledge; they can be said to be really enlightened.

But the Buddhas, having transcended both relative knowledge and right knowledge, have gained a Transcendental Intelligence by reason of which they have entered into a perfect realisation of the emptiness and purity and immutability of Mind-essence; it is they alone who have attained Perfect Enlightenment. That is why they are called, Buddhas—the Perfectly Enlightened Ones; as it is said in the Scriptures: "Those who have an insight into the unreality of all subjectivity, attain to the Wisdom of the Tathagatas."

In the foregoing statement we have referred to the source from which all mentation originates and proceeds. But, in truth, there is no such thing as an origin of mentation, for discrimination and consciousness being purely subjective have no true existence; how can one speak of the origin of that which is wholly imaginary? The great multitude of people are rightly said to be unenlightened, because from beginningless time Ignorance has kept them in bondage to a constant succession of confused subjective states from which they have never been emancipated. In the foregoing we have spoken of the attainment of Enlightenment as though perfect Enlightenment was the goal of a process of mentation. This is not true, because when one succeeds in transcending subjectivity, one then recognises that all particularisation and discrimination and consciousness including relative enlightenment, their appearance, their changes, their disappearance, have no genuine reality. Because these fleeting changes of mentation are all alike dreamlike and unreal, they are neither in spatial nor temporal relation to Enlightenment. When one understands this, one also understands that Enlightenment can neither be accumulated nor manufactured; it can only be discovered, for it is no other thing than Mind-essence itself, universal, all-embracing, undifferentiated, timeless.

* * *

Furthermore, if we liken the nature of Mind-essence considered as Enlightenment to space or a bright mirror, a fourfold significance appears:

The first significance is its Emptiness, in the sense that Enlightenment is absolutely unobtainable by any mode of relativity or by any outward sign of intellection. The second significance is its affirmation in the sense that in their ultimate essence all things are perfect and complete and not subject to destruction; in the sense that all events in the phenomenal world are reflected in Mind-essence in that they never pass out of it, nor enter into it, nor disappear, nor are destroyed; in the sense that they are one eternal and immutable Essence which can not be defiled by any of the defiled things but, on the contrary, Enlightenment perfumes the minds of all beings by its all-pervading wisdom and compassion. The third significance of Enlightenment, when considered as space or a bright mirror, is its Affirmation in the sense of its freedom frcm all hindrances both intellectual and emotional and, although as mind it is implicated in the world of life and death, yet, in its essential nature, it remains pure, clean, calm, immutable and eternal. The fourth significance is its Affirmation because of its freedom from all hindrances, by reason of which it unfolds and undergoes transformations wherever conditions are favorable into the form of a Tathagata or some other form, in order that all beings may be induced thereby to bring their root of merit to maturity.

The first significance is called the mirror of True Emptiness; the second significance is called the mirror of the Perfuming Principle; the third, the mirror of Perfect Freedom; the fourth, the mirror of Perfuming Activity.

* * *

There is a twofold relation between relative enlightenment and non-enlightenment: identity and non-identity. These relations may be illustrated by the simile of the different kinds of pottery that are made from one kind of clay—they are identical in one way and not identical in another way. There is but one universal Mind-essence yet from it proceeds all the various and transient forms of non-enlightenment and relative enlightenment. The scriptures teach that all beings, both the enlightened and the unenlightened, the bad as well as the good, are from all eternity abiding in Enlightenment. In truth, Enlightenment, being an aspect of Mind-essence, cannot be created nor manufactured—it can only be discovered.

As Alaya-vijnana in its purity has nothing to do with material phenomena, and there are no attributes in it by which it becomes tangible, nevertheless, by becoming implicated in the material world it thereby becomes defiled, and this defilement, in turn, becomes the source of all transient forms and manifestations. In as much as these different manifestations have a common Essence, they are identical; but in as much as they differ from each other in appearance, they are not identical. If these differences in appearance are not discriminated, there would be no desire, no grasping, and no attachment. Likewise there is no true distinction between non-enlightenment and relative enlightenment except as discrimination, desire and grasping enter in to condition their perpetuation.

Another relation between non-enlightenment and Enlightenment may be seen as follows: By so-called non-enlightenment is meant that as Primal Enlightenment had not been recognised in its true and all-embracing Oneness, there issues forth an unenlightened mind with its subjectivity, but this subjectivity has no existence independent of Primal Enlightenment. To illustrate: We speak of a man having lost his way; unless he had a prior idea of a right way, he could not be said to have lost it. That is, his confusion of mind has no valid foundation apart from the fact that there is a right way. It is even the same in this matter of non-enlightenment. All beings have an innate knowledge or instinct that leads them toward Enlightenment. They become unenlightened because of their ignorance they yield to the lure of false imaginations which lead to subjectivity and their going astray into non-enlightenment, whereas they intended to go the right way into Enlightenment. Thus their non-enlightenment has no independent existence aside from its relation to Primal Enlightenment. Now because non-enlightenment and its relative enlightenment stand in the same relation to Primal Enlightenment, they have only a relative significance.

Concerning non-enlightenment three aspects may be noted: the first is its blind activity that has been prompted by its well-intentioned impulse toward Enlightenment. This disturbance of the mind caused by non-enlightenment leads it to perceive differences which in itself is neither good nor bad but inasmuch as it leads to desire, grasping and attachment, it becomes the origin of karma and according to the law of causation produces unhappiness and suffering. When Enlightened the mind is undisturbed and at peace.

The second aspect of unenlightenment is the appearance of an ego-subject as over against an external world, which it proceeds to discriminate, to desire and to grasp. When the mind is undisturbed this perception of an ego-subject does not take place.

The third aspect is the appearance of this illusory external world. Independent of the perceiving subject, there is no external world, and when the mind is enlightened it vanishes away.

But conditioned by this imaginary external world, six kinds of phenomena arise in succession: The first is intelligence based on sensation, perception, discrimination and the activities of the mind, by reason of which the mind becomes conscious of differences between the agreeable and the disagreeable. The second is memory by reason of which the sensations are linked up into a continuous stream of subjective states. The third phenomenon is the appearance of desire for the agreeable and aversion for the disagreeable, by reason of which action follows in graspings and clingings. The fourth phenonenon is the appearance of words and ideas which the mind sets up as firmly based on the remembered sensations and experiences which the mind proceeds to establish into habits. The fifth phenomenon is the weaving together of these habits into the characteristic behavior of each personality whence it is recorded on Alaya-vijnana, the All-conserving Mind, as karma. The sixth phenomenon to follow is the inevitable reactions of karma, by which the mind finds itself entangled in conditions of its own preparing and thus becomes limited in its freedom of action.

* * *

The question may be asked at this point, what is the difference between non-enlightenment and "ignorance"?

Ignorance is used in two senses, first as the principle of individuation when it is usually written with a capital "I," and second, ignorance with a small "i" when it refers to the hindrances arising from the principle. Non-enlightenment arises out of the hindrances originating in the physical organism, that is, out of the senses, the sense-minds, the brain and the lower mental processes. It is from these that thirst, desire, grasping and clinging arise and by their attachments and habits establish false imaginations of an ego-personality and its external world, and thus hinder the attainment of enlightenment and right knowledge and obscure the truths of pure Enlightenment. "Ignorance," on the other hand, is an intellectual and intuitional hindrance that arises in the higher mental processes of intellectual thinking and improper meditation, by reason of which true creations of intellect are inhibited, the integrations of unselfish compassion are made difficult or impossible, the practice of dhyana is interfered with, and the mind fails to realise its true identity with Noble Wisdom and Mind-essence.

On account of non-enlightenment, attachments affirm themselves, habits are fixed, karma accumulated, and there arises a distinction between that which apprehends and that which is apprehended. Thus believing in an ego-personality and its external world, both of which have originated within the subjectivity of the mind itself, it becomes oblivious of the oneness that underlies all appearances. Mind-essence is universal and eternal and there being no internal differences within it, is forever calm and tranquil, revealing no sign of change nor becoming. "Ignorance," however, in its blindness is oblivious of pure Enlightenment and, on that account, cannot recognise truthfully all those conditions, differences and appearances which characterise the phenomena of the universe.

CHAPTER THREE

MIND-ESSENCE AS MANIFESTING PERSONALITY

To unthinking minds, personality appears as a conscious entity emerging by some law of natural causation and having relations with just as real an external world. This will now be shown to be an illusion of the mind itself.

Alaya-vijnana, the Universal Mind, in its Essential nature is pure and immaculate, that is, it is not directly the source of individualised appearances. It is only as it becomes defiled under the conditions of non-enlightenment, false imaginations and thirst, that activities take place by reason of which the immaculate face of the Alaya is clouded over by karmaic defilement, and various appearances of differentiation of thinking, thinker and objects of thought, arise. We have already considered the relations that non-enlightenment bears to Enlightenment; we will now consider the development of the thinker and its objects of thought.

If we examine our conscious personality we will note that it is made up of the five grasping aggregates of form, sensation, perception, discrimination and consciousness. The four steps of mentation, sensation, perception, discrimination and consciousness, appear to be localised in the five senses (*vijnanas*), the discriminating mind (*mano-vijnana*), and the intuitive or realising mind (*manas*). Because of thirst, desire and grasping, which have their origin in false imaginations and non-enlightenment, these various mentations lead to attachments and habits the memory of which is stored in the form of defilement upon the face of the Alaya. These karmaic defilements may be considered as divided into two groups: those relating to an experiencing, subjective self, and those relating to an external world of non-self. Through non-enlightenment, the imaginary subjective group comes to be imagined as a substantial and enduring entity, and is thought of as an ego-soul (*atman*).

There are five different names given to this ego-self according to its different modes of operation, namely:

The first name is activity-consciousness, in the sense that, through the agency of ignorance and non-enlightenment, the mind is disturbed or awakened. The second name is evolving-consciousness, in the sense that, when the mind is awakened, there evolves that which senses an external world of objects. The third name is representation-consciousness in the sense that the newly awakened mind names and reflects upon the external world. As a clean mirror reflects images of all descriptions, even so does representation-consciousness, when mind is stimulated by the five objects of sense, weave the five into one image instantaneously and without effort. The fourth name is particularisation-consciousness, in the sense that it discriminates between different things, good, bad and indifferent. The fifth name is succession-consciousness, in the sense that, continuously directed by the awakened attention, it retains and stores these different concepts in memory, and in the sense that it can recall things that have passed and imagine things that are to come. The all-conserving Alaya-vijnana never loses nor suffers the destruction of any karma, good nor ill, which has once been sown and whose retribution, agreeable as well as painful, it never fails to mature according to a universal law of causation, be it in the present or the far off future.

The three domains of thought, namely, the external world of sensual experience, the mind-world of thought and consciousness, and the inner world of egoism, therefore, being dependent upon finite mind, are all alike unsubstantial and unreal. Apart from the activities of the mind, there are no sights, no sounds, no odors, no tastes, no objects, no mental processes, no mental images, no ego-soul. Let me explain.

First, as to the external world: since all things owe their existence to the sensing, perceiving, discriminating mind, and since all the modes of particularisation and discrimination are the self-activities of the mind, all things are thus dependent as to their realness upon the mind's subjectivity which, as we have seen, is unreal itself; therefore, we are forced to the conclusion that all things and conditions of the phenomenal world, being vouched for and established only through ignorance and subjectivity, have no more reality than have the images in a mirror. When the mind is stimulated by contact and excited by desire, the multiplicities of things evolve simply and wholly from the particularising and discriminating consciousness; and when the mind is quieted, the multiplicities of things disappear.

Second, as to the mind-world. Since all ignorant and unenlightened beings through their particularising, discriminating and succession-consciousness, misapprehend the true nature of the six objects of sense and the perceiving and discriminating mind, they build up, grasp and cling to the conception of an ego-self and an external world. Being fed on the products of its own mental activities, its desires, fears, illusions and infatuations, its reliance upon the distinction grows apace and being conditioned by its own ignorance and unenlightenment, it gets farther and farther astray from pure Enlightenment which is its true Essence-nature.

Third, as to the inner world of selfness:

the truth of this ego-self, that it is wholly mind-made and arises from ignorance and unenlightenment, cannot be understood by the minds of common people or novices, or by disciples whose thoughts are bent upon themselves. It is but partially comprehended by those Bodhisattvas who have reached the stage of knowledge that is based on practice, that is, who have learned to restrain themselves, who practise meditation and concentration, and whose goal is Buddhahood. Even those who have reached the highest stage of Bodhisattvahood cannot fully realise its significance. They may attain to a perfect understanding of the facts, namely, that Mind in its Essence-nature is eternally clear and pure and that it is Ignorance that produces the defilement; that Mind in its pure Essence-nature is free from all individuation, though it is from Mind that all the various appearances of existence arise but within its Essence-nature there is no change whatever; and that when this essential Oneness of the totality of all things, through Ignorance, is unrecognised, particularisation of appearances arises, the notion of an ego-self arises, and all the phases of a defiled and disturbed mind are developed. But the significance of it, the significance of multiplicity arising out of Emptiness and leaving Emptiness unchanged, the profound significance of it only the Buddhas can understand. The reason why it is only the Tathagatas who can realise the pure Essence-nature of Dharmakaya, is because it is the Tathagatas alone who are entirely free from the limitations of the life of birth and death.

* * *

In personality we may distinguish two aspects of Mind, namely, Mind as manifested in the changing world of appearances, and Mind in its ultimate nature as Essence and Emptiness. Each aspect constitutes all things and both aspects are so much of a sameness that one can not be separated from the other. Nirvana is Samsara; Samsara is Nirvana. We have already discussed Mind as manifested in the changing world of appearances; we will now consider Mind in its ultimate nature of Emptiness, but in this place, very briefly.

Mind-essence considered in its ultimate nature of Emptiness is the perfect Oneness of the totality of all being; it is the great all-inclusive Whole; it is the quintessence of Truth, uncreate and eternal. Because of our ignorance, our habits of looking at things as subject and object, our accumulated memory of sensual experiences, our attachments to false imaginations by reason of habit-memory, our confused subjectivity, all things appear under imaginary forms of individuation and as not-self. If this confused subjectivity could be overcome, the signs of individuation would disappear and there would remain no trace of a world of objects nor of sentient beings.

Therefore, all things in their fundamental and true nature are inconceivable and inexplicable. In their essence having no marks of individuation they possess absolute sameness; they are subject neither to transformation nor to destruction; they are outside the range of apperception. Fundamentally being simply Essence of Mind they can not be adequately described in any form of language, nor established by any formula of reasoning. All words and reasonings are nothing but representations and their existence also depends on our confused subjectivity. Mind-essence has no attribute of individuation; how can it be distinguished and discriminated? The term, Essence, is the ultimate reach of language and through this term all other terms must be disposed of. In Mind-essence there is neither anything excluded nor anything that can be added; it is final.

Now the question arises: If Mind-essence is final and inconceivable, how can finite beings have any insight into it, realise it, and conform to it?

The answer is: As soon as it is understood that when the totality of existence is spoken of, or thought of, there is neither that which speaks nor that which is spoken to; there is neither that which thinks nor that which is thought about; when there is perfect conformity to Essence, all subjectivity is obliterated, there is perfect insight because it is based on identity.

From the viewpoint of perfect insight, Essence may be considered as having two aspects: The first aspect is that of Emptiness in the sense that it is void of all the attributes or distinctions that characterise the "unreal" objects of the world of appearances. That is, Mind-essence in its aspect of "real" Reality. The second aspect is that of Affirmation in the sense that it contains all things in potentiality. That is, it is Essence in its all-embracing self-existence.

By Emptiness we mean that Mind-essence in its self-nature has nothing to do with conditions; that it is free from all the signs of distinction that characterise the changes of phenomenal transformations; that it is independent of any particularising consciousness. Thus we are to understand that Essence is neither that which is existence nor that which is non-existence; nor that which is at once existence and non-existence; nor that which is not at once existence and non-existence; that it is neither that which is unity nor that which is plurality, nor that which is at once both unity and plurality; nor that which is not at once both unity and plurality. In a word, then, as Essence can not be comprehended by the particularising and discriminating consciousness of all beings, we call it Emptiness. But the truth is that subjectivity does not exist by itself: Emptiness, also, is empty in its nature. Neither that which is declared to be empty nor that which does the declaring, is independent; neither the world of life and death, nor sentient mind, nor Mind-essence are to be separated.

By Essence as Affirmation we mean: that just as soon as subjectivity is realised to be empty and unreal, just so soon is Mind-essence realised to be eternal, immutable, universal, and sole Reality. It is for that reason that we speak of Mind-essence as being Affirmation, nevertheless, there is no trace of affirmation in it because it is not the product of the dualistic activity of a confused subjectivity; it is only by transcending subjectivity that its true Emptiness can be realised.

CHAPTER FOUR
MIND-ESSENCE AS EMANCIPATION OF PERSONALITY

MIND-ESSENCE in its aspect of Enlightenment when implicated in the realm of life and death becomes manifested in two kinds of emancipating activities: first, activities pertaining to Wisdom, and activities pertaining to Compassion.

By activities pertaining to Wisdom is meant those individualised activities which are prompted by the employment of skillful means by virtue of which faith is awakened, false imaginations are avoided or dissipated, true knowledge is sought after, aspiration to realise Enlightenment is quickened, and disciples are encouraged to undertake the discipline of the True Path and thus to accomplish meritorious deeds as a result of which egoism and its evolving subjectivity is broken down and annihilated, while there remains only the pure Enlightenment of Mind-essence.

By the activity pertaining to Compassion is meant that inconceivable activity that is prompted by the pure potentiality of Enlightenment which becomes manifest in all the excellent spiritual states of Bodhisattvahood that culminate in the identification of the lives of the Buddhas with the lives of all sentient beings. That is to say, Mind-essence that in its aspect of Tathagata-womb is the exuberant source of immeasurable manifestations and appearances, is also the source, through its principle of Love and compassion, of never ending and inconceivable spiritual benefits which are accomplished in all beings.

On account of the above activities both conditioned and pure a constant succession of changes is taking place. These changes are conditioned by the perfuming influences of the four different conditioning agencies which are as follows: First, there is the perfuming by the external world which the subjective mind frames from its sense-concepts; second, there is the perfuming by the subjective mind and its activity consciousness; third, there is the perfuming by the principle of individuation, Ignorance and karma; and fourth, there is the perfuming by pure Mind-essence.

By perfuming we mean that while our worldly clothes have no odor of their own, neither offensive nor agreeable, they acquire one or the other according to the nature of the substance with which they are perfumed. Essence of Mind is pure and free from defilement, but in its aspect of Universal Mind, however, it acquires a quality of defilement owing to the perfuming power of Ignorance. On the other hand, just as defilement has no part in purity, so Ignorance has no part in Enlightenment, nevertheless, it serves the purposes of Universal Mind because, in its turn, Ignorance is perfumed by Essence of Mind. Determined by Mind-essence in its aspect of Universal Mind, Ignorance becomes the causal reason of all kinds of defilement. Ignorance perfumes Universal Mind, which in turn perfumes subjective mind, which in turn perfumes Ignorance, from which mutual and reciprocal perfuming Truth is misunderstood. On account of this misunderstanding a conception of discriminated particulars which make up the mind's obsession of an external world, is produced. Further on account of this perfuming influence of subjectivity, various modes of particularisation and discrimination are produced through which, by grasping and clinging, various deeds are done and we suffer, as a result, mentally as well as bodily.

There are two ways in what we call "the perfuming influence of the external world": first, that which strengthens particularisation, and second that which strengthens clinging and attachment. There are also two ways in what we call "the perfuming power of the subjective mind": first, that which strengthens the particularising and discriminating consciousness, whereby all common people are subject to the miseries of being fettered by the prior deeds that make up karma; and second, by that which strengthens the fundamental activity consciousness through which disciples, Arhats and even Bodhisattvas are subject to the sufferings of life and death, even as they advance along the stages of Bodhisattvahood.

There are two ways in what we call "the perfuming power of Ignorance": first, a fundamental perfuming in the sense that the activity consciousness thereby becomes actualised into deeds; and second, a perfuming of thoughts and emotions in the sense that the particularising consciousness discriminates between that which is agreeable and that which is disagreeable, and is attracted to the one and feels aversion to the other.

We may distinguish two phases of the mind's activities which originate through the perfuming power of ignorance. The first is the cruder phase, it being the state of mind interrelated with its environment. This is the subjective condition of common people. The second and more refined phase being less interrelated with its environment is the subjective condition of higher disciples and Bodhisattvas. These two phases of the mind's activities have a reason for their apparent existence and also a cause or condition. Non-enlightenment is the reason, and the mind's differentiation of self and not-self is the condition. When non-enlightenment is annihilated, the condition loses its conditioning power; when the condition is annihilated the mind is no longer interrelated. If Ignorance, which is the principle of differentiation, is annihilated, then the whole process of intellection would be annihilated and the state of a free mind would be impossible.

It may be asked: If mentation is to occur how can there be annihilation? and if the discriminating mind is annihilated, how can there be mentation at all? In reply we say: By annihilation we mean, not the ending of all mentation, but the ending of its particularising and discriminating function. To illustrate: Water shows disturbance when stirred by the wind; if the wind ceases, the disturbance of the water will cease, but the water will remain the same in either case. Let the water itself be annihilated, however, and the disturbance would be ended for all time because there is nothing left through which it can be manifested. It is only so long as the water is not annihilated that the disturbance may reappear.

It is the same with beings. Through non-enlightenment their minds become disturbed; if non-enlightenment is annihilated, the symptoms of mental disturbance will also be annihilated, but the underlying Essence of Mind will remain the same. But if Ignorance, the principle of particularisation, is annihilated then all sentient beings would cease to exist, because there would be nothing by which they could become manifest, but so long as Ignorance is not annihilated, the disturbances accompanying personality may continue. That is, it is not the general principle of individuation that is to be annihilated, but the lesser principle of particularisation and discrimination.

Though all modes of mentation and consciousness are mere products of Ignorance, Ignorance in its nature is neither identical nor not-identical with Enlightenment and, therefore, in one sense it can be annihilated and in another sense it can not be annihilated. This may be illustrated by the simile of the ocean and its waves. The waves can be said in one sense to be identical with the water, but in another sense they are not identical. The waves are stirred up by the wind; when the wind ceases the waves subside but the water remains the same in either case.

Likewise, when the minds of all creatures, which in their essential nature are pure and clear, are stirred by the winds of ignorance, waves of mentation make their appearance, but these three—ignorance, mentation, subjectivity—have no true existence, they are neither unity nor plurality. Neither Ignorance nor Enlightenment has any form or attribute of itself yet they condition each other. It is because Mind-essence in its aspect of Universal Mind which is pure and immaculate in its self-nature, is defiled by ignorance and non-enlightenment that it becomes the source of mental disturbances. When non-enlightenment is annihilated the disturbances that arise from the false imaginations arising from particularisations and discrimination subside and the subjective mind and personality drop out of sight. When "ignorance" is annihilated the higher mind realises its identity with Wisdom and Mind-essence.

Now we come to the important conception of Mind-essence as the source of perfect emancipation. There are two aspects in what we call the "perfuming of Mind-essence." First, there is the deeper, inconceivable perfuming by the potentiality aspect of Mind-essence; and second, there is the perfuming by the activity aspect of Mind-essence.

Mind-essence, embracing as it does within its potentiality aspect and from all eternity, infinite and spotless virtues and incomprehensible and excellent spiritual dharmas that have an incessant and eternal potency, thereby perfumes the minds of all beings. In consequence of this perfuming power of Mind-essence, all beings, in course, are caused to loathe the miseries of birth and death and to long for the blessings of Nirvana, and, believing that they are in possession within themselves of the true and authentic Essence, faith is awakened, spiritual aspiration is quickened and they are encouraged to discipline themselves for its realisation.

Here a question arises: If all beings are uniformly in possession of Mind-essence and are equally perfumed by it, how is it that there are some who do not believe in it, while others do; and that there are such immeasurable stages and inequalities among them from the first stage to the last stage of Nirvana? According to the teaching, there should be equality. This is the reply: Though all beings are uniformly in possession of Mind-essence, the intensity of ignorance, the yielding to particularisation and discrimination, the nature of environment, that have been at work from all eternity, varies in such manifold degrees as to outnumber the sands of the Ganges. It is even so with all the entangling prejudices such as the ego-conception, intellectual and physical capacities, which vary according to the karma previously accumulated by each,—all of which things are comprehended by the Tathagatas in their application of efficient means. Further there is in the teachings of all the Buddhas a distinction between reason and cause, both of which are to be fully satisfied before the final goal of Buddhahood is actualised.

To illustrate: the combustible nature of wood is the reason why it burns and there is fire, but if a man is not acquainted with the fact or, though acquainted with it, does not apply suitable causes, how can a fire be actualised?

It is even so with all beings. Although they are alike in possession of Mind-essence, how can they attain Nirvana if they do not happen to see Buddhas or Bodhisattvas, or wise sages, or even if they meet them, do not respond to their teachings and example by destroying prejudices, practising restraint, exercising wisdom. Conversely, the mere happening to meet good sages is not in itself sufficient to induce them to loathe the miseries of life-and-death, and to long for the blessings of Nirvana, unless they have within themselves the nature of Enlightenment. It is only when both reason and cause are present that Enlightenment can be realised.

Now there is an inherent perfuming principle in one's own Mind-essence which being encouraged and protected by the love and compassion of all the Buddhas and Bodhisattvas, causes all beings to loathe the miseries of birth-and-death and to long for the blessings of Nirvana, to cultivate their root of merit, to habituate themselves to it, and to bring it to maturity. In consequence of this inherent principle and the employment of efficient means, all beings are enabled to see all Buddhas and Bodhisattvas, to receive instruction from them, to be benefited, to be gladened, to be induced to practice all good deeds etc., until in the long last all shall attain to Buddhahood and enter Nirvana.

* * *

As to activity-perfuming of Mind-essence. By this is meant the perfuming influence of all external causes. These external causes are exercised in innumerable ways, but we may distinguish two classes: First, individual, and second, universal.

All beings since the dawning of their first aspiration till the final attainment of Buddhahood are sheltered and protected by the guardianship of all the Buddhas and Bodhisattvas who, responding to the requirements of each occasion, transform themselves and assume actual forms of personality. Thus, for the sake of all beings Buddhas and Bodhisattvas become sometimes parents, sometimes wives or children, kinsmen, servants, friends, sometimes even enemies, sometimes they manifest themselves as spiritual beings or in some other form. Again Buddhas and Bodhisattvas may employ different means; sometimes they employ sympathy, or friendly speech, or kindly action, or friendly cooperation; sometimes they influence by the six paramitas, charity, good behavior, patience, zeal, wisdom; all of which are inducements to all beings to perfect their knowledge and clear their enlightenment.

Thus embracing all beings with their deep compassion, with their meek and tender sympathy, as well as with their immense treasure of perfect wisdom, Buddhas benefit them in such a way as to best suit their individual needs and conditions;

while all beings are enabled thereby to see and hear Buddhas, or to be benefited by some transformation of the Tathagatas, and thus to increase their root of merit. This individual cause is divided into two kinds: that which takes effect immediately, enabling one to attain Buddhahood without delay; and that which takes effect gradually, enabling one to attain Buddhahood only after a long period. Each of these two is again divided into two kinds: that which increases one's root of merit, and that which induces one to enter the path.

As to the first, that which increases one's root of merit. By this perfuming disciples are convinced that they are in possession of an Essence whose essential nature is pure and eternal and they are also able to recognise that all the phenomena of the world is nothing but an illusory manifestation of their own mind. When they come to clearly understand this truth then the way is open for them to practise suitable means for liberation from the fetters of non-enlightenment and to perform those actions which are in accord with truth. By thus always following the truth, the habit of particularising and discriminating is broken, the power of thirst and desire and grasping is broken, attachments fall away, and karma is matured.

As to the second, that which induces one to enter the Path. By the fundamental perfuming common people and the lower classes of disciples are induced to loath the sufferings of life and death, to awaken faith and each according to his capacity is encouraged to move toward right knowledge; while higher disciples and Bodhisattvas courageously making up their minds unhesitatingly move toward Nirvana.

As to the universal phase of activity-perfuming of Mind-essence. Because of their perfect Wisdom and their Pranidana Vows all Buddhas and Bodhisattvas are wholly devoted to the emancipation of all beings. This purpose is constant and spontaneous on their part, and as its wisdom and beneficence is universal all beings without regard to individuality are moved to think of or to recollect all Buddhas and Bodhisattvas, so that sometimes seeing them, sometimes hearing them, all beings acquire a measure of spiritual benefit that will ultimately bring them to the Path. All beings will become able to overcome hindrances as they are met with, will gain insight, will realise Enlightenment, and finally will be able to enter into the presence of all the Buddhas.

The universal perfuming by Mind-essence and its following activities may be divided into two classes: that which is not yet in unison with Mind-essence; and that which is in unison with Mind-essence.

By the perfuming that is not yet in unison with Mind-essence is meant the efficacy of the religious discipline of common people and the lower classes of disciples. While their strength of purpose, conditioned by the ego-personality and its ego-consciousness, enables them to continue their religious discipline, they have not yet attained to a state that is entirely free from particularisation and discrimination, because their faith is not yet in perfect unison with Mind-essence which in its nature is universal, nor have they yet attained to perfect spontaneity because their discipline is not yet in perfect unison with the potentiality of Mind-essence.

In the emancipation of the minds of ordinary disciples, there are six progressive stages: First, there is the getting rid of defilement by reason of attachment to agreeable things, by becoming accustomed through faith to the thought that all things are empty and transitory; this can be gradually accomplished as novices advance into the enlightenment of disciples, Arhats and the younger Bodhisattvas. Second, there is the getting rid of defilement caused by discriminations and comparisons, thinking of this as pure and that as defiled, of this as comfortable and that as painful; this can be gradually accomplished through strenuous effort based on faith as the Bodhisattva advances to the stage of patient sincerity. Third, there is the getting rid of defilement caused by dependence upon the thinking mind; this can be partially accomplished as Bodhisattvas, through the earnest and faithful practice of dhyana, advance along the stages from dependence upon good behavior and right knowledge; and, upon reaching self-realisation of Wisdom, they will be eternally freed from it.

In these three stages, the mind is not entirely free to act because it is more or less interrelated with its environment due to the mind's still clinging to the distinction of self and not-self. In the following stages the mind is freer in as much as this hindrance is now gone.

Fourth, there is the getting rid of defilement caused by dependence upon all material things and conditions; fifth, there is the getting rid of defilement caused by dependence upon all mental notions; sixth, there is the getting rid of defilement caused by dependence on the "will-to-live."

As the Bodhisattva reaches the highest stage of Bodhisattvahood and fully realises his egolessness, the fundamental "will-to-live" is gone and he willingly relinquishes his hope of Nirvana that all others may be emancipated; thus he gains the perfect Wisdom of Buddhahood. For such as these the universal perfuming of Mind-essence is a sustaining influence.

By the perfuming which is already in unison with Mind-essence is meant the efficacy of the religious discipline of the highest Bodhisattvas. They have attained to a state of non-particularisation and non-discrimination, because their discipline is in unison with the self-nature of all the

Tathagatas; they have attained to perfect spontaneity of activity because their discipline is in unison with the wisdom and the self-giving compassion of all the Tathagatas. Allowing themselves to be influenced only by the nature and power of Enlightenment, their discipline acquires a virtue that destroys Ignorance and manifests Enlightenment. The incessant perfuming of Ignorance that goes on universally and eternally, still goes on, but for one who has attained Buddhahood it is ended. The incessant perfuming of Enlightenment that goes on universally and eternally, is destroying subjectivity, on the one hand, and manifesting Pure Enlightenment, on the other hand. Thus the universal perfuming process, demonstrating the self-nature of Mind-essence forever goes on and is forever renewed.

CHAPTER FIVE

THE ONENESS OF MIND-ESSENCE AND PERSONALITY

FROM the foregoing, we understand that it is on account of confused subjectivity that all things appear as individualised forms which, because of ignorance, the mind proceeds to discriminate. From discrimination arise thirst, desire, grasping, habit and conditioning karma, because of which there is established the conception of personality and an external world of particulars, and if this confused subjectivity can be overcome, all individuation and discrimination will disappear and there will remain no trace of an external world or ego-personality. We have also seen that within Mind-essence there is a process of emancipation going on by reason of which this proneness to particularisation and discrimination is overcome.

What then is the true selfness of personality? By the true and essential selfness of personality is meant that in Essence personality is undifferentiated from the Essence that is the uniform totality of all being. That is, personality is Mind-essence and as such is un-born, empty of any self-substance and egoless. To make this clear let us review the nature of the mind-system that makes up personality. One of the names given to Mind-essence is Universal Mind, Alaya-vijnana. This all-conserving Alaya is in its nature pure and immaculate, but because of the particularising-discriminating consciousness of finite minds, its face becomes defiled by the age-long accumulation of karma which thereafter serves to condition the evolving manifestations of finite minds. Influenced by the principle of differentiation, a system of minds is evolved. First, there is the intuitive mind (*manas*) that is dependent upon Alaya-vijnana but is in touch with the lower finite minds and reflects upon their activities. Manas is the mind that belongs especially to the integrating principle and its right use is the goal of the Noble Path; it is the mind of the Bodhisattvas. Below the Manas is the intellectual, conscious, discriminating mind (*mano-vijnana*); and below that the five sense minds (*vijnanas*).

The principle under which this system of minds has evolved is the general principle of individuation, another name for which is Ignorance. Under that general principle there has evolved a subjective mind with all its false imaginations and illusions, its desires and graspings and attachments, its illusions of an ego-personality, that has no affinity with Universal Mind and yet which serves to defile its face. All that ignorance, non-enlightenment and egoistic infatuation can do is but to diversify and multiply appearances which in themselves are empty of any self-substance. This apparent activity is conceived by the minds of ordinary people and even by some disciples as a real world of Tathagata transformations. They do not realise that these objective transformations are merely the shadow, the reflection, the projection of their own evolving consciousness. They falsely imagine that it has substance and so they give it corporeal limits and names, such as this and that, I and myself.

Evolving under the principle of Ignorance, the system of minds becomes conscious of sensation, perceives differences, experiences thirst and desire, is prompted to grasping and clinging, from which result attachments and habits, the illusion of an ego-self and an external world, and the storage of karma upon the face of Universal Mind where it serves to further condition and to perpetuate its bondage to life and death with all its unhappiness and suffering.

But the same system of mind, emancipated by the principle of integration, gets rid of the habit of particularisation and discrimination and grasping and the notion of an ego-self and its external world. Thus the particularising-discriminating subjective mind is obliterated and the purely synthetic faculty of the intellectual mind is free to devote itself to the attainment of true knowledge and enlightenment and, with the assistance of the intuitive mind to the realisation of Enlightenment and to the manifestation of meritorious Buddha dharmas.

But apart from this external activity of particularisation, there is a more significant activity at work. It is the inconceivable activity of integration that in unseen ways is harmonising, unifying, emancipating, until the oneness of all beings in Essence and Potentiality is accomplished. In the phenomenal world of life and death this inconceivable activity is manifest in an ever present principle that draws things together into more and more inclusive and harmonious unities; that draws animate life together into more and more cooperative ways and mutuality of spirit; that draws the thoughts of men away from selfishness of egoism to sympathy and helpfulness, from the false imaginations of ignorance to the realisations of Truth; and thus obliterating the assumptions of Ignorance establishes the truth of Enlightenment.

The particularising activities which are seen by common people in the changing phenomena of the external world are a coarse form of activity that, in reality, is transitory, empty and dreamlike and that leads to bondage and suffering. Disciples and lower Bodhisattvas are able to recognise faintly the inconceivable activity of the Tathagatas, they become conscious that the phenomena of the external world is only a reflected shadow of their own minds, and they begin to understand the true nature of Mind-essence and the eternal and constant activity of the Tathagatas. But they still cling to the notion that the ego-self is in some sense an entity even though it is related to Mind-essence. These lower Bodhisattvas have not yet freed themselves from the finer forms of particularisation and discrimination, because they have not yet fully understood the emptiness of Mind-essence.

The insight of the Bodhisattvas who have arrived at the stage of pure heartedness and sincerity is more penetrating, and they are able to realise still finer forms of Truth, but it is not until they reach the highest stage that their insight is perfect and that they have capacity to fully realise the perfect Emptiness of Mind-essence. When they finally transcend activity-consciousness all traces of individuation are obliterated. Unlike the minds of common people who recognise an external world of differentiated phenomena and form, Bodhisattvas realise an inner world of potentiality that is radiant and luminous, vibrant in inconceivable ways but never coming nor going and ever remaining boundless and inexhaustible. Just as bodies in the imaginary world of space and time have infinite varieties of form, and forms have infinite attributes, and attributes have infinite excellencies, so Bodhisattvas, as they attain self-realisation of Noble Wisdom and move forward to Buddhahood, find themselves endowed with infinite merits, ineffable graces and boundless means.

Under this principle all Buddhas while yet in the stage of discipline, become conscious of a great heart of compassion toward all sentient beings; they treat all others as being themselves, purposing to work out through limitless kalpas of ages an universal emancipation, not as present individuals but as an all inclusive brotherhood, realising truthfully and adequately the ultimate principle of Oneness as including not only all animate life but all Buddhas as well. And finally, forgetting the very notion of self and others, to be lost in the inconceivable rhythm of joy that is the accompaniment of this inconceivable activity of the Tathagatas. That is, Buddhas enter into Sambhogakaya which to them is a "Body of Reward," and through them is forever manifested its boundless potentiality.

When finite mind is disturbed it falls short of true and adequate knowledge, it fails of purity and sincerity, it fails of eternality and spontaneity and freedom, it fails of tranquillity and peace. But in Dharmakaya there is no conflicting differentiation of Essence, in Sambhogakaya there is no limit of potentiality, in Nirmanakaya there is perfect spontaneity of activity because all is in perfect balance. When finite mind is disturbed, it is because it has become conscious of an external world, and, to control that world to its selfish advantage, it seeks to establish an ego-self, all of which reveals the imperfection and defilement of its inner condition. But the very constitution of Alaya-vijnana is its immaculate purity and its storage of all meritorious Buddha-dharmas in perfect synthesis and potentiality. Therefore, in Alaya-vijnana, there is no sub-conscious urge to seek after anything external to itself. On the contrary, in Alaya-vijnana there is knowledge that is adequate and true, there is perfect command of boundless and skillful means, there is perfect tranquillity and blissful peace, because it is free from all stain or limit of necessity or compulsion. It is this pure Mind-essence that is the true selfness of personality.

If the question is raised: If Mind-essence is devoid of variously differentiated forms, how is it that Mind-essence can manifest itself in the world of life and death? The answer is: Mind-essence can manifest itself in a world of corporeal forms, precisely because it is the Essence of form. Matter and mind not being a duality, we may speak of the universe as being a system of rationality, because the real nature of mind is the same as the real nature of matter. Likewise we may speak of the universe as a system of matter, because the real nature of matter is the same as the real nature of mind. But neither the one conception nor the other has any substantial basis, for both alike, being Mind-essence, are characterised by Emptiness. Tathagata, therefore, depending upon its self-nature of Essence and Potentiality and Activity-balance is able to manifest itself and is universally present at all points of space and at all instants of time; and highest Bodhisattvas, according to their capacities and their vows are able to manifest themselves in all Buddha-lands and at the same time, in infinite bodies of transformation, now individualising, now reciprocally merging into the transformations of other Bodhisattvas, spontaneously, naturally and without interruption.

We have referred to the threefold significance of Mind-essence—Essence, Potentiality, Activity—but these three never exist apart for in Tathagata there is perfect Oneness. Tathagata is the unified totality of being, not as the sum of pre-existing multiplicities, but as primal and final, existing in its own authentic right. From Mind-essence as from a Womb emerge all manifestations, appearances, modes and attributes, but these multiplicities do not analyse Tathagata, they but reveal it and emerging they still remain Tathagata. For Tathagata to be, is to be eternally at rest and incessantly active, for in Tathagata all opposites are integrated into perfect Oneness. Ignorance is Enlightenment; Wisdom is Love; Samsara is Nirvana. When highest Bodhisattvas come to a realisation of this inconceivable Oneness, it is not personality's realisation of Tathagata, it is Tathagata's contemplation of itself. As a manifestation of Mind-essence, personality is Mind-essence.

CHAPTER SIX

THE PLACE OF MIND-ESSENCE IN THE UNITARY PRINCIPLE OF TATHAGATA

IN the foregoing explanation of the relation of Mind-Essence to personality, there is to be noted a threefold significance. First, there is the significance of Essence, or Dharmakaya. Second, there is the significance of Potentiality, or Sambhogakaya. Third, there is the significance of Balanced-Activity, or Nirmanakaya.

In its significance as Essence, Dharmakaya is universal, undifferentiated, inscrutable; it was never created in the past, nor will it ever be annihilated in the future; it knows no diminution nor addition, but is eternal, unchanging, absolute. And yet from all eternity it embraces within its unchanging, inscrutable Essence all potentiality and all manifestation. It is the same and ever remains the same whether manifested in common people, novices, disciples, Bodhisattvas, or Buddhas. It is the same whether thought of as the Truth Principle or the blissful peace of Nirvana.

In its significance as Potentiality, Sambhogakaya is potential of all manner of manifestations, yet within it are no marks of heterogeneity; it is free and self-regulating, nevertheless, it is eternal and immutable, it is blessed, tranquil and pure; transcending all conceivability, it is inscrutable. It contains within itself the Radiating Splendor of Noble Wisdom; the Integrating Light of Love that draws all, that illumines all, that holds all in one harmonious Wholeness. Being potential of all, yet containing no dualism of individuation or conflict, it embraces the joy of accomplishment and fruition. Within, it is Mind that knows all, that realises all, that conserves all, and yet it is undisturbed, patient and equitable. It is both Universal Mind, Alaya-vijnana, and Womb of Tathagata.

In its significance as Nirmanakaya, Mind-essence is manifested in the many transformation bodies of all the Buddhas and in all manner of inconceivable activity incident to their work for the emancipation of all beings. It is the Balanced Activities of forth-going Wisdom and incoming Love; it is the eternal rhythm of perfect Peace.

These three significances are in no sense to be considered as independent of each other; we speak of three but there is only One. This threefold significance is Tathagata, inscrutable, ineffable.

Just what this ultimate totality of all may be cannot be conceived, much less expressed in words; at best we can say of it, "It is such as it is." This ultimate Suchness which exists exactly as it is (*bhuta-tathata*), we call Tathagata, "That which has the nature of Suchness in its coming and going." It has such characteristics as, The Radiancy of Noble Wisdom, the Integrating Glory of Perfect Love. It is Mind in its all-embracing, all-conserving Consciousness; it is Womb in its inexhaustible Fertility; it is Nirvana in its blissful, changeless Peace. Its knowledge is true and adequate, its intelligence transcendent, its compassion boundless and eternal; its Mind, pure in its self-nature is blessed, self-regulating and free; its nature tranquil, immutable and serene.

* * *

In the foregoing it has been said that Mind-essence is devoid of all characteristics; how can it now be said without contradiction that Tathagata embraces all these inconceivable and ineffable merits and excellencies? In order to answer this question it is necessary to speak more at length concerning Nirmanakaya. Essence and Potentiality are at once seen as necessary components of ultimate Oneness, but why is Activity included? We think of activity as being bound in with change, waste, exhaustion, pain and death; how can these things be characteristic of Mind-essence and Tathagata?

The first thing is to get a true conception of the meaning of Activity. In this connection, Activity may be considered as divided into two classes.

The first class are the action, reaction and interaction of the phenomenal world that take place in time and space, that are always particularised and dependent upon one another. This class of objective activities appertains to the principle of differentiation and particularisation, and includes the logical sequence of intellection. The second class of activities is the inconceivable activity appertaining to the principle of integration and compassion, an activity that has no beginning and no ending, that takes place without regard to space and time and differentiation and particularity. Its effects are seen in the awakening of faith in the minds of common people, in the clearing of enlightenment in disciples, in the unfolding spirit of Bodhisattvas as they advance along the stages to Buddhahood. At first it appears to be a gradual unfolding like dawn and growth, and then suddenly it is complete and perfect. As the Bodhisattvas advance along the stages to the sixth or seventh they are still entangled in the illusion and infatuation of selfness and egoism, but the hindrances are disappearing, reliance upon things and conditions as they are seen to be manifestations of one's own mind, are left behind, the bonds of desire and fear are gone, the habit of grasping and clinging is broken, and in their place has appeared another spirit of kindness, sympathy, unselfish humility and patient serenity. Suddenly, when the Bodhisattva has reached the seventh or eighth stage, there is an inexplicable "turning about" within his deepest consciousness by reason of which he realises Noble Wisdom. From that time on there is no recession and he finds himself in possession of a trancendental body with its tenfold powers: Now he clearly understands things that had puzzled and baffled him before—how multiplicity can co-exist with unity; why, if the life of birth and death with all its entangling, alluring illusions of self and otherness is wholly imaginary, why it should appear at all. Now he can pass with the speed of thought from one Buddha-land to another; now he can assume appropriate forms and use skillful means at will not necessarily successively but at the same time, forever actualising his wisdom and compassionate vow to emancipate all beings; and now he is in uninterrupted experience of highest samadhis. At the ninth stage he passes into Buddhahood with all its treasures of Wisdom-Love and is able to utter his supreme Pranidana, his final vow of renunciation. He is Buddha, one with all the Buddhas, past, present and future.

The activities of the radiating intellective principle are transitory, empty and unborn; they have no part in the eternal reality of Mind-essence, and yet they are the same thing as the inconceivable activity of the integrating principle of compassion, which is the very Essence of Tathagata. Without one the other could not be, for how could there be compassion without otherness? How could there be Enlightenment without Ignorance? How could there be compassion without suffering? Love is suffering; Enlightenment is Ignorance; Nirvana is Samsara; for Tathagata is perfect Oneness of Essence, Potentiality and Activity.

The first class of particularised activities, it is true, is bound in with change, waste, pain and destruction that is inherent in the world of life and death, but our knowledge of it is dependent upon the particularising and discriminating consciousness in which self is distinguished from not-self and an external world is set over against an ego-personality. All of these things as we have seen are of the nature of "maya" and a dream and being un-born and unreal have no part in Mind-essence which has nothing to do with modes of particularisation and duality and is free from all individuation and change. And yet the external world of life and death with all its dualism in its essential nature is Mind-essence, and all its restless change of appearance and activity is abundantly embraced in Nirmanakaya. How can this be, you ask? Just as Essence lies at the basis of form and matter, so Activity-balance lies at the basis of the world's restless activities. And just as manifestation and appearance are illusions of finite mind, so the outward activities of the principle of disintegration and Ignorance are dreamlike and unreal. It is only the inconceivable activity of the integrating principle of Love that is real and that forever abides in the serenity and peace of the Nirmanakaya of Tathagata.

* * *

And what is Tathagata? Tathagata is the essential basis of all things phenomenal and supra-phenomenal. Tathagata is one's own Mind-essence, and it is through the highest reaches and the deepest depths of one's own Mind that its threefold significance is realised. Tathagata as Essence is the perfect Oneness of the totality of all things. It exists in all things, remaining unchanged in the pure as well as in the defiled; it neither increases nor decreases; it is eternally void of distinction, always one and the same inconceivable Essence.

Tathagata as Potentiality is the source of all conceivable manifestations, relations and meanings. It is Alaya-vijnana, Universal Mind; it is Tathagata-garbha, the Universal Womb. It is both fountain of all exuberance and storage of all meritorious truths; it is the perfect balance of Prajna-paramita, the Wisdom that is Love, the Love that is Wisdom.

Tathagata as Activity-balance is forever manifesting its self-nature in innumerable and immeasurable appearances which, as they are only appearances, are empty of any self-substance, are un-born, transitory, and egoless, having no more reality than a mirage. Tathagata as Activity is also forever manifesting its self-nature in all kinds of meritorious and inconceivable integrations, harmonising all differences, unifying all dualities, embracing all in its perfect Love-Wisdom. So perfectly balanced is its radiation of appearances which is Wisdom and its integration which is Love, that it never loses its perfect Balance, a Balance which is both Activity and Peaceful Rest. Nirmanakaya is Tathagata in its Universal Immanence by reason of which it is present and at rest in every manifestation of Samsara, and is equally present and active in the inconceivable peace of Nirvana.

* * *

This Principle of the Tathagata is the Mahayana—the Great Vehicle—in which all the Buddhas from the beginning have been riding, and, trusting in it, all the Bodhisattvas of the present and future will surely enter into the state of Buddhahood.

* * *

We began this treatise by saying that its purpose was to awaken faith in the minds of all beings; now, before leaving this section, we again desire to emphasise that same purpose, in order to persuade all beings to step forward, away from the mirage of life and death, away from the words of this treatise, along the Path that leads to Buddhahood.

We have tried to make it plain that the first step must be right ideas concerning the dreamlike nature of personality and its external world. The last step is the perfect realisation of the ineffable Oneness of the Principle of Tathagata. Let us recapitulate:

First as to the dreamlike nature of personality and its external world. If we follow the differentiating principle of intellection to its limit in the minds of scientists we come at last to the composition of the atom, and find it to be balanced charges of electricity, but back of electricity he thinks there may be some unitary particle obeying some primal law of rhythm. That is, the scientist's beginning is an hypothesis of points of space vibrating in instants of time. But space and time are only modes of the thinking mind, and all ideas, propositions, syllogisms, have no substantial basis apart from the processes of the mind itself.

As to the ineffable Oneness of the Tathagata. If we follow the integrating principle to its limit in the unitive world of spirit, we follow the course of the Bodhisattvas as they ascend the stages, the limitations of their humanity dropping away as they realise the emptiness of Mind-essence and the wholeness of Buddhahood, and utter their great vow of renunciation, not to enter Nirvana except in the company of all sentient beings. This is the limit of love, as the other was the limit of knowledge. Beyond all-embracing Wisdom and all-enduring Love there is the universality of Essence, the boundlessness of Potentiality, and the perfectly balanced Activity, that is Tathagata, the Suchness that is as it is. Wisdom is like space without its extension; Love is like time without its limiting duration. Space and time and vibration manifest the changing world of appearances, so Wisdom and Love in Activity-balance constitute the unitary principle of Tathagata. Therefore Samsara, the world of space and time and life and death and all their never resting movement, is Nirvana the realm of changeless peace and tranquillity. They are the same in Essence and yet not the same, for Samsara is a realm of "maya," a dream world of transitory and empty appearance with no reality in it; whereas Nirvana is the abode of the universal and Eternal Reality that is Tathagata. But neither are they both the same nor not both the same, for Tathagata transcends all conditionality; it has a threefold significance but there is no triplicity in its perfect and eternal Oneness. Tathagata is such as it is.

* * *

A man that is lost takes the East for the West and goes astray, but the points of the compass do not change on account of his confusion. So beings on account of nonenlightenment become confused as to what is imaginary and what is true and authentic, but when one clearly understands that birth and death are only confused states of one's own mind and that Tathagata—the Essence of one's own Mind—is pure and undisturbed, then there is nothing to hinder one's realisation of Tathagata's bliss and peace.

CHAPTER SEVEN

FALSE DOCTRINES OF PERSONALITY TO BE AVOIDED

FALSE doctrines invariably follow the conception of an ego-soul as having some sort of an eternal value. If one is liberated from that conception, the rising of false doctrines in general will be avoided.

There are two classes of ego-soul conceptions: Belief in the existence of a personal ego-soul; and belief in the existence of a soul in things.

As to the conception of a personal soul as held by common people, five different views of it can be distinguished. First, common people hearing that the scriptures teach that the ultimate nature of the Tathagatas is tranquil and may be likened to space, yet not understanding the significance of the teaching, they cling to the view that in their self-nature Tathagatas are eternal and omnipresent, in the sense that space and time are. This is a false doctrine and in order that the clinging to it may be eliminated, it should be clearly understood that space and time are only modes of mental particularisation and that they have no real existence of their own. Where ever there is a perception of space, there is side by side with it the perception of a multiplicity of things in contradistinction to which space is thought of as existing independently. But in truth, space exists only in its relation to the particularising consciousness. Further, since changes of form are merely particularisations of confused thinking, it is clear enough that time must be also, and, therefore, time can not have an independent existence. In other words, all modes of relativity, which include the ego-soul and its external phenomenal world, arise simply out of confused thinking. If we become disassociated from our particularising and discriminating consciousness, then all modes of relativity will vanish, while there will remain only universal and undifferentiated Mind-essence. The essential nature of Tathagata, therefore, can not be truly likened to the conception of space and time, although in a certain limited and relative sense space and time may be real and eternal.

Second: Hearing that it is said in the Scriptures that all things in the world without exception are characterised by emptiness, and that even Nirvana is also perfect emptiness, and yet not understanding its true significance, ignorant people cling to the idea that Nirvana is absolute voidity. In order that this clinging may be eliminated, be it clearly understood that Dharmakaya or Nirvana or Ultimate Reality, while being characterised by emptiness as far as all differentiations are concerned, is not absolute voidity, because it envelopes within its self-nature immeasurable and meritorious potentialities, the perfect synthesis of which makes up its true nature.

Third: Hearing that it is said in the Scriptures that Tathagata-womb envelopes in full all potentialities which, constituting its true nature, neither suffer augmentation nor diminution, yet not understanding the significance of the teaching, ignorant people cling to the view that there is, in Tathagata-womb, a fundamental distinction between matter and mind. In order that this clinging may be eliminated, be it clearly understood that in Ultimate Reality there is no distinction of differences. Even when we speak of its embracing unlimited and meritorious Buddha-dharmas, there is still not a trace of difference or defilement, all is pure and imageless.

Fourth: Hearing that it is said in the Scriptures that all things in the world are not at variance with Mind-essence, that even the impure and defiled things appear from Tathagata-womb, and yet not understanding its true significance, ignorant people imagine that Tathagata-womb all-containingly envelopes both good and bad. In order that this clinging to a false doctrine may be eliminated, be it clearly understood that Tathagata-womb all-containingly envelopes only pure and spotless potentialities which outnumbering the sands of the Ganges are not at variance with the emptiness and imagelessness of Mind-essence. The prejudices and illusions and defiled objects of the phenomenal universe, that also outnumber the sands of the Ganges, are in truth imaginary and non-entities. Having no self-existence from the beginning they have never been in correspondence with Tathagata-womb. Neither has Tathagata-womb ever been in correspondence with defiled objects and then later on purified of defilement through the virtue of intuitive intellection.

Fifth: Hearing that it is said in the Scriptures that depending upon Tathagata-womb there is both birth-and-death and the attainment of Nirvana, yet not understanding the significance of it, ignorant people imagine that depending upon Tathagata-womb there is a beginning of life-and-death, and since there is a beginning there must be an ending of Nirvana. In order that the clinging to this false doctrine may be eliminated, be it clearly understood that as Tathagata-womb has no beginning, ignorance and birth-and-death, depending upon it but having no self-substance of their own, also, have no beginning.

These different views relating to the conception of a personal ego-soul as being an eternal entity are held by various schools of heretics, they are not taught by the Buddhas. The Buddhas teach that there are no other beings independent of the three realms of form, mind and spirit, and that all manifestations within the three realms are dependent upon Tathagata-womb, which has no beginning and no ending; and that those who attain to an insight into that truth will thereby eternally destroy the seeds and life-and-death, and will attain to Nirvana which also has no beginning and no ending.

As to the false doctrine that there is an ego-soul in things, it is to be said that the Blessed One taking into consideration the limited intelligence of novices and disciples was careful not to say very much about a non-personal ego-soul and because of that fact people have formed a fixed idea of the transitoriness of the five grasping aggregates of form, sensation, perception, discrimination, consciousness, and being terrified at the thought of birth-and-death have cherished an intense desire for Nirvana. In order that this clinging may be eliminated, be it clearly understood that in their essence the five grasping aggregates are uncreate and, therefore, there is no annihilation of them; and since there is no annihilation of them, they are in their essential nature Nirvana itself. If one can be absolutely freed from particularisation and discrimination and attachment, one will come to see that all things both pure and defiled in their essential nature are alike and only have a relative existence. Be it known, therefore, that all things from the beginning are merely imaginary appearances that are neither matter, nor mind, nor intelligence, nor consciousness, nor being, nor non-being; they are un-born, inconceivable and inexplicable. The reason why the Tathagatas nevertheless endeavor to instruct sentient beings by means of words and definitions is because of their knowledge of skillful expediencies. Provisionally they make use of words and definitions to lead all sentient beings, while their real object is to persuade all sentient beings to abandon words and definitions and to enter by intuition directly into Mind-essence. So long as people indulge themselves in reasonings, they more and more become attached to sophistries, more and more depend on their subjective particularising and discriminating mind, and the more they are held in bondage to a supposed ego-soul. How can one, clinging to an ego-soul, ever realise highest perfect Wisdom, or the Emptiness of Mind-essence and Nirvana?

CHAPTER EIGHT
THE TRUE PATH TO BUDDHAHOOD

THERE is a Noble Path that leads to Enlightenment and Wisdom; it is the Path that all the Buddhas have followed and, if a Bodhisattva is ever to attain self-realisation of Highest Wisdom, he must follow it, also. It is the Path of faith, self-restraint, aspiration and discipline. Faith may be awakened by some slight occurrence, but aspiration is awakened by something more than a mere chance ethical stimulus: aspiration is based on some clear recognition of a truth that is already within one's deepest consciousness —the Truth of Highest, Perfect Wisdom; in aspiration there is an element of confidence based on some experience that Highest Truth can be realised through patient, earnest effort.

There are three kinds of aspiration: Aspiration through work; aspiration through knowledge; and aspiration through the self-yielding of compassion; all of which must be preceded by a measure of faith. There is a certain class of people whose root of merit from time immemorial has been poor and weak, whose minds are deeply veiled by many illusions. Such people, even if they see Bodhisattvas and Buddhas and wait on them and make offerings to them, will merely be sowing the seed of men or at best minor gods; they will attain only the enlightenment of novices and disciples. Some of them aspire, or think they aspire, after Wisdom but, owing to instability of character, there will be constant oscillation between progress and retrogression.

Some of them, happening to see Buddhas and Bodhisattvas, may make offerings to them with a measure of sincerity and may practise many meritorious deeds. After a very long time, perhaps ten thousand aeons, they may come into some favorable circumstance and thereby awaken a measure of aspiration. For instance, they may come into personal touch with some Buddha, or may make some gift to the Brotherhood with especial sincerity, or may be instructed with especial tact and wisdom by some novice or disciple, or may be deeply moved by the example of some other lay-man; these circumstances may awaken a measure of aspiration, but this kind of aspiration generally is not very constant for later on they may fall upon less favorable circumstances and just as easily lose all they have gained.

But among these more or less inconstant beginners, there will be some whose root of merit is more firmly grounded; deeply and sincerely believing in the efficacy of karma, in their heart of hearts loathing the sufferings of this life, and seriously practising the ten precepts of good behavior, they will sincerely aspire after highest Enlightenment. Then, coming in contact with Buddhas and Bodhisattvas, they will wait upon them with humility, make offerings to them in sincerity, and will discipline themselves in many meritorious ways and, after the lapse of a tenth of the time required by others, they will awaken a perfect faith.

Among these of more perfect faith there will be a few who, either by virtue of the instruction received from Buddhas or Bodhisattvas, or because of their sincere compassion for all animate life, or because of their earnest zeal in preserving and circulating the Scriptures, will awaken pure aspiration to realise Highest Wisdom. With aspiration now fully awake, they become members of the group of constancy who never relapse but, always abiding in the thought of Buddhahood, they will ultimately become identified with its pure Essence.

A distinction is thus made between the awakening of faith in the mere notion of Enlightenment and the awakening of pure aspiration to attain its self-realisation. As faith becomes stronger, there are three faculties of the mind that must be awakened and quickened before pure aspiration is established. First, there is rightness of comprehension by reason of which the mind is able to truthfully contemplate Mind-essence. Second, there is right decision of purpose to meet all the conditions of behavior and knowledge that such right comprehension demands. Third, there is greatness of compassion by reason of which all attainments and merit are freely devoted to the emancipation of all beings from their sufferings incident to life and death.

It may be asked whether there is any need for one to discipline himself in all good deeds in order to save mankind, since all sentient beings, abiding in the oneness of the universe, have logically nothing to do but calmly to contemplate Mind-essence.

In reply we answer: Yes, there is need. The mind may be likened to a precious jewel which is pure and bright in its essence but is buried in gross veinstone. There is no reason to suppose that one can make it manifest in all its purity and brightness by merely thinking about it. It is even so with Mind-essence. Though it is pure and bright in Essence and embraces all potentiality, yet it is hidden, deep buried in external defilements. There is no reason to suppose that a man can realise its all sufficient perfectness without first clearing away the defilement. Earnest thinking about it, alone, will not do it; there is need to awaken every faculty,—clear, true thinking, earnest purpose and a great heart of compassion for all animate life. To awaken these faculties and to quicken them into active aspiration, there is need to employ all wise means and patient self-discipline. If these many defilements, hindrances and attachments that becloud Mind-essence are to be cleared away so that perfect Enlightenment may shine forth, it must be done for all sentient life, therefore it is necessary that all good merit should be accumulated—that each should have compassion for all—in order that all may be emancipated.

With regard to skillful means, there are four classes: The first and most important is the need for self-discipline in the practice of concentration of mind on the fundamental truth of the Emptiness of Mind-essence which, being uncreate and free from particularisation, is independent of the changes of life and death. By keeping in mind that all things arise from the concurrence of causes and conditions, and that the reactions of karma are irrevocable, by keeping in mind these things one will awaken compassion within his deepest consciousness by reason of which he will be encouraged to discipline himself in all good deeds for the emancipation of all beings, even to the extent of giving up his own hope of Nirvana. Realising that Mind-essence has nothing to do with either Nirvana nor birth and death, this attitude toward all beings is in accord with the nature of Mind-essence and is, therefore, the means of practising Fundamental Truth.

The second is called, the means of abeyance. Since Mind-essence is free from all distinctions of imperfection, one should develope feelings of shame and remorse to aid him in checking all evil deeds and thoughts, and thus, to keep them from growing into deeds and habits.

The third is called, the means for strengthening the root of merit. By always cherishing reverential feelings for Buddha, Dharma and Brotherhood, by always revering, paying homage to, praising, rejoicing in, making offerings to, the Three Treasures, one confirms his faith and awakens aspiration for the self-realisation of perfect Enlightenment. Through the protection of the Three Treasures, one's karma hindrances will be matured and cleared away, and one's root of merit will become firmly established. Because Mind-essence is free from all hindrances and envelopes all potentialities, the practice of good deeds is in full accord with Mind-essence.

The fourth is called, the means of the Great Vow. That is, by making his Great Vow to give up his own hope of Nirvana, which is free from the miseries of life and death, one brings his own life and purpose into accord with the nature of Mind-essence which, being free and embracing all without partiality, is free from all attachments to this or that, self or not-self.

When a Bodhisattva by reason of the foregoing means is able to aspire to highest Enlightenment, he receives a partial insight into the Essence of Buddhahood and according to the power of his Great Vow, is able to perform eight things, namely, to descend from the palace in the Tushita heavens; to enter into a human womb; to remain there; to be born; to utter his Great Vow to attain Buddhahood; to demonstrate in his own person the highest reach of the Dharma by voluntarily yielding up his own personality in the effort to integrate all personality, and by so doing to fulfill the final condition of Nirvana; and, finally, to attain his Parinirvana. As yet, however, he is not to be thought of as absolute Dharmakaya, for he has not yet completely matured all karma that has been accumulated during numberless incarnations in the past. Perchance, by reason of this remaining karma, he may suffer a little more, but he will suffer only for a short time and not because he is fettered to it, but because of his Great Vow he has voluntarily assumed the karma of all.

* * *

It is sometimes said in the Scriptures that even those Bodhisattvas who aspire to highest Enlightenment, sometimes become inattentive and forgetful and fall into lower paths, but later on regain control of themselves and recover the lost ground. But this was only said to encourage those novices who occasionally give themselves up to indulgence and thereby stray from the Path and fail to follow the right order, although they may not have really fallen onto lower paths, and because of it become discouraged and give up trying to follow the True Path.

But the true Bodhisattva from the time of his first sincere aspiration continually disciplines himself in those ways which are beneficial both to himself and others and thereby his heart becomes free from timidity. Even the thought that he might fall down to the stage of evil paths does not cause him to tremble or falter, much less does the thought that he may slip back into the stage of the novices and disciples. If he learns that he may not be able to attain Buddhahood until after assiduous observance of various rules of austerity and mortification during immeasurable aeons of time, if he is a true Bodhisattva, he will not fear nor falter. Having gained a firm faith in the truth that from the beginning, all things in their nature are Nirvana itself, how could he ever again cherish the fears of novices and disciples? Much less, how could he ever again fall into the depths of evil? The degree of aspiration to which the Bodhisattva has thus attained is more excellent than the earlier degrees. For him the first long aeon of Bodhisattvahood is drawing to its close and, because his acts are no longer stained by any sort of attachment, he has attained a partial realisation of Mind-essence.

As he knows that the nature of Mind-essence, being free from any stain of attachment, is the extreme of pure and disinterested charity, he, in conformity with it, practises the ideal of charity (*danaparamita*).

As he knows that the nature of Mind-essence being free from the lure of seeing, hearing, tasting, touching, discriminating, and having nothing to do with sexual passion, is the perfection of pure and undefiled morality, he, in conformity with it, practises the ideal of behavior (*sila-paramita*).

As he knows that the nature of Mind-essence, being free from the hindrance of malice and having nothing to do with hatred, is the perfection of pure and tranquil patience, he, in conformity with it, practises the ideal of patience (*kshanti-paramita*).

As he knows that the nature of Mind-essence, being free from physical and mental limitations and having nothing to do with indolence, is the perfection of pure and undefiled activity, he, in conformity with it, practises the ideal of earnestness (*virya-paramita*).

As he knows that the nature of Mind-essence, being free from prejudices and favoritism and having nothing to do with grasping and clinging, is the perfection of pure and undefiled tranquillity, he, in conformity with it, practises ideal tranquillity (*dhyana-paramita*).

As he knows that the nature of Mind-essence, being free from the uncertainties and illusions of ignorance, is the perfection of pure and undefiled Wisdom, he, in conformity with it, practises the ideal of Wisdom (*Prajna-paramita*).

What is the "object" toward which the Bodhisattva has been aspiring from the earliest stage of sincerity, and to which he has attained in the final stage? The "object" is no less than the self-realisation of Mind-essence, which is the ineffable Dharmakaya. We speak of it as an "object" in deference to our passing consciousness but, in truth, when the Bodhisattva attains to self-realisation of Prajna-paramita there is no object to be seen, neither is there any subject to see it. The Bodhisattva, having passed beyond all individuation and particularisation, has transcended the distinctions of subject and object, and intuitively realises Mind-essence, which is beyond the range of demonstration and argumentation, by becoming identified with it.

Thus, having become identified with Mind-essence, there is instantaneous passing over all the Buddha-lands to make offerings to all the Buddhas and to beseech them to expedite the emancipation and enlightenment of all beings. In Mind-essence there being but one undifferentiated ultimate Principle there is but one purpose, namely, to benefit and enlighten all beings; hence there is no giving up to the enjoyment of the felicities of the heavenly mansions, nor is there any resort to words and symbols. Instead there is incessant zeal in the attainment of highest, perfect Wisdom by reason of which the lapse of immeasurable ages is instantaneously annihilated. Or in order to awaken and quicken indolent people there is the slow attainment of Buddhahood through long discipline and the sufferings of immeasurable ages. The reason why there is resort to all these innumerable skillful means is because the self-nature of Dharmakaya and the sole purpose of Tathagatahood is to benefit all beings. But, in truth, there are no innumerable methods of emancipation and enlightenment; they are only spoken of to awaken aspiration and zeal within the limits of human comprehension. As there appear to be differences in the various states of existence, differences as regards the objects of seeing, hearing, etc., differences between subjective personalities as to faculties and desires and character, so there appear to be as many different forms of religious discipline. But, in Mind-essence, intrinsic nature, faculties, intellectual attainments, spiritual aspirations, of all Bodhisattvas are of one sameness; in Mind-essence there are no scales of gradation. In Mind-essence there is such perfect integration that all these seeming differences merge into one perfect Emptiness; which at the same time is the perfect Oneness of Wisdom.

In aspiration through intuitive self-realisation, three different operations of the mind are revealed. First, there is pure consciousness that arises within the mind as it becomes free from its habits of particularisation and discrimination. Second, there is a superconscious Wisdom that arises within the mind which discloses the true nature of all things and all conditions and which reveals for their eradication unlimited skillful means. Third, there is a radiating activity that transcends all consciousness by reason of which there is the spontaneous doing of those deeds which are of benefit to others, in inconceivable and effortless ways.

A Bodhisattva having attained pure consciousness, and with it its ornaments of perfect bliss and transcendental intelligence, attains also an astral body that transcends time and space. Having annihilated ignorance and attained transcendental intelligence, he intuitively identifies himself with perfect Enlightenment. Having attained perfect Enlightenment, he is enabled to see all forms and manifestations in their essential emptiness and oneness; and with this omniscience he spontaneously achieves inconceivable activities, revealing himself in immeasurable worlds and effecting in unseen and effortless ways the universal emancipation of all beings.

* * *

A question arises here in regard to this omniscience by reason of which he spontaneously achieves inconceivable activities. As space is infinite, worlds are infinite; as worlds are infinite, beings are infinite; as beings are infinite, modes of mentation are also infinite. Now, as all these objects and conditions are infinite, they can hardly be fully known and perfectly understood. But when this ignorance is annihilated, with it will go all those particularised modes of mentation, and if they go, how is the Bodhisattva to perfectly understand all things and thus be able to complete his omniscience?

In reply we say: All these imaginary objects and distinctions in their primal origin are of the one Mind-essence which is wholly free from imagination and particularisation and subjectivity. As beings falsely imagine the existence of an external phenomenal world, it imposes limitations upon their minds. As they thus ignorantly cherish these false imaginations and subjectivity, which are not in accordance with the essential nature of Mind, they are hindered from perfectly understanding the true nature of Mind. All the Buddha-Tathagatas, however, are free from these false and imaginary perceptions and, therefore, are able to see things in their true nature, and thus they perfect their omniscience. There is but one ultimate Principle of Mind-essence. When the Bodhisattva's mind is fully in accord with that Principle, it sees all things clearly and truly. From that ultimate Principle of Mind-essence, which is both wise and beneficent, there radiates a light that illumines all conditioned manifestations revealing their true nature of Emptiness. The Bodhisattva, seeing all things in this Light, attains a transcendental intelligence that carries with it highest Wisdom and perfect Compassion and command over infinite and skillful means, by reason of which there is the spontaneous doing of those deeds which are of benefit to all beings according to their capacities and necessities. Thus it is that ignorance is annihilated and omniscience is attained.

Another question now presents itself: If all Buddha-Tathagatas are in possession of infinite expediencies and can spontaneously benefit all beings in the ten quarters, why is it that the latter cannot always see the Buddhas in person, or witness their transformations, or hear their instruction in the Dharma?

The reply is: Tathagatas are really in possession of those expediencies, and are only waiting for all beings to purify their own Mind-essence, to reveal themselves. When a mirror is covered with dust, it can not reflect images. It is even the same with all beings: if their minds are not clear of defilement, Mind-essence cannot reveal itself in them. But if their minds are free from defilement, then the Dharmakaya will be revealed. The Dharmakaya of all the Buddha-Tathagatas is universal and pervades all beings, but being free from compulsion it waits until conditions are perfect, then it manifests itself in the minds of all beings.

CHAPTER NINE

THE RIGHT PRACTICE OF THE TRUE PATH

IN the foregoing sections a distinction has been made between the awakening of faith and the awakening of aspiration. The first stage of awakening must necessarily be based on partial knowledge. Faith is a trust in something at first dimly apprehended, or accepted on authority, or merely hoped for. As knowledge increases there is the awakening of aspiration to become identified with Truth itself. The goal of aspiration is the spiritual realisation of this identity of the self with the perfect Oneness of Mind-essence. Thus it can be said that faith leads to the transcendence of the non-enlightenment that characterises the physical plane, while aspiration leads to the transcendence of ignorance which characterises the mental plane. Enlightenment is therefore seen to be the goal of an unfolding process that clears away hindrances and illusions, and reveals actuality. It is not a process of accumulation, but a process of getting rid, first of false imaginations and attachments, and second of getting rid of all particularisation and discrimination. These things having been gotten rid of there is realisation of Wisdom.

* * *

This part of the discussion is intended for those who have not yet entered into the order of Constant Truth. It is devoted to the elucidation of the practice and discipline that first awakens faith and then through aspiration leads on to Enlightenment.

Four aspects of faith may be distinguished. First, there is instinctive belief in the wisdom and goodness of Ultimate Reality by reason of which one thinks confidently and joyfully of it. Second, there is a belief in Buddha as manifesting Ultimate Reality and as enfolding within himself efficient and sufficient merits to warrant one in joyfully and confidently paying homage to him, making offerings to him, listening to his teachings, disciplining oneself according to his teachings, and aspiring after full realisation of Ultimate Truth.

Third, there is a confident belief in the Dharma as embodying all Truth that encourages one to joyfully practise the Paramitas. Fourth, there is sincere belief in the Brotherhood, as embodying true morality, that warrants one in trusting it, making generous offerings to it, allying oneself with it and accepting its discipline as being beneficial both to oneself and others.

Again, faith will be changed into confident certainty by the sincere and earnest practice

of the Paramitas: charity, good behavior, patience, zeal, concentration, and Wisdom.
How should one practise charity?

If some one comes and asks for anything, disciples, as far as they are able, should grant the request ungrudgingly and in a way to benefit them. If disciples see any one in danger, they should try every means they have to rescue them and impart to them a feeling of safety. If any one comes to disciples desiring instruction in the Dharma, they should as far as they are able and according to their best judgment, try to enlighten them. And when they are doing these acts of charity, they should not cherish any desire for recompense, or gratitude, or merit, or advantage, nor any worldly reward. They should seek to concentrate the mind on those universal benefits and blessings that are for all alike and, by so doing, will realise within themselves highest perfect Wisdom.

How should one practise good behavior?

Lay disciples, having families, should abstain from killing, stealing, adultery, lying, duplicity, slander, frivolous talk, covetousness, malice, currying favor, and false doctrines. Unmarried disciples should, in order to avoid hindrances, retire from the turmoil of worldly life and, abiding in solitude, should practise those ways which lead to quietness and moderation and contentment. They should practise the ten precepts of the bhikshus: dependence upon charity, no permanent home, a single suit of castoff clothes, one meal a day and no eating between meals, sleeping on a hard bed, avoiding the use of cosmetics, never attending entertainments, living a solitary life, meditating under a tree, having nothing to do with money or valuable things. They should feel shame and regret over even small violations of these precepts. They should endeavor by their conduct to avoid all disapproval and blame, and by their example incite others to forsake evil and practise the good.

How should one practise patience?

As one meets with the ills of life he should not shun them nor feel aggrieved. Patiently bearing evils inflicted by others, he should cherish no resentment. He should neither be elated because of prosperity, praise, or agreeable circumstances; nor depressed because of poverty, insult, or hardship. Keeping his mind concentrated on the deep significance of the Dharma, he should under all circumstances maintain a quiet and equitable mind.

How should one practise zeal?

In the practice of good deeds one should never become indolent. He should look upon any mental or physical suffering as the natural following of unworthy deeds done in previous incarnations, and should firmly resolve that henceforth he would only do those things which are in keeping with a spiritual life. Cherishing compassion for all beings, he should never let the thought of indolence arise, but should ever be indefatigably zealous to benefit all beings. Because of the hindrances of evil karma accumulated in previous existences by the violation of important precepts, a disciple may sometimes be annoyed by evil thoughts, by entanglement in worldly affairs, or by sickness. Such things will naturally disturb the course of his purpose and cause him to neglect the practice of good deeds, but he should dauntlessly, energetically, unintermittently, all six watches, day and night, pay homage to all the Buddhas, make offerings to them, praise them, repent and confess to them, aspire to the highest Wisdom, make great vows, thereby maturing and annihilating old karma and accumulating a better.

How should one practise Dhyana?

Intellectual insight is gained by truthfully understanding that all things follow the law of causation, but in themselves are transitory and empty of any self-substance. There are two aspects of Dhyana: the first aspect is an effort to suppress idle thinking; the second, is a mental concentration in an effort to realise this emptiness of Mind-essence. At first a beginner will have to practise these separately but as he gains mind control the two will merge into one. Those who practise Dhyana should retire to a solitary place and, sitting erect, should definitely seek to tranquillise the mind. Do not fix the thoughts on the breath, do not think of individualised forms or colors, do not fix the thoughts on space limits, nor on time concepts, nor on earth, water, fire, nor ether; do not let the thoughts dwell on what you see, hear, learn or memorise. All particularisations and discriminations, all recollections and imaginations should be excluded from conscious thought; even the idea of exclusion should be excluded, because the mind, if it is to be tranquillised, must be like Mind-essence, that is, devoid of all attributes, free of all distinctions, calm, unchanging, eternal.

In all conscious thinking, thoughts are preceded by perception, perception is preceded by sensation, sensation by some external stimulus; so one who is seeking to tranquillise his mind should first abandon the notion of an external world, that is, he should concentrate attention on the emptiness aspect of Mind-essence. Then in all mentation, there is something that precedes and something that follows, therefore he should avoid all discursive thinking. In short, as his attention is distracted by everything pertaining to the external world, he should turn to the inner world of his mind and seek by intuition to realise its true nature. If even this effort seems to awaken a succession of thoughts, he should let them pass without becoming attached to them, because, independent of Mind-essence, they have no existence of their own. This practice of concentration of mind is not to be limited to special periods of Dhyana practice: one should seek to discipline himself in concentrated attention of mind at all times whether sitting or standing, moving or thinking or working. Gradually attaining tranquillisation, he will unconsciously enter the more receptive state of Samadhi and in that state prejudices and hindrances will vanish, faith will be awakened, aspiration will be strengthened, realisation will be attained. But to those who are doubtful, sacrilegious, destitute of faith, encumbered with hindrances of karma, arrogant, indolent, the door is closed.

To those who faithfully and earnestly and perseveringly practise Dhyana certain benefits will surely accrue during this life: they will always be remembered and sustained by all Bodhisattvas and all Buddhas; they will be unmolested by evil spirits; they will not be led astray by false doctrines, nor hold true doctrines lightly. Gradually their serious tendencies and karma hindrances will diminish; gradually their doubts, sinful recollections and imaginations, will disappear; they will become emancipated from enthraling-fear and gloomy remorse; faith in the spiritual state of Tathagata will be strengthened; they will become courageous and unflinching in the face of birth-and-death. Becoming free from the pride and presumption of egoism, they will become meek and patient and will be revered by all the world; if busy about their affairs, prejudices and inclinations and acquisitiveness will no longer assert themselves; if practising Dhyana, they will not be disturbed by external things such as voices, discomforts, etc.

But if the disciple is trained only in cessation of thought, his mind will easily sink into stupidity and, acquiring a habit of indolence, he will become self-centered, will no longer take pleasure in doing good deeds, will forget to be sympathetic and compassionate; therefore he should discipline himself in the concentration of mind upon the emptiness aspect of all things. In this discipline, the disciple should contemplate the fact that all things of this world are subject to constant transformations, are empty and transitory. Being transient all things are dependent and conditional and therefore empty of any self-substance; being dependent and conditional they inevitably lead to disharmony and suffering. He should contemplate the fact that all things that have passed are as a dream, those that are passing are as lightning, those that are to come are but clouds that obscure the moon. He should contemplate the fact, that although all things are transitory and empty yet, nevertheless, on the physical plane they have a relative value to those who are cherishing false imaginations; to these ignorant ones, suffering is very real—it always has been and it always will be—immeasurable and innumerable sufferings. Ignorant beings having been immersed in suffering all their lives, and knowing how difficult it is to escape from suffering, are unconscious that all things and suffering itself are transient and empty and dream-like, all of which makes their condition the more pitiable.

Because of all this, there is awakened in the mind of every earnest disciple a deep compassion for the suffering of all beings that prompts him to dauntless, earnest zeal and the making of great vows. He resolves to give all he has and all he is to the emancipation of all beings. He resolves: "May my mind be free from all discriminations; may I cease to particularise; may I attend on all Buddhas and Bodhisattvas, paying homage to them, making offerings to them, revering and praising them; may I ever listen to them as they proclaim the good Dharma; may I earnestly and sincerely discipline myself according to their teachings, and to the end of my life may I never be negligent to this self-discipline; may I be endowed with innumerable skillful devices that I may effectively emancipate all beings and save them from this ocean of misery, and bring them to the highest bliss of Nirvana."

After these vows, the sincere disciple should at all times and as far as his strength and mind permits, practise those deeds which are beneficial alike to others and to himself. Whether moving, standing, sitting or lying, he should assiduously concentrate his mind on what should be wisely done and wisely left undone. This is the active aspect of Dhyana.

But if the disciple only practises the active aspect of Dhyana, his mind may lack tranquillity and become too susceptible to doubt and uncertainty; it may become out of accord with highest Truth; it may not attain to the wisdom of not particularising and not discriminating; therefore the two aspects of cessation and activity should be practised side by side. He should continually keep in mind that no thing is self-existent, that all things are uncreate, eternally tranquil, are Nirvana itself. But at the same time he should not forget to reflect on the truth that karma and its retribution, both for good and ill, being produced by the coordination of principle and conditions, will never be lost nor destroyed, but will inevitably come to a final balance. He should thus ponder upon the law of causation, both in its good and retributative karma, but at the same time let him not forget that all things in their essence nature are uncreate, empty of any self-substance, void of any ego-soul, in other words, they are Nirvana.

By the practice of cessation, common people will become convinced of the futility of seeking pleasure in worldly things and worldly activities; while true disciples, will get rid of that feeling of fear and anxiety that follows the thought of birth-and-death. By practising the active aspect of Dhyana, common people will be encouraged to cultivate their root of merit and lay up good karma; while disciples, will eradicate the tendency to narrowmindedness and egoism whereby there is left no room for compassion and aspiration. Therefore, cessation and activity are not antagonistic but are complementary to each other. If either one of the two are missing or out of balance the disciple will be unable to attain highest perfect Wisdom.

It will often happen that novices, being immersed in this endlessly changing world of appearances, may suffer ills that are beyond their control, such as are caused by climate, famine, or contagion; or seeing so many about them that ignore the good Dharma and are giving themselves up to immorality, fears and selfish infatuations, or enslaved in lust, hatred and egoism, or chasing after false doctrines, and are thus sinking deeper and deeper into evil habits, may become discouraged and feel impotent in their own strength, and doubt whether they will ever be able to see Buddhas and Bodhisattvas, or to actualise their faith and aspiration by the attainment of perfect Wisdom. Such faint hearted disciples should cherish the thought of all the Buddhas and Bodhisattvas dwelling in all the Buddha-lands who by their vows have attained command of unlimited and efficient means for the emancipation of all beings, and who have wholly devoted themselves and all their merits to that purpose. By so doing their faith and aspiration will be strengthened, their insight into the Dharma will be cleared, their assurance of ultimate oneness with all Buddhas will become unshakable, and their earnest and faithful practice of Dhyana will, in due course, be rewarded by self-realisation of Noble Wisdom.

How can one practise Wisdom?

When one by the faithful practice of Dhyana attains to Samadhi, he has passed beyond discrimination and knowledge, he has realised the perfect oneness of Mind-essence. With this realisation comes an intuitive understanding of the nature of the universe and its relation to Dharmakaya. He now realises the perfect Oneness of Essence, Potentiality, and Activity in Tathagatahood. That is why this early Samadhi is called the Samadhi of Oneness. By disciplining himself in this Samadhi, the Bodhisattva is enabled to always see things in their true nature and thus be able to subjugate all momentary impulses to foolish and egoistic thoughts and action, gaining time for deliberation and the reestablishing of unity and harmony and thus to leave behind all mental disturbances and unrest. Mere trance and ecstasy can not do this, because they too often lead to egoistic satisfactions and hallucinations that are the very opposite of tranquillity.

Some early disciples, being scantily supplied with a root of merit may yield to the lure of false imaginations; sometimes they assume frightful forms and frighten one; sometimes they manifest beautiful forms that entrance and fascinate one; but if the disciple recalls that all phenomena are subjective, the manifestations will disappear of themselves and will no more trouble him. Sometimes these manifestations that accompany imperfect Samadhi take on good forms, the forms of good spirits, of Bodhisattvas, and even of a Buddha, with all their surpassing virtues and charms; they may speak magic words and phrases that promise to dispel evil and misfortune and to bring happiness and prosperity; they may offer instruction as to various means and methods for attaining emancipation; they may declare apparently wonderful teachings, such as: there is no hatred, no friendship, no causation, no retribution; they may declare that all things in the world are absolute emptiness, that they are in essence Nirvana itself; or they may reveal to immature disciple his own past or future states of existence, they may teach him how to read the thoughts of others, they may grant to him incomparable power of eloquence, they may induce him to crave covetously for worldly fame or riches or power, with which to do good. Now all these things may be good in themselves and may be the legitimate fruits of Bodhisattvahood in their due time, but if the thought of them, the vision of them raises perturbation of mind and desire and unrest, they are out of place and unwise. Prajna Paramita is highest, perfect Wisdom; its fruitage comes unseen, without effort, spontaneously; it merges all seeming differences whether they be evil or good into one perfect Whole.

Further, through these early and imperfect Samadhis, the disciple may become inordinately susceptible to emotional moods of delight or fear or dissatisfaction; he may sometimes become misanthropic and again exceedingly philanthropic; he may sometimes be unbearably drowsy, and again not care to sleep for a long time; he may sometimes be susceptible to contagion, at other times apparently immune; he may sometimes remain in a discouraged and indolent state for some time, and then suddenly rise into excessive energy, only to relapse into indolence again; he may sometimes be over sceptical, and at other times prone to believe anything he hears; he may sometimes be excessively religious and at other times give himself over to frivolous occupations, indulge in worldly affairs, and openly seek to gratify his passing desires and inclinations. Such an unstable disciple may attain to the raptures and ecstasies and trances of psycho-pathic unbelievers and, remaining in such a state for a day or two, or even a week, and imagining himself supplied with delicious food and drink, and feeling very comfortable both physically and mentally, feel no sensation of hunger nor thirst. At other times, apart from these raptures and trances, he may be very misogynistic and at other times yield easily to female attractions; sometimes being irregular at meals, sometimes eating over much, and at other times living abstemiously; sometimes his countenance will reflect these changing states and be handsome and attractive, or repulsive. All these changing states of mind are not the indication of Wisdom, but reveal lingering attachments and hindrances of an immature karma. If the Bodhisattva yields to these changing moods, he will but lose the gain that has been made in previous incarnations, perhaps at great cost, and make his practice of the Path still harder. Noticing these changing moods, he should zealously renew his practice of Dhyana, especially being mindful of the evil source of these temptations that are taking advantage of his unguarded deficiencies and accumulated karma hindrances.

There are many other samadhis practised by outsiders, but they invariably have some characteristic of egoistic imperfection which prevents the one practising them from coming into the presence of Buddhas and highest Bodhisattvas in whom is no egoism whatever. All these emotional disturbances are nothing but mental hallucinations, having no other basis than undisciplined subjectivity. When these thoughts are clearly appreciated, false imaginations will instantly disappear and, being freed from their hindrance, the Bodhisattva will realise true Samadhi. In true Samadhi there are no images, no individuations; with the disappearance of false imaginations, even the memory of discriminated notions will disappear, yes, even the notion that Ultimate Reality is Mind-essence will disappear. When the Bodhisattva rises from true Samadhi, there will be no surviving memory of image or likeness to encumber his mind, for the illusion of difference has been destroyed at its root by the realisation of perfect Wisdom. Thereafter all hindrances without exception being eradicated, he will manifest only those deeds which are in conformity with the pure self-nature of Mind-essence and which, appearing spontaneously and without effort, will never become exhausted. With perfect Love has come perfect Wisdom, for perfect Wisdom is perfect Love.

In this full concentration of spiritual potency, Bodhisattvas make their Great Vow,—to forego Nirvana for the sake of all beings. This is the final obliteration of that which bound them to the world of life and death—the final ending of the illusion of selfness—they are now ready to be reborn in some transcendent Buddha-land where, in company with Buddhas and highest Bodhisattvas, they will have passed beyond the reach of change and retrogression, being of the pure Essence of Tathagatahood.

Therefore let all disciples who aspire

after highest perfect Wisdom, which is Prajna-paramita, assiduously apply themselves to the discipline of the Noble Path for that alone will lead them to perfect realisation of Buddhahood.

CHAPTER TEN

THE REWARDS OF THE TRUE PATH

IN the foregoing treatise there has been explained the profound significance of the Tathagata Principle, which is before all, embraces all, explains all.

In order that there may be no hindrance in the Path, those who desire to awaken a pure and efficient faith in its central Dharma, those who aspire to perfect knowledge of it, and to deepest realisation of it, should diligently study this treatise, meditate upon its teachings, and discipline themselves in its practice. By so doing they will surely attain the goal of their faith, which is self-realisation of this highest Principle.

If upon first hearing the teachings of this treatise, a person does not react in fear, he is qualified to inherit its Buddha-seed and to become a partaker of the Buddha's prophecy of those who shall finally realise highest perfect Wisdom both for themselves and all beings. If one might conceive a person so potent that he is able to convert all beings in three thousand great universes of worlds and to persuade them to observe the ten precepts of good behavior, his merit is intrinsically less than the merit of a single disciple who for a single second comprehends this treatise and becomes conscious of awakening faith in it. For when one considers the ultimate end of faith—the emancipation of all beings—the merit of a true disciple is seen to be immeasurably and inconceivably great.

If one but practise the discipline as it is presented in this treatise earnestly and sincerely for a single day and night, the merit thereby accumulated will be so immeasurable, infinite, inconceivable, that, though all the Buddhas of all the Buddha-lands taking turns in praising it, the praise could not be exhausted in innumerable kalpas of kalpas of ages. As the merit of Tathagata has no limit, so the merit of this discipline has no bounds. On the other hand, those who hold this Dharma lightly or who slander it, commit an immeasurable fault, for thereby they block the emancipation of all beings and themselves suffer with them for innumerable kalpas. More than that, its neglect and destruction would mean the destruction not only of one person but the destruction of all animate life, even the destruction of the Triple Treasure, of Buddha, Dharma and Brotherhood. You may ask, how can the evil act of one, condition the destruction of all? The answer is this: Just as the awakening faith of one leads on to Buddhahood with the Buddha's saving love for all animate life, so the evil of one who might have become a Buddha means the destruction of all animate life.

By earnestly practising this Dharma, all the Buddhas of the past have realised highest perfect Wisdom; by practising this Dharma, all Bodhisattvas have obtained an insight into the Essence of Tathagatahood; by practising this Dharma Bodhisattvas of the past have consummated, and Bodhisattvas of the future will consummate pure and spotless faith in the Principle of Tathagata. Therefore, those who desire to become Buddhas should diligently study this treatise.

HERE ENDS THE ELUCIDATION OF
THE PROFOUND AND SIGNIFICANT
PRINCIPLE OF TATHAGATA.

MAY ITS MERITS BE SHARED BY ALL
BEINGS AND LEAD THEM TO
BUDDHAHOOD.